YOUNG CHILDREN,
PARENTS
AND PROFESSIONALS

book is to

YOUNG CHILDREN, PARENTS AND PROFESSIONALS

Enhancing the links in early childhood

Margaret Henry

London and New York

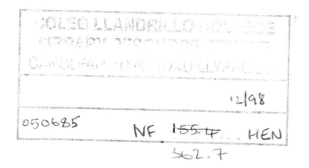
First published 1996
by Routledge
11 New Fetter Lane, London EC4P 4EE

Simultaneously published in the USA and Canada
by Routledge
29 West 35th Street, New York, NY 10001

© 1996 Margaret Henry

Typeset in Palatino by
J&L Composition Ltd, Filey, North Yorkshire

Printed and bound in Great Britain by
T J Press (Padstow) Ltd, Padstow, Cornwall

British Library Cataloguing in Publication Data
A catalogue record for this book is available from the British Library

Library of Congress Cataloguing in Publication Data
Henry, Margaret Bertha McNamara, 1931–
Young children, parents and professionals:
enhancing the links in early childhood / Margaret Henry.
p.   cm.
Includes bibliographical references and index.
1. Child development.   2. Child rearing.   3. Early childhood education.
4. Child care workers.   I. Title.
HQ767.9.H46   1996
305.23′1–dc20   96–7285
CIP

ISBN 0–415–12831–5
ISBN 0–415–12832–3 (pbk)

To
Emeritus Professor
Betty Watts

CONTENTS

FIGURES

TABLES

ACKNOWLEDGEMENTS

This book builds on a doctoral thesis in which I formulated the three dimensions of caregiving behaviour which lie at the heart of the present work. I should therefore begin my acknowledgements, much as I did in the thesis, by saying that, for me, no practitioner of these dimensions could embody them more positively than has my husband. I am also indebted always to my parents, my children and my grandchildren for helping me to understand these dimensions more fully over the years.

I must also again express my appreciation, as I did in the thesis, to the members of the Brisbane family day care community – practitioners, parents and children – whose experiences provide strong evidence for the three dimensional model of caregiving behaviour outlined in the book. That model took shape over many years in which I worked with teachers, parents and children at the local state school, and later with Aboriginal parents, children and colleagues at Inala. My thanks to all of them, and to John Dwyer and Ross Clark, members of the Queensland Department of Education, who stood behind the Inala program.

To the Queensland University of Technology and especially the Head of the School of Early Childhood, Professor Gerald Ashby, I owe a great debt for ongoing support during the work leading to this book. My colleagues and students have been unfailingly interested and encouraging. In particular I want to thank Kym Irving and June Kean for their help, and Beverley Broughton, Debbie Gahan and Judy McDonell for valuable exchanges of ideas. My thanks, too, to Meg Roberts and Leon Frainey.

When one moves from early childhood settings into a university, one would be deprived of the lively interaction one enjoyed with parents, children and other professionals were it not for continuing contacts with in-service students, in my case practising teachers, child care professionals and parents, who keep one in touch with the real world. Nine of these students have kindly allowed me to tell and discuss a number of stories based on events drawn from their own real life experiences. These are events of great significance to readers, and my deep thanks go to Alan Bowmaker, Margaret Bowman, Jean Carden, Dian Jones, Deborah Miller, Sue Panuccio, Rhonda Tibbits, Sally-ann Turner and Nereda White.

Author and publisher have approached all holders of copyright. They would be grateful to hear from any they were unable to contact. Acknowledgement for permission to use material is made to Addison Wesley Longman Australia; Allen & Unwin; the Australian Early Childhood Association Inc.; the Australian Institute of Family Studies; Cornell Cooperative Extension; the Department of Applied Social Studies and Social Research, Oxford University; the Department of Education, Queensland; *Early Childhood Research Quarterly*; Falmer Press; Gordon and Breach Science Publishers; HarperCollins Publishers, Australia; Harvard University Press; the High/Scope Educational Research Foundation; the Institute for Responsive Education, Boston; John Wiley & Sons; *Merrill-Palmer Quarterly*; the National Association for the Education of Young Children; Penguin Books Australia; Penguin Books UK; Queensland University of Technology and *The Australian Journal of Indigenous Education* (formerly *The Aboriginal Child at School*).

For the cover photograph, kind acknowledgements go to the Kelvin Grove Community Early Childhood Centre, Creche and Kindergarten Association of Queensland.

INTRODUCTION

Who is this book for?

Is it for you?

If you saw any of these figures under threat, which one would you most want to help?

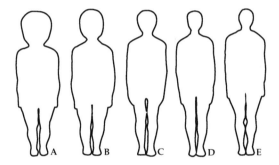

If Figure A is the one you most respond to, you share your empathy with many others. Large groups of students (Alley, 1983) agree with you, finding that this stylisation of a new born baby (B, C, D and E are of increasingly later stages of development), with its large, rounded head and short stubby limbs, has immediate appeal for them.

We adults – not just parents – appear to be genetically programmed to want to assist, to meet the needs of, very young children. This is a book about meeting the basic needs of young children, a topic on which there is still profound ignorance and confusion, so perhaps it is a book for all of us.

But it is also a book about meeting the basic needs of those caring for young children: parents and professionals. The book produces evidence that these sets of needs are interlinked and that there are parallels between the behaviours required to meet the needs of young children, and the behaviours we adults require to meet our own needs for care and education.

If you are interested in meeting young children's needs and your own as a professional or parent, the book may be for you.

But there is a further qualification, related to the meeting of needs. In order to meet needs, you must be able to recognise them, and then to respond to them. In real life what this requires is contingent reciprocal interaction. Two partners respond to each other by taking turns to act (reciprocal interaction), where each turn is not merely related in time to the other's previous action but is dependent on a precise aspect of the meaning of the other's action (contingent reciprocal interaction).

In this book you and I have not been able to interact in this way. I have had to do something against which the book cautions above all: I have had to address your inferred, not your expressed, needs. The language used in the book points up the issue. I have used a good deal of professional language, although the book cautions against this too. The reason is easy to see from the previous paragraph. Here a basis of responsiveness is explained in professional terms (three words, 'contingent reciprocal interaction') and in everyday ones (a whole paragraph).

To achieve the scope required in the book, I have sometimes used professional language, fewer words but more packed, sometimes the more diffuse language of the everyday.

So while this is a professional textbook, I hope that it will also meet the needs of nonprofessional people willing to attend to the variety of ways in which it makes its points: explanations, evidence, real life stories, models.

I hope, then, the book is for you.

Margaret Henry
Centre for Applied Studies in Early Childhood
School of Early Childhood
Queensland University of Technology

1

THE TIMES OF THEIR LIVES

Like the citizens in Charles Dickens' *Tale of Two Cities*, young children in today's Western societies are living in the best of times and the worst of times.

THE BEST OF TIMES

For young children, these are the best of times because we know now more than has ever been known about how to help them become, and remain, predominantly happy, healthy, productive and caring of others. Views of children which ideologised them as repositories of original sin and which helped to perpetuate the long nightmare of childhood recorded from earlier times (de Mause, 1974) have been offset, in this century, by study after study of the actual behaviour of the young and of its causes. Bringing the scientific method to their investigations, researchers such as Gesell, Piaget, Isaacs, Erikson, Patterson, Ainsworth and Rutter have not merely philosophised about young children. They have observed them, and recorded how they function, and can function more joyously.

In addition, these are the best of times for young children because the resources potentially at their disposal are vastly enhanced. Take, for example, the resource of mothers. Mothers, so the tradition goes in Western societies, are there to be resources at home lavishing love on little children. Yet as Edgar (1981) points out, this 'tradition' is so short that, if we think of the life of humanity as a 24-hour day, 'the middle class traditional nuclear family, of Mum at home with two or three kids and Dad the breadwinner, barely precedes the midnight chimes' (p. 4). Before that, and for many families since, a variety of arrangements operated: young children were with parents at work, or with other members of the kinship group, or with paid servants (Aries, 1962; Shorter, 1976). It was the Industrial Revolution, bringing rising standards of living to the West, which permitted middle class (and increasingly working class) mothers to stay at home with the children. But since

1

World War 2, further social and economic changes have propelled many mothers out again. By 1995, notes Ochiltree (1994: 2), 'two-thirds of children under the age of six in the United States will have mothers in the workforce', while in Australia in 1993, 48 per cent of mothers with children aged 0–5, 68 per cent with 5–9 year olds, and 72 per cent with 10–14 year olds, were in the workforce (Australian Bureau of Statistics, 1993).

If half of the mothers of very young children in Australia are employed and half are not, what does this mean for mothers as resources for their children? In the book *Mothers and Working Mothers*, Harper and Richards (1986) discuss their conversations with over 200 employed and non-employed mothers. Typical responses from each set of mothers are these:

> *Working mother (clerk)* I do what I want to do within the circle of the family . . . I need my family but I must have other people as well. I must have other friends, I must have other interests.
>
> *Non-working mother* I always put the children before housework . . . At home I can give them unrestricted time and attention. If I worked, they would have to fit in with my timetable, which is not a child's timetable. I'd spend less time with them.
>
> (Harper and Richards, 1986: 245, 117)

If, as Freud (1961) said, the two resources that make life worthwhile are love and work, we see evidence of both in these two different, but satisfied, maternal responses. The Working Mother requires the 'other interests' found at work to complete the fulfilment of the family circle. The Non-Working Mother sees the family itself as her work and finds her fulfilment therein. At this point it is worth noting Berthelsen's (1994: 295) conclusion that 'empirical evidence of any differential outcomes for children of employed versus non-employed mothers has not been forthcoming'. The fact that Western society at present offers both the option of working and the option of not working outside the home to women with differing needs helps to make this the best of times for them, and by enhancing them, for their young children.

Further, it is the best of times because it is increasingly recognised that mothers need not be children's only resources as caregivers. Take, for example, fathers. An early study that demonstrated fathers' importance in young children's lives was the mid-1960s' examination of the 'development of social attachments in infancy' by Scottish researchers Schaffer and Emerson (1964). Their observations showed that although mothers, not fathers, were the primary caregivers of the toddlers in the study (i.e. spent most time with them), it was the fathers to whom about a third of the children were primarily attached (as well, in many cases, as being attached to other figures who enriched their lives). These fathers inter-

2

acted differently from mothers – often with more pizzazz, adored by the children, a finding confirmed in many later studies (Lamb, 1976).

But as well as their rough-and-tumble fascination for infants, fathers have also demonstrated their capacity for warmth and nurturance (Lamb and Oppenheim, 1989; Russell, 1983). Fathers have shown this particularly when they have taken on sole responsibility for young children, adopting patterns more like those of 'traditional' mothers. A father who, as Ochiltree (1994: 12) puts it, 'takes a more nurturing role due to separation, or illness of the mother, or because he chooses to stay home and care for the children while the mother is in paid work' augments immeasurably the available resources and helps to make this the best of times for young children.

Russell (1983) has speculated that fathers might become more like mothers if their tasks were the same, and suggests that it is the demands of the task in a particular setting that are responsible for such a shift in behaviour patterns. Years ago, writing of school settings and their ability to impose similarities on the behaviour of those operating within them, Gump (1964: 177) made the same point: 'The nature of the settings themselves may coerce social interaction patterns as much as teacher personality variables.'

Are there other home-like settings that exist for young children in these best of times, settings that are available to them as resources when mothers, fathers and other family members are unavailable? Of course there are. There are family day care homes and child care centres. What is best for young children in child care depends on the two factors mentioned by Gump: the 'nature of the settings' themselves and the 'personality variables' of the staff.

In an article entitled 'Is day care as good as a good home?' Prescott (1978) answers yes to her own question, provided that 'the nature of the settings' in day care can meet a number of standards commonly achieved at home. Home is a setting seen by Prescott as having evolved, in part, to meet the needs of young children for nurturance, sensory exploration and the fostering of autonomy and initiative. Similar results will be achieved in centre settings, she believes, provided that staff keep in mind home-like measures of child initiation of activity, measures of 'softness', freedom from structured routines, problem-solving conversation with adults and active engagement with the environment.

As for the 'personality variables' of teachers in child care, these have sometimes been seen as deeply different from those of parents, sometimes as strongly similar. Katz (1980), for example, emphasises differences, maintaining that parents' roles are diffuse yet optimally intense, while those of teachers are specific but optimally detached. Yet in the same paper, Katz has noted that the younger the child, the broader the scope and responsibility assumed by any caregiving adult. Powell (1989: 55), too, has concluded that 'the work of early childhood practitioners is likely to be viewed as similar to the tasks of parenting'.

So what are the behaviours that both practitioners and parents perform that help to create the best of times for young children? Here is Schaffer's (1971: 135) description of the operative adult behaviours that he found elicited attachments on the part of very young children to both mothers and others: 'in the first place the individual's responsiveness to the infant's signals for attention, and in the second place, the amount of interaction which the adult spontaneously initiated with the infant.' (It was that spontaneous initiation of rough-and-tumble that lifted fathers to top place on their toddlers' attachment scorecards.)

In a similar description of the qualities that she found 'predicted good child development in centers and family day care homes', Clarke-Stewart (1987: 113) has written of 'activity areas oriented to the child's activity' and of 'a caregiver whose interactions with the child were responsive, accepting and informative'.

THE WORST OF TIMES

With more knowledge and more resources (settings and people) available than ever before to get young children started, why are these best of times also the worst?

The reason is largely because parents cannot win. Not just mothers (Harper and Richards, 1986), but fathers too, in many areas of Western society, are caught within a thicket of confusion and guilt. This confusion sprouts around the roles of those looking after young children.

For women, the dual roles of engaging in family-related love and work appear to have been happily resolved in the two quotations (see p. 2) from a Working Mother ('I must have other interests') and a Non-Working Mother ('I always put the children before housework'). But the voices of these two contented role models from the Harper and Richards' (1986) gallery are drowned out by the array of women in their study crowding forward to express anxiety and resentment. A home wife speaks of her working sisters:

> They don't worry about their kids. So long as they're getting ready for work, they just ignore the kids. They just don't care. They're always in a hurry.
>
> (Harper and Richards, 1986: 28)

One of the workers agrees:

> I intended to stay home. I had a grandmother's attitude. But I didn't have children for a long time, so I kept on working. Financially it

4

made a big difference. When I did have a child, I decided I couldn't bear not to go on working. I feel guilty at having left her at an early age. I regret not having the sole care of her when she was young.

(Harper and Richards, 1986: 55)

A home wife reflects on the people that stigmatise her:

They sort of look at you now as if to say, 'You're not capable of anything else. What would you know? What would you know, Libby, you only stay home.' I'm not capable of reading a newspaper because I stay home and look after a baby and wash and iron.

(Harper and Richards, 1986: 42)

The dreary housewife, the selfish worker (with condemnation softened by an excuse 'if it's really necessary') – these are the alternative stereotypes. They are held not only by many members of the public but also by many of the women concerned. The ill effects on young children of living in a climate of domestic unease and anxiety have been well documented (Hock *et al.*, 1988).

It is not only mothers whose lives, with those of their children, are pricked and scratched by the tangle of confused emotions surrounding their family roles. Fathers, too, are beset. Over the years, studies conducted in Australia and elsewhere have shown that the contribution of fathers to the everyday tasks of family life has been miniscule in comparison to that of mothers. Russell's (1983) Australian findings that mothers were performing 90 per cent of child care tasks and 70 per cent of family work have been virtually replicated in the USA (Demo and Acock, 1993) across all family types, irrespective of whether mothers were employed or not. Mothers have called for a greater sharing of such family work (Russell, 1984) and fathers have increasingly expressed agreement (Glezer, 1991). However, attempts to achieve greater equality within the home have struck obstacles. Russell (1994: 17) has noted that: 'In some families fathers were dissatisfied because mothers were unwilling to allow them to take over more responsibilities for child care and housework.' Russell speculates on 'the barriers presented by mothers themselves, many of whom struggle with the ambivalence of overtly seeking paternal involvement but covertly experiencing an "encroachment" on their domain of perceived power and expertise'.

Such feelings of 'encroachment' on one's own domain may also underlie the uncertain relationships that often exist between the adults from the 'old' setting for young children, the home, and those from that 'new' setting, the child care centre. Not all parents, of course, feel encroached on by the child care worker. Some of the mothers interviewed by Harper and Richards (1986) embrace her presence with delight, such as this mother speaking of family day care:

5

I'm very happy with it. She's a better mother than I am. More patient. My little girl has someone else to play with and sees a different home environment. I can forget I've got kids while I'm at work. I've got no worries. I know they're being well looked after.

(Harper and Richards, 1986: 64)

But many mothers – sometimes apologetically – see their own territory threatened if 'outsiders' acquire a stake in their children's upbringing:

We have a thing about not leaving our children with anybody but family. I suppose, you know, I'm really sorry I still sort of think that way. But I can see the error of my ways, in that they should be able to mix with everybody, or go along with everybody. I still, I myself have got this thing; I prefer them to be with the family.

Harper and Richards, 1986: 121)

Another mother speaks of the impossiblity of anyone but herself looking after her young child:

I'd have to find someone who shares my thoughts on child-raising. I would always be apprehensive, because I don't believe anyone else could give her the mental stimulation I do.

(Harper and Richards, 1986: 131)

Mothers who see themselves as being squeezed out of their rightful nest by the upstart cuckoo of child care have their counterparts in the centres, where many professionals have their own sets of negative attitudes to offer. A powerful insight into such attitudes comes from a questionnaire administered by Kelly (1986) to 84 final year students of early childhood teaching. These students were asked what their future work preference would be if they were in full-time employment and were going to have a baby. A quarter of the students said that they would stay at home till the child was aged three or four, while another 45 per cent said that they would not work till the child was at school. Asked, further, for their preferred type of child care if money were no object and they wanted to work full-time, 54 per cent opted for care by relatives or friends only. Not till the baby was 18 months to two years old would a sizeable proportion (38 per cent) consider care in a child care centre, the setting where many of them were about to work. As Kelly (1986: 9) notes, our present child care policy 'erects some buildings and staffs them with people who basically believe that women and babies belong at home together'.

As Kelly points out, such attitudes reflect the most conservative view of child care for the very young – namely that it should not exist – or the second most conservative view – that it is a necessary evil, a band-aid measure for those who 'really need it' financially or through some special family problem. They are not attitudes that see in child care 'a valuable supplement to the family's resources' like baby health centres, or which prize 'the contributions which non-parental caretakers make to children's development' (Kelly, 1986: 4).

Possessing these attitudes, it is not surprising that child care staff have been heard to make both self-denigratory and parent-denigratory remarks. As a mother drops off her toddler, the group leader looks around the room for which she is responsible and says: 'It's so sad that she wants to leave him in a place like this.' A staff member dismisses the departing parent of an upset child with: 'Don't worry, off you go, *we'll* look after her.'

Such attitudes of denigration and patronisation between staff and parents exist not only in child care but also in kindergartens, pre-schools and the early years of primary school. A study by Powell and Stremmel (1987) found that early childhood teachers hoped that parents to whom they gave information about their children would come to trust them more, would use the information at home to bolster classroom learnings and might, indeed, use it to improve their own interactions with their children. In turn, teachers hoped that parents would give them valuable information about children, but as Powell (1989) notes:

> Teachers were troubled by the absence of information from parents. It was difficult for staff to determine whether parental silence reflected a lack of interest in the program and/or the child, or a lack of trust in the center staff.
>
> (Powell, 1989: 67)

An example from Powell (1989) of the uneasy basis of some teacher–parent relationships perhaps helps to explain many a parental silence:

> A teacher who makes the observation, 'Your child put on her coat by herself today so well,' intends to inform or remind the parent of child skills the parent is not encouraging, at least during parent–child interactions at the early childhood program. However, there are several other logical interpretations a parent might apply to the teacher's comment: 'The teacher can get my child to do things I can't. The teacher's better than I am. The teacher must think I'm a bad mother.' Or, 'Why does my child do things for the teacher that she doesn't do for me? There must be something wrong with my relationship with my child.' Presumably these are not interpretations a teacher would want a parent to apply to the comment. Yet the covert intent of the statement provides considerable latitude to the parent in determining the teacher's intent.
>
> (Powell and Stremmel, 1987: 125)

While good will is often overtly expressed by both parents and professionals towards one another, it is hardly possible for either to avoid sensing the denigrating and patronising attitudes frequently expressed – as here – by the other. Further, if many parents and professionals distrust each other as people, it is hardly surprising that each should frequently also have doubts about the competence of the other. Many parents of young children, for example, are critical of the failure of early childhood professionals to *teach* their children. In Australia, as elsewhere, the push continues to become the clever country, the information superhighway advances apace, yet parents see the teachers of young children continuing to preach the virtues of play. 'They should be teaching my child to read, to write,' lament the parents of the four-year olds. Teachers, on the other hand, cannot understand why parents fail to appreciate all the learning – physical, socioemotional, cognitive – wrapped up in, for example, sociodramatic play. 'Socio-what? What sort of learning?' mutter parents, uncomprehending. In a study by Power (1985), elementary teachers rated their own competence sigificantly more highly than did parents. Returning the compliment, caregivers across a variety of studies have been found to 'perceive much larger discrepancies between ideal and actual parenting among center parents than the parents themselves perceive' (Powell, 1989: 68).

THE WIDER CONTEXT

So far this chapter has focused on young children and the effects, both on them and on one another, of their mothers, their fathers and their other immediate care providers. In a seminal model of the ecology of human development (see Figure 1.1 for an adaptation) Bronfenbrenner (1976, 1989) has written of the individual, in this case the child, at the centre of the system, arriving with some intrinsic characteristics, such as sex, age and aspects of health. Surrounding the child, parents and other care providers constitute part of the microsystem, the system made up of those entities immediately influencing the individual. The relationships between these influences constitute, in Bronfenbrenner's model, the mesosystem. So far in this chapter, we have noted that these mesosystem relationships (among parents and care providers) are sometimes for the best, often for the worst. Outside the microsystem is a wider system – the exosystem – made up of influences that affect the members of the microsystem, and beyond that again, a still broader macrosystem of overarching institutions of the culture or society.

In a later version of the model, Bronfenbrenner (1989) has added a further system on which all these systems rest: the chronosystem, which relates to the changes occurring over time in the elements making up individuals, and the micro-, exo- and macrosystems that influence them. The title of this chapter, 'The times of their lives', reminds us of the everchanging nature of events in human development.

The positive and negative attitudes reviewed so far in this chapter are

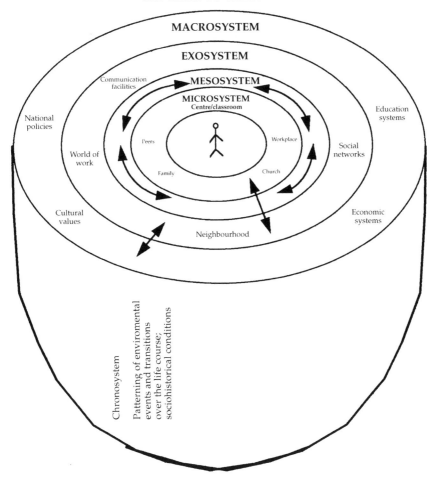

Figure 1.1 Bronfenbrenner's ecology of human development
Source: after Santrock and Yussen, 1992

not constructed by parents and professionals alone. Both groups may be assuaged into acceptance or nudged further into negativity by the pronouncements of public figures in the exosystem who help to solidify a society's climate of beliefs.

As noted already, a climate of uncertainty presently surrounds the whole area of child care. In her book *Children First*, Penelope Leach (1994), the Doctor Spock of the late twentieth century, bases her manifesto for a more humane and loving society firmly on her view of the need to abolish child care, as currently constituted, for under-three year olds. Like the care provider who deplored a mother's leaving her toddler 'in a place like this', Leach sees no value to the baby or toddler in any kind of group care. Such care she sees as utterly inimical to the baby's need for close one-to-one attachment, a topic to be treated at some length in Chapter 2.

Why can such an attachment not be developed between a caregiver and a baby or toddler? Because, Leach believes, caregivers' roles are quite different from those of a parent:

> Whoever it is who cares for infants, they need to have permanence, continuity, passion and a parent-like commitment that is difficult to find or meet outside the vested interests and social expectations of family roles and cannot be adequately replaced by professionalism.
>
> (Leach, 1994: 83)

Basically, Leach suggests, what motivates professionals is money. For very young children, money is indeed the root of all evil. Few others will care for them 'as well as most parents because nobody will ever do as much for money alone as they will do for that atavistic mystery we call parental love' (p. 97). Many parents who leave their babies with professionals sense this, Leach believes, and thus, in addition to the stresses that accompany the swapping of mother hat for working-woman hat:

> There is a broader, vaguer unease that many parents share but most rarely voice: a sense of loss, even foreboding, arising from leaving much of their children's socialisation, education and acculturation to paid labour and the values of the marketplace.
>
> (Leach, 1994: 22)

The reader may wonder why a number of other paid professionals, whose jobs are commonly thought to require warmth as well as expertise, have managed to escape the Leach lash. Why are parents not also warned off nurses, doctors and the teachers of their older children, all of whom are 'paid labour' and consequently likely to be promulgating 'the values of the marketplace'?

'The labourer is worthy of his hire' said Christ (Luke, 10: 7) and this precept applies as firmly to the labour of professional child care as it does to the practice of nursing, medicine and teaching. The problem is that more worldly arbitrators than Christ have not extended the precept to the labour of women in the home. Thus the work of professional child care providers can be stigmatised (by writers such as Leach) as mercenary when compared with the saintly – or slave – labour of their fellow carers, the unpaid mothers.

Leach's censure of caregivers *because* they are paid – as are nurses and doctors – to help parents to do an essential job may seem too absurd to warrant further comment. It will, however, be taken seriously by many readers, as are all the works of this bestselling author. Much of the book should be taken seriously. But the sections about very early child care will add to the 'broader, vaguer unease that many parents share' about professionals, while professionals who care for young children will labour under greater anxiety, or be angered at unwarranted slurs. In sum, such comments add further to the confusion that many parents of young children and professionals feel about their roles and relationships. It is this confusion that contributes to making our times, which should be among the very best for young children, among the worst.

Parents are uncertain about their own roles in relation to the family and the world of work. Many mothers and fathers are uncertain about their relationships with each other, and they are in a state of peak uncertainty about the often unknown 'other half' of their children's lives – the professionally staffed child care centre, pre-school or school settings. As for the relationships of the professionals with the people who should be their greatest supports, the parents, these relationships are often so uncertain as to be, like the customs of Hamlet's day, more honoured in the breach than the observance.

SUMMING UP

Western societies have added immeasurably to the resources available to promote the wellbeing of young children. But with the growth of parental emancipation, child care and early education, anxious questions are increasingly asked. Parents of very young children ask: 'Am I doing the right thing with child care?' Parents of slightly older children ask: '*When* are they going to start teaching my child to read?' Professionals ask: 'Why can't parents understand what we're doing for their children?' Community members ask: 'Is it any wonder those young people are out of hand when they've been deprived of maternal attachment?' Oracular figures such as Penelope Leach ask: 'Why don't you put children first?' All of these questions increase the guilt – and often the defensiveness – of the groups at whom they are directed.

Seldom asked is the more basic question: What are the fundamental needs of young children? parents? professionals? And the further question: How is it possible to meet the needs of each of these sets of people in ways that allow the others' needs to be met? To suggest some answers to these questions is the purpose of this book.

2

NEEDS MUST

WHAT ARE THE FUNDAMENTAL NEEDS OF YOUNG CHILDREN?

In Chapter 1, a serious criticism of early child care was noted. This criticism, related to the notion of attachment, has been made not only by Leach (1994) but by respected early childhood researchers such as Belsky and Rovine (1988). The concern is that because of their instability, unpredictability and qualities of 'strangeness' for young children, many child care settings and personnel cannot meet very young children's attachment needs as can stable, predictable and familiar parental (or family) figures; thus child care is more likely than home to produce 'insecurely attached' children with consequent behaviour problems.

Because 'secure attachment' is currently perceived in our society as a basic need, and child care is commonly suspected of not fulfilling it, the issue of attachment requires consideration before we look more broadly at the needs of early childhood.

ATTACHMENT AS A BASIC NEED

Although the term 'attachment' began to seep into the society in the 1970s, largely through John Bowlby's (1969, 1973, 1980) massive trilogy *Attachment and Loss*, a treatise whose name reverberates like one of the great world novels (*War and Peace, Crime and Punishment*), hints of the importance of enduring and consistent ties between adults and the very young had emerged decades earlier. Skeels (1966) and Spitz (1945) had provided enthralling studies of the effects of maternal deprivation and suggestions for countervailing measures to offset such deprivation.

Perhaps my own continuing interest in the theme of attachment derives from my role as a subject in one of these measures, an inadvertent one, when, as a toddler of almost two, I was hospitalised for six months with scarlet fever and a potentially lethal ear infection. The hospital forbade parental visiting and parents could only look, heart-

12

rent, at their child through a window. As my mother's autobiography records, after several weeks the matron called her in.

> 'We are going to give your child a Special,' she said. 'We are really worried. She is going down hill fast. A Special could perhaps help.' I had never heard of the merciful measure of providing a special nursing sister to devote herself solely to the care of a dangerously ill child, but I blessed the name of the wise large-hearted matron who, with those hundreds of sick children in her care, had decided that this one child needed a Special. From that time on, Sister X, a charming sweet-faced young woman, was our Margaret's own and sole nurse, feeding and washing her, sitting by for hours at a time to soothe and stroke her and talk to her . . . [After six months] the hospital staff and the medicos were amazed at the stamina of our frail little girl, who at last was declared well enough to go home.
>
> (McNamara, 1979: 177)

Since antibiotics were decades away, what changed a two-year old 'going down hill fast' into a child with stamina may largely have been what was brought by the 'sweet-faced young woman . . . feeding and washing her, sitting by for hours at a time to soothe and stroke her and talk to her'. Doing, in other words, the things that Schaffer (1971: 135) described as fostering attachments in very young children: 'in the first place the individual's responsiveness to the infant's signals for attention, and in the second place, the amount of interaction which the adult spontaneously initiated with the infant'.

Are we justified in ascribing an increase in stamina (and later, optimism) in a disastrously ill child to the beneficent effects of attachment? Certainly a multiplicity of studies continue to support both the short and longer-term benefits to children of secure early attachment to responsive adults. As summarised by Sroufe (1985:1), such studies indicate enhanced performance on the part of these children in 'peer competence, coping with failure, coping with novelty, enthusiasm and persistence in problem-solving, independence and infrequency of behavior problems'.

Insecure attachments, on the other hand, are characterised by Ainsworth et al. (1978), who developed the diagnostic 'Strange Situation' to categorise them, as either avoidant or resistant reactions on the child's part to an adult whose behaviour towards the child is either over- or underinvolved. Ainsworth's categorisations were constructed by correlating the adult–child relationship in the Strange Situation with long observations of the same adults and children interacting in the natural setting at home.

Secure and insecure attachments have been associated not only with more or less competence, as noted in the description above by Sroufe

(1985), but also with what Bowlby (1980) called 'internal working models' concerning our responses towards other people. Attachment theorists (Bretherton, 1985) believe that these working models form the basis of our expectations about how people behave, and about how we behave towards others. Crittenden (1985) has an analogy for these working models: they are like an economy of plenty or an economy of scarcity. Inhabitants of a country where resources are scarce must husband or hide their possessions since others will have designs on them, while those from a country with plenty to go round can afford to be generous. So it is with our close relationships.

For Leach (1994) the child care centre is the scene of the scarcity economy. The resource in short supply is one-to-one love and attention. Compared with the child at home, very young children in child care must be deprived of attachment opportunities, Leach holds, since caregivers, those paid employees, are on roster, they come and go, and in any case have numbers of children to care for. They cannot give maximum attention or maximum sensitivity to each child, as can a mother.

On a highly emotional issue, as this one is, readers should be like researchers: they should not rush to conclusions through reading one book or visiting one centre, but should attempt to gather relevant information from more than one source and by using more than one method. For example, readers might actually observe some parents and children in several homes, and do the same with care providers, babies and toddlers in several centres; and they might read a number of research publications related to very young children's attachment at home and in child care. The likelihood is that observers/readers who carry out such a variety of attachment-related investigations will come up with a variety of findings.

On the controversial issue under discussion, is it true that, in child care but not at home, the resource in short supply is one-to-one love and attention? What do wider readings and observations show? From the literature it would seem that, for young children, one-to-one love and attention may or may not be present in child care and they may or may not be present at home.

A father interviewed by Harper and Richards (1986) comments on what can happen at home, even when there is only one child:

> I've got a friend who says his wife won't go out to work because he wants the wife to grow up with the child. He doesn't want someone else to see the child growing up. But all his wife is doing is sitting around the house and the child's growing up, probably in another room or out in the yard, so there's no point in what he says.
>
> (Harper and Richards, 1986: 116)

In Western societies, families generally have more than one child. As a car advertisement says, Australian families currently have 2.3. As Amato (1987) points out, 'parental time and energy are finite resources . . . parental support for children tends to diminish as family size increases.'

In a striking example of that principle, a study by Lewis and Feiring (1982) of families at the dinner table showed that, in the families of three, four and five members studied, with every extra child parental exchanges of information, warmth and affection with a target three-year old were sharply reduced. For example, over the observational period, exchanges of information between mother and the target child decreased significantly from a mean of 14.6 exchanges (family size three) to 9.4 (family size four) to 4.8 (family size five). Proportionally similar reductions occurred for father–child interchange.

Similar effects appear to hold in family day care, as Fosburg (1982: 251) noted in a review of the National Day Care Home Study: 'As the number of children in the home increased, interactions of virtually all types between the caregiver and individual children decreased.'

On the other hand, in the same review of family day care, Fosburg (1982: 257) drew out the finding that caregiver training was strongly related to responsiveness to children in groups of varying size and age mix. Similarly, Watts and Patterson (1984: 144) reported from the Lady Gowrie Child Centre in Brisbane that caregiving staff, all holding an early childhood qualification, maintained or increased their responsive behaviours to very young children as groups became somewhat larger.

Despite Leach's (1994) dismissal of professionalism as a factor in promoting loving relationships with the very young (see p. 10), there is strong support from the literature that caregiver training can enable caregivers to overcome the tendency to reduce responsive interactions even if numbers rise somewhat.

In a review of the work of the Munro Centre, catering specifically for 0–3 year olds in Brisbane, the review team (a'Beckett et al., 1988) found agreement between their observations of the centre and what parents said about it. Interviewed about the goals they saw being achieved for their toddlers, parents used phrases such as 'love and security – as at home', 'a sense of confidence in a loving, caring community', 'fun and happiness', 'independence'.

Reporting on the daily life they saw in the centre, the team wrote:

> There were several caregiver behaviours which were consistently reported by the observers. These personal characteristics and behaviours were responsible for the open atmosphere of the Munro Centre. The range of observed behaviours included:
>
> - eye contact
> - physical contact, i.e. touching, cuddling, carrying children

- smiling
- talking, extended conversation
- attentiveness
- responsiveness and imitation
- greeting adults and children
- following children's leads

The interactive styles of caregivers towards children were mediated to accommodate the varying developmental levels of the children. Caregivers tended to follow a wholly child-centred approach with the babies. That is, interactions with babies were usually very individualistic, personal and intimate. The infants' sleep/feed/play times were on a highly personalised timetable.

Toddlers' and two year olds' developmental characteristics and behaviours were accounted for in the interactive approaches of their caregivers. These children were exploring the environment more actively and, consequently, were prone to risk taking, social conflict and independent behaviours. Caregivers of this age group accommodated these behaviours by adopting developmentally appropriate practices, e.g. encouraging self-help, mediating conflict and promoting confidence and competence. Caregivers were observed assisting children's attempts to follow routines during toileting time, to share materials in outdoor play and to express themselves in creative activities.

(a'Beckett *et al.*, 1988: 24)

There are, of course, many child care centres where the behaviours needed by young children to develop attachment – that is to say, the responsiveness and stimulation (Schaffer, 1971) that permeate this description of an under-threes centre – are not found. The same thing can be said of many homes. The purpose of this book is to add to the number of places (both homes and centres) where we can find what parents said they found at the Munro Centre: 'love and security', 'a sense of confidence in a loving, caring community', 'fun and happiness' and 'independence'. In other words, places of secure attachment.

These positive epithets from parents about their centre may be considered in the light of a more recent, broader view of attachment that is gaining ground, as attachment theorists study young children's emotional ties to persons other than their mother or father. Children's attachments to careproviders are increasingly being investigated (Goossens and van IJzendoorn, 1990; Oppenheim *et al.*, 1988) in an extension, at long last, of Schaffer and Emerson's (1964) study of the parents and others in very young children's lives who helped to enrich those lives. Ochiltree (1994) is among those who have suggested that a view of attachment which encompasses non-parental attachment figures is far more in keeping with a broad evolutionary perspective on the survival of the species than one that is focused, like the view of Bowlby (1953) and Ainsworth *et al.* (1974), specifically on infant–mother attachment. Ochiltree (1994) writes:

> In this version, it is accepted that humans are still evolving and that different but viable attachment patterns will emerge adapted to new pressures in the environment, and that optimal caregiving arrangements for children should consist of a network of stable and secure attachments . . . In the ethological–evolutionary version of attachment theory children in non-parental child care have the opportunity to extend their attachments to other significant people, and child care may be viewed as a positive experience, or at least neutral in its effects, rather than potentially negative because of separation from mother.
>
> (Ochiltree, 1994: 69)

In the review of the Munro Centre (a'Beckett *et al.*, 1988), no formal assessment was made of the quality of children's attachment either to their centre care providers or to their parents. In this context, however, some further comments from their parent questionnaire are interesting. Asked about the effect of the centre on their own daily lives, the overwhelming response of parents was of: 'heightened appreciation of children, of "more freedom during the day" fostering "better attention when home", of "improvement in family relationships" and of "learning from staff knowledge and activities leading to stimulation and enjoyment of our children"' (a'Beckett *et al.*, 1988: 10). In the parents' view, then, a major effect of the child care experience was its strengthening of their own emotional ties to their children. As one father wrote: 'We all appreciate each other more for the break.'

This appears to be an implication also of a study of Burchinal *et al.* (1992) into good quality infant day care compared with the home rearing of 6–12 month old babies. The authors found that, among their sample:

> the only significant association between maternal responsiveness, routine nonmaternal care, and attachment indicated that mothers of children receiving extensive nonmaternal care became more involved with their infants between 6 and 12 months of age, whereas mothers providing exclusive care of their children did not. This result, observed when maternal education was controlled statistically, suggests that daycare does not hinder and may even enhance the quality of the mother–infant interactions among mothers interested in placing their infants in daycare.
>
> (Burchinal *et al.*, 1992: 394)

An underlying reason for this finding may be just the one given by the Munro Centre father. Working parents and children may have 'appreciated each other more for the break'.

Two features in the design of this study by Burchinal *et al.* (1992) may be of critical importance in the debate about the relationship of child care to secure attachment, clouded as this debate still is by confounding factors: for example, parental attitudes, child gender, temperament and age, type and quality of child care, intactness of the family. In the study of Burchinal *et al.* (1992), two of these factors were controlled.

The first was the age of the children at entry to child care. Entry to child care before the age of 12 months has been stated by, for example, Belsky (1986) as carrying a slightly increased risk of insecure attachment to mother. Yet creating an arbitrary cut-off point at one year may itself cloud the issue. For it is at about 7–8 months of age that the development of recognition and recall among babies results, for many of them, in the onset of painful separation anxiety and stranger anxiety. Babies who meet and become familiar with new careproviders before 7–8 months are likely not to see them as threatening strangers, babies who meet them at or after that time may well do so. Increased anxiety undermines the chances of secure attachment to mother (Hock *et al.*, 1988).

By ensuring that all the babies in their study who entered child care did so before they were 7 months old, Burchinal *et al.* (1992) eliminated one area of anxiety and so of risk. They did the same for another key risk area by ensuring that all the mothers in the study agreed at the birth of their baby to place the infant in child care if this were made available. One group of babies was then randomly assigned to child care. Since all the mothers had agreed to accept this, all were known to feel relaxed, rather than anxious, about the possibility of supplementary, nonmaternal care. Controlling for self-selection of the mother and age of entry of the child may well have eliminated two of the major risk factors contributing to anxiety and hence to insecurity of attachment.

ATTACHMENT AND THE NEEDS OF YOUNG CHILDREN

A glance back at the behaviours observed in infants, toddlers and two-year olds at the Munro Centre will show us why attachments – the close ties formed with support figures – are so important in leading on to the meeting of other needs. On p. 16 we read of the babies in this centre having 'individualistic, personal and intimate' interactions with their caregivers. What is being alluded to here is not merely the meeting of major obvious needs – for a dry nappy (diaper), for food, for sleep – but the moment-to-moment contact that constitutes 'responsiveness to the infant's signals for attention' (Schaffer, 1971: 135).

These signals may be very subtle: like the wind wafting across the

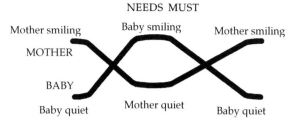

Figure 2.1 Mother and baby smiling
Source: after Open University, 1979

grass a smile may pass from child to adult, or the adult's coo may return an answer to the baby's chirrup. It is these responses to small signals that make up the behavioural dance that developmentalists call 'interactional synchrony' (Isabella and Belsky, 1991). Such a dance, where one partner moves, then allows room for the other's response, then proffers a further reciprocal link in the interactional exchange, is illustrated in Figure 2.1.

This diagram is framed in terms of the 'dance' of mother and child, but as we have seen in the Munro Centre, a sensitive nonmaternal carer who is consistently there for the child can also strike a deep rapport with a young partner in the interactional ballroom.

Besides expressing the moment-by-moment signals that underlie these interchanges, babies also have stronger signals to express: powerful needs which can be met only, as noted in the Munro Report, through 'individualistic, personal and intimate' contacts with their adult care-givers. Since babies have no language to make their wants known, and since, as seen in the Munro Report, their 'sleep/feed/play times were on a highly personalised timetable' (that is to say, unique, and initially unknown and unpredictable), each caregiver, just like each parent, must exercise all those aspects of sensitivity and attentiveness listed on pp. 15–16 – engaging in eye contact, touching, cuddling, carrying, smiling, talking – in order to follow the baby's lead and interpret (Everingham, 1994) the baby's requirements. All mothers, many fathers, and the band of caregivers know how difficult successful inter-pretation of a baby's needs can be. But having achieved it again and again and again, and having engaged again and again and again in the reciprocal steps of interactional synchrony, the adult has laid the basis for secure attachment.

TRUST: RELATIONSHIP TO ATTACHMENT

What attachment can lead to has been suggested by Bowlby (1969) and simply but effectively demonstrated by Hanks and Stratton (1988) in a model of the offshoots of attachment (Figure 2.2). A more general form of the sequence is shown in Figure 2.3.

Baby hungry	→	baby cry	→	mother feed	→	baby satisfied	→	baby play

Figure 2.2 Example of a caregiving sequence
Source: Hanks and Stratton, 1988: 248

Stress	→	demand	→	caregiving	→	assuagement	→	latitude

Figure 2.3 General form of the attachment sequence
Source: Hanks and Stratton, 1988: 248

Hanks and Stratton describe what is happening here:

> under some kind of need or stress, a child will indicate the need and make a demand on caregivers. If the demand is not met it will be escalated until some form of resolution is achieved. If appropriate caregiving is provided the stress will be relieved or the demand met, a state that we call assuagement. In this state the child has surplus capacity and is able to engage in activities that foster development rather than focusing on the needs of the moment. This state of surplus capacity we summarise with the term latitude.
>
> (Hanks and Stratton, 1988: 248)

This model shows us that the establishment of secure attachment leads directly on towards successful outcomes in what Erik Erikson (1950) has called the first challenges of childhood. First, the many-times-repeated responsive meeting of a baby's needs builds up the baby's trust rather than mistrust: a confidence on the baby's part in the predictability and consistency of the adult. 'Resolution is achieved [through] appropriate caregiving' (Hanks and Stratton, 1988: 248). Next, the model shows the development of a second and a third kind of confidence: the second, confidence in him or herself as having brought about (through, for example, crying) this splendid access of adult support. Through the baby's own efforts (crying), a state of ease or 'assuagement' has been reached. Third, with the original need now satisfied, there is room (or space or latitude) for confidence in exploration of the outside world, for example through play. 'In this state the child has surplus capacity and is able to engage in activities that foster development' (Hanks and Stratton, 1988: 248).

Some striking examples of the development of these three kinds of confidence have come from Mary Ainsworth and her associates. In a series of now classic studies, Ainsworth and her colleagues (e.g. Ainsworth *et al.*, 1974; Stayton *et al.*, 1971) investigated the significance for all aspects of young children's development of parental responsiveness to their signals – the ability of 'a parent to work with the grain of her baby's repertoire, rather than against it ' (Ainsworth *et al.*, 1974: 107).

Studies of infant crying in the first year of life (Bell and Ainsworth, 1972) and infant compliance with maternal commands (Stayton *et al.*, 1971) showed that what distinguished the less from the more fussy and the more easy from the less compliant infants was not maternal training directed towards the learning of obedience, but rather maternal responsiveness to infant signals. Similarly, in the realm of intellectual development, Ainsworth and Bell (1970, 1974) found that infants' early exploratory behaviour as well as IQ at the end of the first year were significantly associated with maternal sensitivity, availability, acceptance, and cooperation with the infant.

Long before Hanks and Stratton (1988) brought out in their simple model the links between attachment and the overall development of trust, Ainsworth and Bell (1974) summed up their findings with a similar point:

> a baby whose signals are responded to promptly and appropriately builds up a sense of competence – a confidence that he can through his own activity control what happens to him – and this confidence carries over into his transactions with his physical environment.
>
> (Ainsworth and Bell, 1974: 108)

Underlined in this quotation is the importance of the establishment of secure attachment in planting seeds which will grow over the years into an overarching protective canopy. This is the canopy that safeguards the young children who move successfully through what Erikson (1950) sees as the negotiation of the three major needs, or challenges, of early childhood: first, the establishment of trust versus mistrust; second, confidence in one's own power to affect the world (autonomy versus shame and doubt); third, confidence in one's own transactions with the world itself (initiative versus guilt).

Erikson (1950) has proposed that the meeting of these challenges by young children takes several years to accomplish. He sees the basis of trust being laid down in the first year, autonomy throughout the venturings of toddlerhood, and initiative in the creative outpourings of the preschool years. While it is easy to observe the manifestations mentioned by Erikson over this period, we can also see (for example, in the work of Ainsworth and the model of Hanks and Stratton, just discussed) that the foundations of these three major aspects of human personality are all being laid down very early, within the first months of life.

Earlier we read the description of how care providers in one child care setting, the Munro Centre, helped 0–3 year olds to meet these challenges during their days at the centre. The carers' strategies for helping the babies at the centre to build up trust by meeting their 'individualistic, personal and intimate' demands have already been discussed. Let us now look again at p. 16 for examples of how the second and third needs expressed by the growing children were met, and how caregivers helped them.

AUTONOMY

What comes through the description of life in the Munro Centre is not only the changes in needs as the children grew, but also the continuities. Just as the babies of a few months old – whose lives were largely occupied consolidating their feeling of trust in the environment – were also germinating seeds of autonomy and initiative, so the older children, intent on power and exploration, still needed to consolidate their sense of trust and predictability. So, on p. 16, we see a specific mention of their 'attempts to follow routines' and of caregivers' assistance to build in that predictability. But primarily, we are told, the toddler age is one of 'exploring the environment more actively and, consequently, [of] risk taking, social conflict and independent behaviours. Caregivers of this age group accommodated these behaviours by . . . encouraging self-help, mediating conflict and promoting confidence and competence.'

How did they do this? Caregivers' accomplishments included:

- 'Encouraging self-help' by permitting toddlers many small choices that were genuinely theirs to make: which of the two shirts in their bag they would put on, whether to eat the banana next or the sandwich. Successful choices that built feelings of confidence and mastery reduced the need to be negative.
- 'Mediating conflict' by giving toddlers many opportunities to 'do their own thing' within limits which were few but firm. These were limits that protected safety and property. When caregivers said 'No', children could see that it was their action that was unacceptable, not themselves: 'No hitting. There's your bike', rather than 'You're a real bully'.
- 'Promoting confidence and competence' by building up toddlers' feeling of trust in both themselves and the caregivers. At the centre, toddlers did not have to be afraid of making a mistake. Like all of us, they could learn from their mistakes as well as their successes. Often, rather than punishing, caregivers offered to help fix the problem, giving a hand to squeegee up the spilt drink. Caregivers knew that swinging back and forth between the need to return to the 'secure base' of trust and the need to strike out on one's own can be frustrating, both to children and to carers.

In helping to foster autonomy in the children rather than shame or doubt, these caregivers were backed by a great body of developmental literature that has proposed, as a fundamental premise of human well-being, a behavioural dimension of personal outgoingness, or engagement with the environment.

In the psychosocial school, Erikson's (1950) stages of autonomy and initiative may be viewed as expressions of young children's impetus towards active engagement with the environment, following the establishment of basic trust.

From a biological viewpoint, attachment theorists such as Bowlby (1969) and Ainsworth (1967) see the child's active exploration from a secure base as having species survival value and being built in to the genetic code.

Bandura (1977), extending the work of earlier learning theorists (Skinner, 1953), sees children not merely as recipients of reinforcements from outside agents, but, through their own activity, as reciprocally determining those reinforcements.

In the cognitive–developmental school, Piaget's (1954) cognitive stages – and the levels posited by his successors, the information processing theorists (Siegler, 1983) – may be thought of as children's increasingly complex attempts to be active explorers of their world, organising, structuring and learning from their own experience.

When young children's attempts at some control or mastery over their environment are successful, according to a seminal study by White (1959), they experience pleasurable feelings of efficacy or 'effectance', self-perceptions of competence and further motivation for mastery activity. On the other hand, repeated failure to exert contingent influence on the environment, as in the case of emotionally deprived children (Dennis, 1973; Rutter, 1981), has been shown to result in child apathy and passivity.

INITIATIVE

Erikson (1950) sees the stage of initiative (discovering and trying out new ideas) as extending through the pre-school years. While the children at the Munro Centre were younger than this, 0–3 year olds, mention has already been made of their 'attempts to express themselves in creative activities' (another example of the continuity of the needs of early childhood). The children's creative expression involved sand, water, blocks, books, paint, playing with toys, singing songs, exchanging chat with caregivers and with other children.

Such chat, especially with adults, has been shown to be strongly associated with young children's development and learning (Carew, 1980; Clarke-Stewart, 1987; McCartney, 1984). What these studies have shown is that children demonstrating more advanced language development have had caregivers who interacted and talked more, and more responsively, with them. Included among the 'responsive, informative and accepting caregiver behaviour' identified by Clarke-Stewart (1987) was 'reading from books' (p.38), as caregivers and children were often seen doing at the Munro Centre, in quiet, soft-furnished corners of the playroom.

If talking to adults has increasingly been shown to be critical to young children's development, the evidence is equivocal on the effects of communication between very young children. While the Brontë sisters' practice, from infancy, of a shared secret language may have foreshadowed their later verbal prowess, other children may be less remarkable. McCartney (1984) found two-year olds' peer conversation, by contrast with that between child and adult, to be a negative predictor of language and IQ scores. Her explanation is that time spent conversing with peers diminishes that spent with facilitative adults (not an issue for the Brontës). Clarke-Stewart (1987), on the other hand, sees older peers as also facilitative, and proposes (as does Brownell, 1990) that the effects of peer interaction are age-related: 'The opportunity to watch and interact with older children was related to higher competence; the presence of younger children and infants was related to lower competence' (Clarke-Stewart, 1987: 39).

The watching of others mentioned by Clarke-Stewart, indeed the watching or monitoring of the environment in general, has come into prominence as an indicator of intellectual competence – 'steady staring' it is called by White *et al.* (1979). Bandura (1977) has made it the foundation of his theory of observational learning, while imitation, one of the major processes identified by Bandura in such learning, has also received considerable attention from cognitive developmentalists. Piaget (1952), for example, identified the developing ability to engage in voluntary imitation as one of the essential accomplishments of the 0–2 year old period. Imitation figures in the Munro Centre list of frequent adult behaviours, and the mutual modelling of child and adult in very early childhood, where one partner observes the other, then acts, to be followed in turn by the other (Brackbill, 1967; Bruner, 1975; Schaffer, 1971), appears to be one example of what Gordon (1975) describes as the ping-pong processes of reciprocity through which growth occurs.

Learning by watching other people, talking with them and doing things with them – these are the foundations of initiative, the third great need of early childhood. These are clearly not solitary activities. As Edgar (1993) has noted, the demand for young children to:

> master certain skills, alone, and perform tests which show individual mastery . . . flies in the face of how children actually learn and is mocked by the real world outside the school. Children learn and

grow in competence with other people – mother, father, siblings, friends. Few tasks are done alone.

(Edgar, 1993: 8)

If young children need the people listed by Edgar (among whom we might specify caregivers and teachers – in other words, professionals) to accomplish their major developmental challenges, what – and whom – do parents and professionals need to help them with theirs?

WHAT ARE THE FUNDAMENTAL NEEDS OF PARENTS AND PROFESSIONALS?

What, in other words, do parents and professionals need in order to do their jobs?

Erikson (1950) has pointed out that the challenge of meeting needs is never finally resolved. Meeting the needs that are fundamental to young children's productive lives – needs for trust (confidence), autonomy (a sense of power and independence), and initiative (ability to carry through new ideas) – remains a challenge for adults as well. This may be readily seen if we set Maslow's (1954) lifelong hierarchy of needs beside Erikson's (1950) first three challenges of early childhood (Figure 2.4).

If as adults, in Maslow's terms, our basic physiological needs have been met, along with our needs for security, belonging and esteem, then we are free to move out from that secure base (of trust, according to Erikson) to feel confidence in our own capacities (self-esteem, Maslow; autonomy, Erikson) and, further, to operate productively in the world (self-actualisation, Maslow; initiative, Erikson).

Adult needs for trust, autonomy and initiative are subsumed, in Erikson's life stages, within the major challenge of the middle years, that of generativity. Parents and professionals generate and pass some-thing on to the future, and they need resources to do it. Let us look first at the resources needed by parents.

Parental resources, and the demands or stresses offsetting them, have been presented as a kind of see-saw or balance beam in a model of parental childrearing framed by Gowen (1979) (Figure 2.5). In this model, parents are at the heart of the system that advances the child's development. A young child's status at any moment is seen as a function of the child's past history (the biological endowment and past experiences of the child) and the child's environment. For Gowen, parents are the main providers of the childrearing environment, and their ability to perform this role is a function of the ratio of the demands made on them and resources available to them.

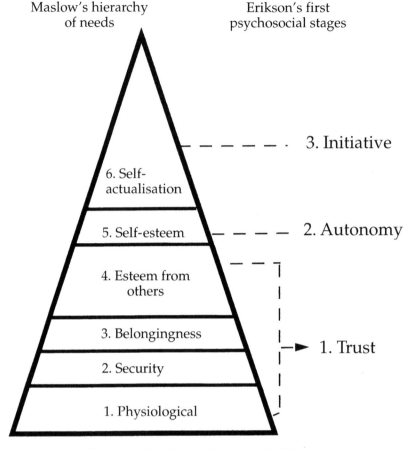

Maslow's hierarchy of needs

Erikson's first psychosocial stages

3. Initiative

6. Self-actualisation

5. Self-esteem — — — — 2. Autonomy

4. Esteem from others

3. Belongingness

2. Security

1. Physiological

1. Trust

Figure 2.4 Meeting needs across the lifespan

Parental resources, Gowen suggests, may be of three kinds:

1 Internal resources, e.g. childrearing skills, knowledge and attitudes, problem-solving skills, physical and mental health, intelligence.
2 Intra-household resources, e.g. economic resources, models for good parenting, cooperative household helpers, supportive interpersonal relationships.
3 Extra-household (community) resources, both formal (e.g. employment, educational, health, child care, welfare opportunities and available social organisations) and informal (support from friends, relatives, neighbours).

Where the resources possessed by parents exceed the demands made on them, the positive end of the 'see-saw' in Gowen's model rises. That is, the probabilities are increased that children's development will be facilitated.

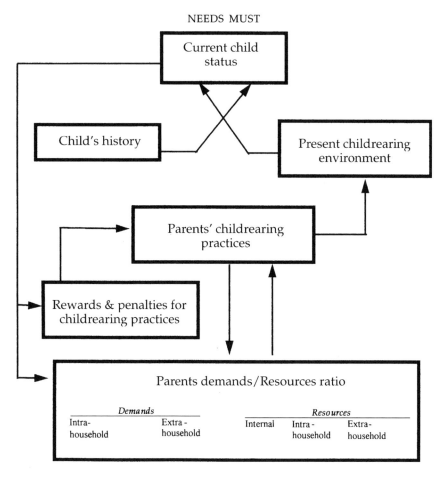

Figure 2.5 Childrearing system for pre-school children
Source: Gowen, 1979

Where demands overwhelm resources (for example, in situations of poverty or prejudice), the positive end of the see-saw falls, and children's development is likely to be hindered. Thus Gowen's model, with its emphasis on the balance between resources and demands, might be seen as embodying the immortal principle of Charles Dickens' Mr Micawber, namely: 'Annual income twenty pounds, annual expenditure nineteen nineteen six, result happiness. Annual income twenty pounds, annual expenditure twenty pounds ought and six, result misery.'

If we are parents (from *parere*, to give birth), our primary role is to advance the interests of those beings we have brought forth, that is, our family. When professionals are responsive to our resource needs, they can help in the building up of those resources both within and beyond the family, along with our personal growth (our internal resources). All

27

three categories of resources mentioned by Gowen may be enhanced. In brief, as parents, we may acquire from our contact with professionals: supportive figures to help us in our task, and further information relevant to family matters. Members of the extended family – our mothers, our grandmothers – used to offer these resources. Today, in a mobile society, they are frequently far away, or our values have changed and we find their advice unsympathetic (Berger, 1988). We need other supporters. The logical people to look to are the professionals who are also dealing with our children from a broader, less intense perspective than our own (Katz, 1980).

If we are professionals (from *profiteri*, to declare publicly), our primary role is to profess a body of important knowledge, to advance our understandings and skills in our field. As members of the helping professions (in this book teachers and child care personnel), we may add to the resources we need for this task by acquiring more information from and about the people we are attempting to help (children and their families), and by acquiring more supportive relationships with them. To enhance our resources, the logical people to look to are the parents of the children, who are dealing with them from a closer, more intense perspective than our own (Katz, 1980).

Thus parents and helping professionals not only need one another but also have useful differences in their approaches which can complement the value each has for the young child and which can enrich their own and one another's respective repertoires.

PARENT AND PROFESSIONAL ROLES

This discussion concerns not only the needs of parents and professionals but also the roles (functions) that parents and professionals perform in relation to one another. Professionals (e.g. Petit, 1980) have often viewed parents' roles in education as hierarchical, ranging from more passive at the bottom of the hierarchy to more active at the top. One professional, however, who has seen all parental roles as important and declined to place them in ascending or descending order, is Ira Gordon, who framed a model of parental roles as a wheel, with each role a spoke (Figure 2.6). According to Gordon and his associates (1979), only if some parents play each of the roles, that is, if all the spokes are strong, will the wheel of parent–professional (e.g. home–school) collaboration turn.

In this model, Gordon sees parents (not in any order) as:

- *Learners* of new skills and understandings, especially about children's development and learning.
- *Teachers* of their own child.
- *Classroom volunteers*, assisting other children.

Figure 2.6 Parent roles in parent involvement
Source: Gordon *et al.*, 1979

- *Paraprofessionals* (teacher aides), including in their function the inter-
  pretation of community culture to professionals.
- *Audience*: informed consumers on community matters.
- *Decision makers* on policy and management.

Students with whom I have worked have found it useful in expanding
their perspectives on parent roles (Henry, 1984) to broaden three of
Gordon's six roles, and to add a seventh. These amendments have
attempted to retain the fundamental meaning of Gordon's model, while
making it more universally applicable (Figure 2.7).

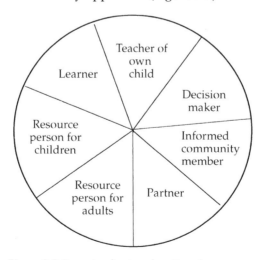

Figure 2.7 Parent roles in educational programs

29

The amended model retains Gordon's roles of parents as *learners, teachers* of own child and *decision makers*. In this model, parents are:

- *Learners about child development.* Many parents are eager for the support and information that a sensitive professional can help to provide: for example, through day-to-day conversation, observations in centre/school, library borrowings, membership of discussion groups.
- *Teachers of own child.* Whether they are aware of it or not, all parents are contributors to their children's development. They need support from professionals to begin (or continue) seeing themselves as vitally important to that development.
- *Decision makers.* Parents who are supported by professionals (through informal consultation and on management committees) in using their decision-making capacity strengthen their sense of being, in the phraseology of de Charms *et al.* (1965), origins rather than pawns. Parents are likely to transmit their own sense of self-direction and competence to their children (Schaefer, 1987).

The amended model substitutes:

- *Informed community members* (instead of audience). The centre or school is for children but it can also be a community centre, where parents and professionals can share community information (e.g. visiting medical care, library hours, local exhibitions). Parental choices become more informed, enhancing parents as citizens.
- *Resource persons for children* (instead of classroom volunteers). Parents may broaden their support of professionals so that other children besides their own benefit. Parents may raise funds for equipment, take part in working bees, provide materials, help in classrooms.
- *Resource persons for adults* (instead of paraprofessionals). Parents, who know their children more intimately than anyone else, have a store of information and insights on which professionals are wise to draw. Through such a sharing of ideas, professionals and other parents may modify their own practice.
- *Partners* (or colleagues), a relational role, linking parents and professionals, without which none of the other roles will occur.

Amending Gordon's model in this way brings out the capacity of parents and professionals to enrich one another's roles by meeting one another's needs for information and support. This capacity has received too little emphasis. A host of writers (e.g. Berger, 1995) have written about the value to children of, as Bronfenbrenner (1974: 51) puts it, 'bringing the two halves of the child's world together'. Very few have discussed the value for parents, professionals and children of changing (hopefully enriching) those two halves of the child's world by having them meet and interact with each other.

I believe this omission has occurred because writers about parent–professional relationships have fixed their sights primarily on the child as the fundamental beneficiary. This book, however, is about enhancing all the links, including those between parents and professionals, not only their reciprocal links with the child. Only if parents and professionals are recognised as equal players and if the relationships between them are examined in some detail will the child, in the end, be best served.

PROFESSIONAL–PARENT INTERACTION

Writing of the need for professional–parent interaction in the field of child health, Schaefer (1982) has proposed a model (Figure 2.8) which would lead to optimal outcomes for the child. In this model (to whose outcome, of child health and development, Education has been added for our purposes), Schaefer (1982) points out:

> parent and family characteristics are related both to parental care of the child and to parent–professional interactions. Similarly professional and institutional characterstics are related to professional care of the child and to parent-professional interaction. Both parent and professional care of the child have direct effects upon child health and development, but the model emphasizes that parents and professionals also have indirect effects upon the child through their interaction with one another.
>
> (Schaefer, 1982: 3)

In commenting further on his model, Schaefer notes that the complementary and mutually reinforcing processes emphasised in the model frequently do not take place. Parents' questions are often ignored and unanswered and many parents report that they have not discussed their concerns with professionals. He suggests that professionals often

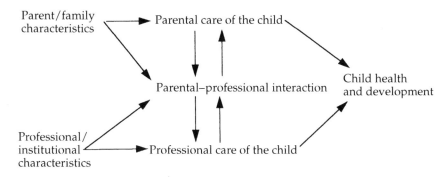

Figure 2.8 A model for parent and professional care and interaction
Source: Schaefer, 1982

emphasise delivery of services to the isolated child rather than attempting to strengthen and support the most powerful and pervasive force operating on the child's behalf – family care. Nevertheless, Schaefer sees the model as a useful representation of how beneficial change for children can and should take place.

Note that in Schaefer's model the recipient of change is the child. Parents and professionals are change agents, both directly and indirectly, but, in this model, they do not change themselves. What is required, to do justice to the reality of their interaction, is a modification of the model as in Figure 2.9. Adding arrows pointing back to the parent and the professional indicates the effects that interaction can have, not merely on parent or professional care of the child at a particular time, but also on the characteristics of the parents and professionals themselves.

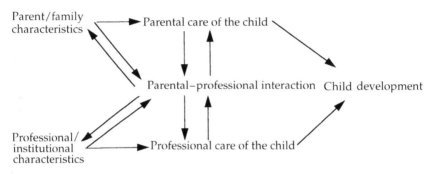

Figure 2.9 A model for parent and professional care and interaction: modification 1
Source: adapted from Schaefer, 1982

SUMMARY

This chapter has focused on the key needs of young children: trust, autonomy and initiative. While Erikson (1950) has proposed that these challenges emerge in sequence, to be met over the first five or so years, evidence has been presented here that all are needs of children from early babyhood on. Parents can meet them, primarily through the mechanism of establishing secure attachments, but there has long been evidence that others too can help to meet very young children's needs, and that building up secure attachments to nonparental caregivers does not disrupt – but may enhance – the attachments already established with parents.

To meet the needs of young children, and indeed their own ongoing needs for trust, autonomy and initiative, adults require resources from other adults. In the case of the parents and professionals who share the fostering of young children's development, there is a particular responsibility to add to one another's resources of information and support. The changes that parents and professionals can thus bring about in one another may be long term, and they may have long term effects on young children.

In the next chapter, we take an odyssey in company with some parents, professionals and children, to examine what some of these changes are.

3

IN SEARCH OF A MODEL

In the past twenty-five years I have worked first with young children and professionals as a parent, second as a professional with children and their parents, and third as a professional teaching other professionals.

In this chapter, a brief review of a project from each of these three stages will help to trace progress towards a model encapsulating more productive ways (that is, ways which meet rather than violate the needs discussed in the last chapter) in which professionals and families can work together so as to promote their mutual interests and the interests of young children.

PROJECT 1: FOCUS ON CHILDREN, PROFESSIONALS AND PARENTS

Years ago, when my children were small and going to the local primary school, another mother and I had a chat about the 'Arts and Crafts' program. We had been to the school to see the head teacher and had found, as I noted at the time (Henry, 1969), a milling shoal of fifty boys:

heaving and pulsating round the teacher while he struggled to interest, control and supervise them. He surfaced and came towards us.

'How on earth does any woodwork get done with a class this size?'

'It's a struggle.' He grinned ruefully. 'We've only got one complete set of tools, and a few odds and ends. A fair bit of time gets wasted.'

(Henry, 1969: 49)

In this three-teacher school, on Tuesday afternoons, one teacher took the under-sevens in singing, another taught sewing – aprons with lace borders – to the older girls, and the head teacher ran a woodwork class for the older boys. In these crowded, under-equipped groups, there was, as our head teacher said, 'a fair bit of time wasted'.

We mothers went home and asked each other how we could help.

34

From our cogitations and consultations, first with the head teacher, then with other parents at the school, emerged a group of voluntary craft leaders, mothers with some training and a little time to spare. 'Marvellous idea,' said the head teacher, as he heard of the talent that had been unearthed: a weaver, two potters, tapestry experts, puppeteers, a fine arts lecturer, painters, a writer, a singer, and lay helpers who volunteered as odd jobbers. A lively session with the Parents and Citizens' Association resulted in workable compromises over funding.

Children were also consulted. Every family received a letter explaining the project, setting out the available groups and asking for the children's preferences. Each child was offered a change of group at the end of the term, but a measure of the project's success was that most children chose to stay with their original group. Group leaders stayed too. With a few replacements, these women, for six delightful years, worked with the teachers and small groups of eight and ten children so that (as a report on the project noted):

On Tuesday afternoons the school took legs.

Some members of the writing group might be seen strolling among the other groups, reporting on what they saw for the magazine they were compiling. One Grade Sixer wrote:

All the children were painting,
The patterns they painted were lovely.
One little girl felt like fainting,
Mrs Underhill was motherly.
The noise coming from the painting
group was laughing and sighing.
Mrs Roe was helping some children
in their painting, lovingly.

Others had adjourned to the library to try out the recorder on which they would tape the plays they had written for the puppet group – 'Grandma's Suspicion' and 'The Pharaoh's Reward' . . . [This play] had been directly inspired by the stories and pictures of ancient Egypt and Persia brought along by the mother whose field was the History of Art. Sitting on the grass at her feet while she spun the globe and held up pictures of the past, her group were a goggle-eyed, updated version of The Boyhood of Raleigh.

One of the puppeteers might be seen flying up to the painting group to find out if the backdrops were ready yet, and colliding with one of the woodwork boys coming to check on the dimensions of the puppet stage which his group was making. The woodworkers were also making a series of little stools, for which the weavers were hard at work on the seats. Under a tree, an idyllic group of tapestry-stitchers were nodding and chatting over their needles like dear old grannies and gaffers in the sun. In another corner stood a spreading poinciana tree, and thereby hung several tails – of string, wire and kaleidoscopic shapes, all suspended from the branches: mobiles that the paper-folding group were experimenting with as decor for the hall. Shouts of joy or despair would go up from the potters as the secrets of the kiln were revealed – pots and bowls done to a fine turn, but, alas, a jug whose handle had fallen off and the sad pieces of a frog who had met the same fate as La Fontaine's: he had blown up and burst. 'Too many fruit boxes too fast,' our potting mother would pronounce. 'Have to heat it slower next time.'

(Henry, 1969: 52)

In the six years that this project persisted, what did we all get out of it?

First the children. In the last chapter, children's early needs were discussed: needs for trust, autonomy and initiative, or, put another way, for confidence in the familiar (trust), allied, as children grow, with a drive (autonomy) to carry out the new and unfamiliar (initiative). It seems that the Tuesday groups gave the children many chances to fulfil these needs, needs now brought together in what Erikson (1950) has called the school-age challenge of industry versus inferiority.

In terms of the need for trust, look at the change in the format of the clientele. Fifty boys in a milling shoal are unable to establish any sense of familiarity or predictability in their dealings with a teacher; eight to ten children can establish a relationship of trust. The Grade 6 writer of the poem about the painting group confirmed the children's feelings when he described one leader as motherly, the other as helping, lovingly.

A sense of children's autonomy, their power to affect their environment, imbues the description of the project. Instead of 'a fair bit of time getting wasted', there was an immense amount of work getting done. At the beginning of the project, the teachers made it clear that the set syllabus of woodwork and sewing must still be carried out, so children alternated, week and week about, their stints in these classes with their voluntary groups. Despite thus spending only half as much time as previously on their tea-pot stands or lace-bordered aprons, they completed their work, and, as well, put together what the delighted Education Department Inspector called 'one of the best displays of children's arts and crafts I've ever seen'. When we (adults or children) feel we are having an effect, remarkable effects can occur.

So children made paintings that caused 'the noise coming from the painting group [to be] laughing and sighing', they wrote plays about pharaohs, created origami kaleidoscopes and were on fire with their firings. They were in touch with people who inspired their initiative.

These people were both the teachers and the parents. Looking back at the project twenty-five years later, it is regrettable that the written record (Henry, 1969), concerned with the changes that teacher–parent interaction had sparked in the children, was mostly silent about the changes taking place in the adults themselves. For they too were developing.

A major change in the teachers was that of increased flexibility. At the beginning of the project, two requirements were sacrosanct. One was the stipulation about children completing their compulsory arts and crafts syllabus, the other was an insistence that, in order to safeguard 'Education Department property', the voluntary groups must operate not in classrooms but in the grounds or in spaces under the high-set school building. In the interests of the project, parents readily acceded to both requirements, and as time went on, the sense of trust and mutual respect growing between the two sets of adults was such that the supposedly immovable foundations of the project's operation began to stretch and give:

> The group activities have turned out to be of so high a standard that official blessing has been given, and the compulsory provisions about woodwork and sewing largely waived. So the woodwork group, now of manageable size, still under the guidance of the head teacher, becomes one among all the other groups . . .
>
> So relaxed has the whole atmosphere become on Tuesday afternoons that no longer are groups banished to the four winds . . . Escorting a visitor on a tour of the school the other day, I found the head teacher on his hands and knees puddling grout for a mosaic table his boys were making; he rose with a grin, excused himself for not being able to shake our hands with his sticky ones, and directed us to a classroom where a lively charcoal sketching class was in full swing.
>
> (Henry, 1969: 55)

Flexibility, too, was the watchword in the changes that took place in the participating parents. They too found new trust and respect in their dealings with the teachers, each group of adults drawing needed information and, especially, support from the other. As well, parents broadened their horizons as contacts with the community were struck up. A 'real' local potter joined the scheme, a Little Theatre company in the city donated a model theatre and advice to the marionette group, other schools called on parents' expertise in establishing vacation schools and festivals. Over time, some of the mothers used the groups as launching pads to new careers, propelled by the confidence they had acquired. Perhaps just as satisfying, those that stayed found their creativity burgeoning from their contact with their own children:

> The children's painting groups have spilled over into a *mothers'* painting group, meeting once a week and inspired by the excitement

the mothers found in seeing the children's experiments. 'It's ten years since I painted seriously, but I got infected by those kids!'

(Henry, 1969: 55)

Looking back at the Tuesday groups, it is clear that Schaefer's (1982) model, Figure 2.8, accurately portrayed the fact that while teachers can affect children, and parents can affect children, the interaction between parents and teachers can also powerfully affect children. The arrows added in Figure 2.9 were important, too, in representing another area of reality evident in the Tuesday groups. This was the area where teachers and parents influenced one another.

The areas where particular influences are evident in the Tuesday groups are portrayed in Figure 3.1. The key indicates important shading features in subsequent modifications of Schaefer (1982). Definition (shading) is given to the arrows leading directly from parents and professionals to children. Thus, from the description of the project we know that the children were able to meet their needs for trust, for autonomy and for initiative, and that from this meeting came a flowering of productivity. Further, we know something of what the teachers and the parents actually did to help this occur. We have seen the potting mother cheering on disconsolate potters, and a pupil has told us that Mrs Underhill was motherly and that Mrs Roe helped lovingly. We have

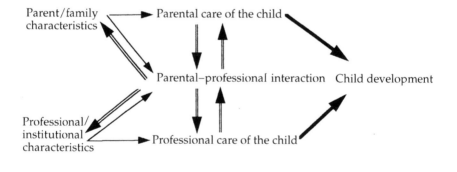

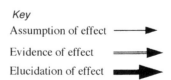

Key

Assumption of effect ⟶

Evidence of effect ⟹

Elucidation of effect ➡

Figure 3.1 A model for parent and professional care and interaction: modification 2
Source: adapted from Schaefer, 1982

noted that the head teacher, no longer caught in a struggle 'to interest, control and supervise' fifty boys, was instead happily working on his hands and knees with a small group of them.

But if one tried to describe the Tuesday groups' adult–adult processes in terms of Schaefer's model, one would not be much the wiser. The arrows linking parents and teachers remain shadowy, they have very little content. What behaviours do they include? We know that adult flexibility was a watchword, but we should like to know more than that.

PROJECT 2: FOCUS ON PARENTS AND CHILDREN

The period I spent as a primary school teacher did little to elucidate the connections between Schaefer's parent/professional arrows, since parent participation played little part in that teaching situation. It was not until I worked in two early intervention programs with Aboriginal families that the arrows began, for me, to gain some definition. The dimensions of behaviour embodied in one of these arrows, the one which in Schaefer's (1982) model, Figure 2.8, leads from parent care to child status, was specifically investigated in one of the programs (Henry, 1981). Some attention, too, was paid to an explication of the central portion of the model, that concerned with parent–professional interaction. This program is worth revisiting as part of the odyssey towards a comprehensive model.

In *Speaking Free*, an Aboriginal student newspaper of the 1970s, and later in the journal *The Aboriginal Child at School*, Karen Martin, a seventeen-year old mother in the program, gives an enthusiastic, thoughtful summary of the program (Martin, 1979):

> I am one of a group of young Inala mothers who are involved in a playgroup in which we teach and learn with our children through their stages of growth.
>
> Each Thursday we are visited by Margaret Henry and Jeannie Barney. They offer me advice concerning different and new methods of play or sometimes we exchange methods of play and communication.
>
> The play involved doesn't require a set time or any expensive toys. Cotton reels, plastic containers, etc. can provide hours of fun. However, we are fortunate enough to have a toy and book library from which our kids can select a toy or book for the week.
>
> Once a month we all meet at the Inala Family Education Centre and there we mothers have the chance to talk, and our children to play. In general, we discuss and experiment with suggestions and ideas, and we get the chance to show off our creativity in the making of an item of play for our sons and daughters.

The advantages of such a program are many. We are not only teaching our children but we're learning with them and they shall have some form of preparation for kindergarten. But for me, there is nothing more fulfilling than to see my son repeat something I've shown him, and enjoy doing it.

(Martin, 1979)

This program was based on an earlier Aboriginal parent program (Watts and Henry, 1978) which grew out of the belief that Aboriginal families, in the city as elsewhere in Australia, had been undersold by the education system, so that Aboriginal parents had been robbed of the central and respected role in their children's upbringing that they held in traditional communities. Wolfendale (1983: 15) was later to characterise the patronising view that many professionals have held of parents (all parents, not only Aboriginal ones) as the 'client approach':

- Parents are dependent on experts' opinions.
- Parents are passive in receipt of services.
- Parents are apparently in need of redirection.
- Parents are peripheral to decision-making.
- Parents are perceived as 'inadequate', 'deficient'.

Yet it had long been recognised by writers such as Bronfenbrenner (1969) that:

it is the parents and other close companions of the child who are the primary determiners not only of what the child learns but of what he fails to learn.

It follows that any appreciable, enduring improvement in the child's development can be effected only through an appreciable, enduring change in the behaviour of the persons intimately associated with the child on a day-to-day basis.

(Bronfenbrenner, 1969: 10)

The question was: how might the kinds of changes envisaged by Bronfenbrenner be achieved?

The director of the Aboriginal parent program (Watts and Henry, 1978) on which the Inala program was based, Professor B. H. Watts, believed that change in parents' behaviour and children's development could occur through what Wolfendale (1983: 15) would later call the 'partnership' approach:

- Parents are active and central in decision making and its implementation.
- Parents are perceived as having equal strengths and equivalent expertise.

40

- Parents are able to contribute to as well as receive services (reciprocity).
- Parents share responsibility, thus they and professionals are mutually accountable.

In the earlier program (Watts and Henry, 1978) urban Aboriginal mothers were encouraged to become more effective educators of their four and five-year old children. In the later program, the focus was on still younger Aboriginal infants and their mothers, based on the growing evidence of the importance for development of the first few years (Staines, 1974; White, 1975). The program operated from the Inala Family Education Centre, in a Brisbane suburb with a high Aboriginal population, where Education Department professionals shared the 'partnership' approach. The participants, as Karen Martin notes in her article, were infants and their young mothers, several of whom had known at school the person who was to be the key 'change agent' in the program. This was Jeannie Barney, a parent participant in the earlier Watts and Henry program, now a teacher aide at Inala and a respected local sports coach. It was with Jeannie that I, as consultant to the program, worked closely throughout the year and to Jeannie that I handed over the program. For over fifteen years it has continued, still operated by members of the Aboriginal and Islander community.

During the year that we worked together, Jeannie's teacher aide job continued part-time; thus the program was also part-time for her, necessitating a small case-load of participants. We had planned just six, but in fact eight young mothers took part, several known to Jeannie from school and others arriving by word of mouth. On our initial visit to each mother, we explained that:

> the Family Education Centre was setting up the program because a number of young mothers had expressed interest in finding out more about the sorts of things babies do as they develop and the sorts of things mothers and families can do to help them. We indicated that we believed parents were the most important teachers of their children, above all when they were babies, and it was clear from the thoughtful expressions of the listeners that this was a novel and stimulating thought. Without exception the teenage mothers said they would like to participate.
>
> (Henry, 1980: 12)

We explained the components of the program (visits at home, group meetings, the library), the plan for Jeannie to take over more and more of the visits, and the need, 'if the program were really to be of use to them (and perhaps later to other mothers), to see how it was working as time went on' (Henry, 1980: 12). So we would assess, through interviews and

41

unstructured home observations to which the mothers readily agreed, how well the program was carrying out its basic aim: to enhance the mothers' understanding of, responsiveness to and enjoyment of their children. Thus evaluation, carried out at the beginning and the end of a year, would attempt to clarify at least one arrow in Schaefer's (1982) model (as we saw in Figure 2.8), that leading from parents to child outcomes.

Precisely what behaviours, then, were we looking at, in these interviews and observations, as the young mothers, in the words of Karen Martin (1979), sought to 'teach and learn with [their] children through their different stages of growth?' In order to answer this question I found myself constructing a model about the influences that parents have on their children (Henry, 1988). It turned out to be a useful model with a wide reach, worth spending a little time on before we see what answers it led to about the young mothers and their babies and toddlers at Inala.

PARENTS AND CHILDREN: DIMENSIONS OF PARENTAL BEHAVIOUR

Some years before the Inala program began, US researcher Robert Hess published two articles which reviewed studies up to that time which had linked parents' behaviour with children's competence. The first of these articles (Hess, 1969) looked at the relationship of parental behaviours to young children's school achievement. In the second, Hess (1971) broadened his focus to examine parental links not only with children's intellectual accomplishment but also with their personal and social development. The findings for parents remained the same. Hess's reviews suggested that parental behaviour which encourages children to be socially and emotionally competent is good for them intellectually as well.

The key facilitative parental (or, in keeping with the times, maternal) behaviours that Hess (1969) extracted from the research of the time were (in the order presented by Hess): encouragement of high achievement, maximisation of verbal interaction, engagement with and attentiveness to the child, maternal teaching behaviour, diffuse intellectual stimulation, warm affective relationship with the child, feelings of high regard for child and self, encouragement of independence and self-reliance, quality of disciplinary rules, and use of conceptual rather than arbitrary regulatory strategies.

Ira Gordon (1972), another researcher concerned with parental behaviour, published a review along very similar lines, and in subsequent years further empirical studies (see Amato, 1987, Table 3.1) have continued to focus on the same parental behaviours as being important in encouraging children's development and learning.

At the time when the Watts and Henry (1978) Aboriginal parents program was being devised, these were the parental behaviours which served as a backdrop for the framing of activities with the mothers and children in the program. By the time the Inala program was being developed, I had begun to see the behaviours assembled by Hess (1971) as providing not only a backdrop for activities (that is, a curriculum) but also an appropriate framework for evaluating the program's effectiveness.

Why appropriate? Because these variables, it became increasingly clear to me, were not merely facilitative parent–child interactional behaviours which studies had demonstrated helped children's development. They were behaviours that were also fascinatingly aligned with the dimensions that researchers in another whole literature were looking at, the literature of general interpersonal interaction. Researchers in this field had long recognised two major dimensions within which one might categorise human behaviour. These were:

Dimension 1 – behaviour expressing warmth or solidarity;

Dimension 2 – behaviour expressing status or power.

Bales (1950), for example, classified student behaviour into categories of socio-emotional support versus antagonism (Dimension 1), and giving guidance versus asking for help (Dimension 2). La Forge and Suczek (1955) and Triandis (1964) respectively used the terms love/hate and associative/dissociative for Dimension 1, and dominance/submission and superordinate/subordinate for Dimension 2. Later Maccoby and Martin (1983) would similarly postulate accepting/rejecting for the first dimension and demanding/undemanding for the second.

How do the Hess variables listed above relate to these dimensions of solidarity and power? Several of them fit neatly. Thus:

Dimension 1
- Warm affective relationship with child.
- Feelings of high regard for child.
- Engagement with and attentiveness to child.

Dimension 2
- Quality of disciplinary rules.
- Conceptual rather than arbitrary regulatory strategies.
- Encouragement of independence.

Four of Hess's key parental behaviours, however, do not fit within these dimensions. These are: encouragement of achievement, teaching behaviour, maximisation of verbal interaction, and diffuse intellectual stimulation.

One can see that these four behaviours are qualitatively different from the others. The six behaviours which we have allotted to Dimensions 1 and 2 are concerned, as are their dimensions, with *the ways* in which

43

parents act towards children, in terms of warmth or control. But the remaining four behaviours are about *content*. They are not about *how* parents interact but about *what* they actually *do* in interaction. Parents keep children on track in tasks, they talk with children and share information, they draw resources to children's notice.

Thus the pot-pourri of Hess variables culled from life may be seen to form themselves into three dimensions, two concerned with the 'how' of parent practice, one with the 'what'. In Table 3.1, I have set out a model of these three dimensions, aligned with the relevant behaviours from

Table 3.1 Facilitative parental behaviours associated with caregiving dimensions

Dimension	Interactional variables	
	From Hess (1971)	*From Amato (1987)*
RESPONSIVENESS	Warm affective relationship with child	Have an emotionally warm and supportive relationship with children
	Demonstration of high regard for child	Reward children for competent behaviour
	Engagement with and attentiveness to child	Participate in joint activities with children
CONTROL	Consistency of regulatory strategies	Use authoritative rather than authoritarian or permissive styles of parenting
	Explanatory rather than arbitrary regulatory strategies	Point out the consequences of behaviour to children; avoid the use of harsh physical punishment
	Encouragement of independence	Encourage independence in children
INVOLVEMENT	Encouragement of achievement	Hold high educational expectations and aspirations for children; encourage children to do well
	Maximisation of verbal interaction	Frequently engage children in conversation
	Parental teaching behaviour	Provide assistance with school work
	Diffuse intellectual stimulation	Encourage children to explore and manipulate their environments

Presage variables from Hess, 1971; Gordon, 1972

Parental self-esteem

Parental sense of control

Hess (1971). Below these appear two major parent characteristics found by Gordon (1972) and his associates to be related to parental functioning: parents' sense of self esteem, and parents' sense of internal control (or sense of being able to affect the things that happen in one's life). Gordon called these two parental characteristics presage variables, since they are not interactional behaviours but rather characteristics which presage or foreshadow the ability of parents to encourage their children's development. Alongside Hess's list of facilitative behaviours for very young children are the findings assembled years later by Amato (1987), in a further review of what parents do to help their school-age children. The ongoing correspondences are illuminating.

Looking at Table 3.1, readers will see that I have moved away from the classical terminology of 'warmth' or 'solidarity' and 'power' or 'status' and have called these two parental dimensions 'responsiveness' and 'control'. For the third dimension I suggest 'involvement'. This appears to be a suitable portmanteau within which to pack the four behaviours identified by Hess which summarise the things parents do in company with their children that broaden their horizons. 'Control' (or management or guidance) is what the Hess behaviours included under the second dimension are about – ways in which parents try to get their children to behave or not to behave and, importantly, how they encourage children to learn to control their own behaviour.

Replacing a 'warmth' dimension with one of 'responsiveness' allows us to include in this dimension, along with warmth and regard, engagement/attentiveness to the cues of the child 'as a separate, active and autonomous person, whose wishes and activities have a validity of their own' (Ainsworth and Bell, 1974: 1). Substituting 'responsiveness' for 'warmth' allows the differentiation of facilitative from interfering or indulgent adult practice. In addition, a dimension of 'responsiveness' builds into the model the flexibility to encompass the changes in parental control and involvement that occur over time with children's increasing age (Bronfenbrenner, 1989; Maccoby, 1980).

Figure 3.2 presents a visual impression of what such a three dimensional model of parental behaviour might look like (Henry, 1988). On the basis of the model set out in Figure 3.2, it is possible (Henry, 1988) to differentiate a variety of parental behaviours, as indicated in Table 3.2.

The parental behaviours found by Hess (1971) to be significant for children's development (which we saw in Table 3.1) may be integrated within a responsiveness/control/involvement model of parent behaviour as indicated in Table 3.3.

In the schema proposed in Table 3.3, both the involvement and the control or management dimensions are shot through and interpenetrated by the responsiveness dimension, with implications for children's development. For example, rules may be enforced with clarity and

45

Responsiveness

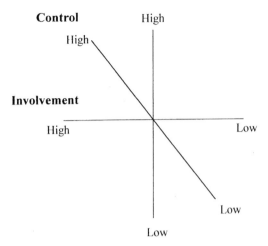

Figure 3.2 Responsiveness/control/involvement model of parent behaviour
Source: Henry, 1988

consistency in either a responsive (authoritative) or non-responsive (authoritarian) way (Baumrind, 1971). Again, verbal interaction may be responsively or non-responsively maximised, as in a parental teaching task described by Monrad (1978). In this task, children had to place cards with verbal help from their mothers. The children whose mothers talked a great deal to them as they carried out their placements did not perform as well as the children whose mothers 'provide[d] appropriate feedback after the children's card placements' (p.90). As Donovan and Leavitt (1978) put it in the context of early parent–infant interaction:

Table 3.2 Patterns of parental behaviour differentiated by a responsiveness/involvement/control model

Parental behaviour	*Dimensions*		
	Responsiveness	*Involvement*	*Control*
Developmental	High	High	High
Overprotective or authoritarian, punitive	Low	High	High
Rejecting, abusive	Low	Low	High
Neglecting, ignoring	Low	Low	Low
Indulgent, permissive	High	Low	Low

Source: Henry, 1988

Table 3.3 Integration of parental variables significant for child development within a responsiveness/control/involvement model of parent behaviour

Responsiveness v. non-responsiveness	*Firm v. lax control*	*Parental involvement v. no involvement*
Warm affective relationship with child	Encouragement of independence	Encouragement of achievement
High regard for child	Consistency of regulatory strategies	Maximisation of verbal interaction
Engagement with and attentiveness to child	Explanatory regulatory strategies	Parental teaching behaviour
		Diffuse intellectual stimulation

Source: Henry, 1988

> The significance of responsiveness is underlined in our data by the finding that quantity of maternal stimulation was not as important as quality of stimulation in its relationship to infant development. How the mother distributed her signals was more important than the actual number of signals.
>
> (Donovan and Leavitt 1978: 1253)

What is the evidence that the proposed three dimensions, responsiveness, control and involvement, really reflect the range of parents' behaviour towards their children? We may find such evidence in a variety of other formulations of parent–child interaction. Here are three.

In an assessment of parental influence on pre-schoolers' competence, White *et al.* (1979) summarised three functions of parents that they saw as essential to 'well developing children'. These functions are, first, the parent as consultant to the child's needs, second, the parent as controller of the child's conduct, and third, the parent as designer of the child's world. 'Consultant to the child's needs' expresses well the solidarity that resides in responsiveness to cues; the relationship of 'controller of the child's conduct' to the control dimension hardly needs further comment; and 'designer of the child's world' brings out the creative involvement of parents as they take the child further, in an active engagement with the environment.

A second piece of evidence comes from one of the most validated US predictors of children's intelligence, the Home Observation for Measurement of the Environment (HOME) (Caldwell and Bradley, 1978) which uses a checklist to gather information about children's lives at home with their parents. In the pre-school version of the checklist, the sub-scales are as follows (Bradley *et al.*, 1988):

1 Pride, affection and warmth.
2 Avoidance of physical punishment.

3 Language stimulation.
4 Stimulation of academic behaviour.
5 Stimulation through toys, games and reading material.
6 Modelling and encouragement of social maturity.
7 Variety in daily stimulation.
8 Physical environment: safe, clean, and conducive to development.

While this schedule is in no way concerned with the three dimensions being proposed here, they are strikingly obvious in the headings. Sub-scale 1 relates to the responsiveness dimension, sub-scales 2 and 6 relate to the control dimension, and sub-scales 3, 4, 5, 7 and 8 relate to the dimension of parental involvement in stimulating activity.

Let a final piece of substantiation of the relevance of these dimensions come from children themselves. In a study by Goodnow and Burns (1985) of the views of over 2,000 Australian children on aspects of their home and school lives, one of the questions asked of the children was: 'What makes a good parent?' While Goodnow and Burns have used a different analytical schema, the children themselves clearly bring out the value of having parents who attend to their special cues, who use non-arbitrary guidance, and who are involved with them in stimulating ways. Here are examples from each dimension:

Responsiveness

'They care for me because I'm the only one in the world like me.'
'I go to my mum; my dad never listens.'
'They cook the things you like.'

Control

'If they tell you off for something and they don't let you go because it's only for your own safety, you might get hurt or something. I still like them.'
'[They] listen to both sides.'

Involvement

'I like going out in our boat with them because they teach you new things and if you're wondering what island that is and it's the first time you've seen it and you want to know – well, the next time you go around it you say, "Oh, that's the island that my mum and dad told me about."'

(Goodnow and Burns, 1985: 15, 18, 22, 21, 22, 11)

Before leaving this analysis of a three dimensional model of facilitative parental behaviour, it is important to clarify just what facilitative parental behaviour is. It is behaviour by parents that encourages children's development, makes it more likely that children will reach their potential. It is not behaviour that makes this inevitable. As I wrote some years ago:

> parents can influence their children's development, but they cannot inevitably determine it. Parents need not feel, and should not be made to feel, totally responsible for how their children turn out. Parent-child interactions are dependent in part on the child's own attributes (Bell, 1974) and on a host of other environmental variables, including socio-economic and cultural factors.
>
> (Henry, 1988: 9)

Both Bronfenbrenner's (1989) model (Figure 1.1) and Gowen's (1979) model (Figure 2.5) support this statement by including a variety of influences on young children besides parental influences. What the list assembled from Hess, Gordon and Amato in Table 3.1 suggests is that certain parental behaviours increase the probabilities of children's competence being enhanced.

Postscript to Inala

After a year at Inala during which Jeannie and I enjoyed ourselves as we worked with families – having fun with library books and toys, making some of our own at group meetings, building always on what parents, fathers, grandmas were *already* doing that encouraged children's interest in their world – we repeated the interviews that had been carried out with the young mothers at the beginning of the year. Similarly an observer made a second audiotaped record of parent–child household doings, as she had done at the start of the year.

In a comparison of the beginning-of-year and end-of-year parent–child interactions of the eight mothers within the dimensions of responsiveness, control and involvement, significant increases were either observed or reported in the following areas (Henry, 1986):

Responsiveness
- Instances of enjoyment of children (reported).
- Instances of mutual activity (reported).
- Proportion of parents' responsive talk (observed).
- Duration of interactional episodes (observed).

Control
- Proportion of child-initiated interactions (observed).
- Encouragement of children's self-reliance (observed).

Involvement
- Instances of talking to children (observed).
- Instances of looking at books with children (reported).
- Use of household resources for play (reported).

What did these results mean? For the families, they were a short-hand for toddlers and two-year olds getting on well with their lives, children having increased input into family doings, parents sharing more time and round-the-house resources with them. For Karen Martin, for example, it meant that there was 'nothing more fulfilling than to see my son repeat something I've shown him, and enjoy doing it' (Martin, 1979).

In telling us something about the program or about professional–parent relationships, however, the findings meant very little. One reason was the small sample size. Another was the absence of a control group. As the program report (Henry, 1980) noted of the 'increased instances of talking to children' (a notation whose principle applied across the findings):

> To what extent is this likely to be due to normal development, quite irrespective of the program? Because children are becoming verbal at about the age of eighteen months, and increasingly so thereafter . . .
> we should expect the amount of talking between the mothers and the children to increase as a matter of course. In the absence of a control group it is impossible to disentangle normal developmental from program effects.
>
> (Henry, 1980: 44)

In relation to Schaefer's (1982) model, the Aboriginal parent program at Inala provided evidence that parent influences on children's development could be categorised in terms of Hess's (1971) behaviours, within a responsiveness/control/involvement framework. It showed that looking at behaviour in this way allowed some further definition, some solidification of the arrow in Schaefer's model leading from parent care to child outcomes (Figure 3.3).

The program also provided tantalizing possibilities (no more) that parent–professional interaction (the central portion of Schaefer's model) had had at least a short-term effect on parent–child interaction. But to make any kind of definitive statement in this area absolutely required the opportunity to work with larger numbers and a control group.

PROJECT 3: FOCUS ON PROFESSIONALS AND CHILDREN

An opportunity for larger numbers and a control group occurred for me when, a few years later, I was working in a project, not with parents and

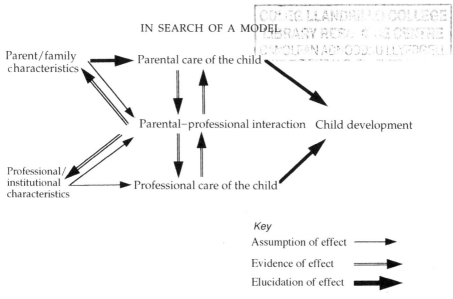

Figure 3.3 A model for parent and professional care and interaction:
modification 3
Source: adapted from Schaefer, 1982

their young children this time, but with professionals, providers of family day care.

The family day care project came about because, as I now worked at an institution where early childhood personnel (teachers and careproviders) received their tertiary education, I was in contact with a variety of child care workers, some of whom were family day care providers. Informal discussions with members of the Brisbane family day care community had confirmed that there was a perceived need for help to sustain care providers in their task. Family day care coordinators and providers alike suggested that providers needed:

1 To understand better the behaviour that young children display.
2 To find solutions to some discipline problems.
3 To add to their repertoire of things to do at home with young children.

Particularly interesting to me was the relationship of these recurrent issues to the three dimensional model of parental behaviour discussed in the last section. This model, confirmed in the actual behaviours of young Aboriginal mothers and their toddlers described in the program report (Henry, 1980), was now again being reflected in the needs expressed by family day care providers. How to account for mystifying shifts in children's behaviour, how to deal with exasperating fighting or

51

recalcitrance in toddlers, how to keep children more happily occupied round the house – all these were seen as areas of need by parents and family day care providers alike.

Karen Martin's overview (on p. 9) of the Aboriginal parent program indicated that that program had helped to meet her needs in relation to her toddler as it responded to these needs with information and support, key resources required by parents, as identified in Chapter 2. In the present section, we shall see whether professionals – in this case family day care providers – were able to do their job better if they, too, were offered information and support in relation to their needs.

The conjunction of the family day care providers' concerns with the concerns of the parents in the Aboriginal parent program (Project 2) strongly suggested that the three dimensional model of parental behaviour might apply more widely than to parents only. In terms of the three dimensional model, the providers' concern to understand children's behaviour better clearly relates to the responsiveness dimension (since in order to respond appropriately to children's signals one must be able to discern them accurately); while finding solutions to management problems and doing more interesting things round the house relate to the control and involvement dimensions respectively.

Thus the expression of needs by the family day care providers raised the possibility that the three dimensional model reached beyond parents' behaviour to caregiving behaviour in general, and that it had application to facilitative adults in general, not only parents, who could:

- *Promote trust* in children by nurturing and valuing them and *responding* to their cues.
- *Promote autonomy* in children by *guiding* their behaviour, while fostering independence.
- *Promote initiative* in children by active *involvement* with them in stimulating ways.

A project thus presented itself with the following three aims:

- To frame and carry out a program which would meet the expressed needs of a number of family day care providers.
- To assess whether, at the end of the program, there had been some enhancement of providers' *responsiveness*, their capacity for effective *guidance* of children's behaviour, and their enjoyable *involvement* with the young children in their care. In addition, at the end of the program there should have been some gain in the children's behavioural dimensions: personal outgoingness (a reflection of trust), sociability (reflecting autonomy in relationships) and intellectual functioning (reflecting initiative).

It is important to appreciate the significance of such results, were they to be achieved. In terms of the Schaefer (1982) model, enhancement of the family day care providers' functioning allied with improvements in child functioning would help to solidify the arrow leading from 'professional care' to 'child development'. It would help to demonstrate, in other words, that professsionals can help very young children to develop, something which critics of early child care, such as Leach (1994), have strongly disputed.

• To investigate the processes linking the first and second aims. A close examination of the processes occurring during the interactions of professionals (mainly myself) with less qualified colleagues (the family day care providers) would produce a firmer definition of the central, interactive, adult–adult area of Schaefer's model. Were care provider and child functioning shown to be enhanced during the project, such an examination would enable us to describe the processes leading to that enhancement. Powerful implications might be drawn for the construction and operation of a variety of other in-service programs concerned with caregiving and education.

What follows in this chapter is a fairly brief overview of the program and its results, particular facets of which will be teased out in greater detail in subsequent chapters.

CHANGING IDEAS IN FAMILY DAY CARE: SUPPORTING THE DEVELOPMENT OF YOUNG CHILDREN AND THEIR CARE PROVIDERS

Since the model encapsulating three major dimensions of caregiving behaviour (responsiveness, control and involvement) appeared to reflect the providers' expressed needs, this model became the framework for a twelve-session, one night a week, in-service program which ran as part of the Continuing Education service of the Queensland University of Technology.

Program procedures

The program was attended by twenty-one family day care providers of under-three year olds (the age-group where support seemed particularly likely to be welcomed) from seven family day care schemes in Brisbane. All schemes were sited within a twenty-minute drive of the University, allowing approximately equal access to the program. There the providers met with me in two groups, ten on one night of the week, eleven on another, to allow for more congenial small-group discussion.

Sufficient expressions of interest, spread across the schemes, had been received from those caring for under-threes to permit the formation of twenty-one pairs of providers matched on age, education and socio-economic status. Members of the pairs were randomly assigned either to the group undertaking the program or to a control group. To ensure equal motivation and contact, it was explained to members of the latter group that numbers were such that a second offering of the program, to which they were invited, would be made later (a promise that was kept). Meantime they were offered involvement in an alternative task of equal time and interest, unrelated to the aims of the program, in which they and I held regular telephone conversations as they evaluated health pamphlets. All control group members readily accepted this offer.

The project had no control over the continuity of the day care children, who came and went according to the demands of the field. A child present at the beginning of the study might well have left child care or moved elsewhere by the end. Thus it was not possible to be sure of following a given child through the study. Accordingly, in each family day care home at each assessment point, a target child was randomly selected from among all under-three year olds in attendance for at least eight weeks (to allow for the establishment of familiarity in the environment, Long *et al.*, 1985). Approximately half of these randomly selected children remained the same, demonstrating a considerable degree of continuity as well as change in the family day care clientele.

At the beginning of the project, the mean ages of the target children in the program and control groups were 22.0 and 22.6 months respectively, at the end of the project 27.7 and 28.6 months.

Perhaps the best way of summarising the program curriculum is by reproducing one of the handouts used in the group (Table 3.4), based on the findings of Robert Hess discussed in the last chapter. This handout, which operationalises the responsiveness, control and involvement dimensions set out in Table 3.1, served, night by night, as the basis for discussion, epecially for the interchange of providers' own experiences. In addition, discussion encompassed new material which was introduced on developmental milestones, films and workshop activities.

Not only was the program curriculum based on the three dimensional model of caregiving behaviour, but procedures devised to assess the effectiveness of the program also derived directly from these relevant caregiver dimensions. These were a Provider Interview (Appendix 1) and a Provider Behaviour Schedule (Appendix 2), both administered before and after the program. A similarly administered Child Behaviour Schedule (Appendix 3) was devised to address the personal, social and cognitive dimensions found in young children. The adult instruments were refinements of those designed for the Aboriginal parent program described on p. 41, while the Child Behaviour Schedule was a new measure (Henry, 1992).

Table 3.4 How do adults help children to develop well?

Researcher Robert Hess looked at a host of studies of children and parents. His findings suggest that children who

- • get on well with others
- • are mostly positive and happy
- • are intellectually able

have parents who:

- are responsive to their children

- • They relate warmly to their children.
- • They have a high regard for their children.
- • They are attentive to and engaged with their children.

- guide their children's behaviour

- • They encourage independence in their children.
- • They are consistent in their guidance methods.
- • They explain *why* their children should behave in certain ways.

- are involved with their children

- • They encourage their children to achieve.
- • They talk *with* rather than *to* their children.
- • They engage in 'by the way' teaching of their children.
- • They have interesting things around for children.

Does this apply in child care too?
We can appreciate and encourage these behaviours in parents and in ourselves.

Program outcomes

The survey of program outcomes that follows highlights significant differences emerging between the two groups of care providers: those who undertook the discussion program (the program group) and the control group. Similarly, descriptions are given of significant differences that became evident over the course of the program in the two groups of target children in care. Readers will find statistical support for these changes in the appendices at the end of this book. A very few instances of statistical support appear in the text.

With the presence of a control group, it was possible – as it was not in the Aboriginal parent program (Project 2) – to be confident that significant changes occurring among the participants over the period of the program were attributable to the program itself. There were a number of such changes, and these will be analysed in more detail in the next three chapters. Here the results as a whole are overviewed.

Family day care providers: reported outcomes

Following the program, a number of significant differences emerged between providers in the program group and those in the control group. These were differences in the understandings, the attitudes and the behaviours towards children reported by the two sets of providers in their pre-program and post-program interviews. As had been hypothesised, program group providers (but not control group providers) markedly broadened their repertoire with respect to responsiveness to children's cues, effective guidance of children's behaviour and involvement in activities enhancing children's development. Results also indicated gains among the program providers (but not the control group providers) in aspects of self-esteem and sense of internal control: the presage variables.

By means of a questionnaire administered after the program, these interview responses were checked against program participants' own assessments of what they were thinking, feeling or doing differently as a result of the program. The interview findings support providers' own assessments. These two sets of findings are given below: first, in italics, the providers' own global assessments from the questionnaire; next, in précis, their interview responses. A juxtaposition of the two sets of findings may serve as a summary of major outcomes of the program.

Presage variables: sense of self-esteem and control

Global comments about having a 'better feeling of self-esteem', becoming 'more aware of what I was already doing', 'being made aware that my job is worthwhile' and a sense that 'handling the children better makes me *feel better'* were confirmed by the interview findings of an improvement in overall job satisfaction and in the sense of internal control on the part of the program group providers.

Responsiveness

A large majority of program group providers said they had become 'more understanding of children's needs and growth patterns'. In their interview responses the program group demonstrated a sharpened awareness of the developmental changes taking place in very young children's capacities, embedding the particular cases cited within developmental norms.

General warmth towards children was perhaps taken as a given by the providers since it was not mentioned in the global assessments; these did, however, refer to increases in 'being pleased at the positive things they do' and feeling able to 'join in without feeling out of place'. The interview responses, too, suggested an already existing warmth (which did not change) coupled with an increase in responsiveness: many more detailed instances were articulated both of children's enjoyment in a broadened range of activities and of providers' own enjoyment in mutual activity.

Control

Provider assessments indicated 'new ideas on how to handle situations', and a greater appreciation of the 'importance of accentuating the positive'. Providers wrote of increasingly 'praising even tiny acts of cooperation and seeing good results', 'using more explanations' and 'not saying no all the time'. Interview corroboration of greater effectiveness in the control dimension comes from the decrease in the control measures – especially punitive measures – that providers reported needing to use, and the increase in the positive strategies they detailed to encourage children's cooperation and independence.

Involvement

Becoming 'more involved with the children, giving them more freedom in play' was another way in which program participants felt they had changed. This greater involvement was borne out, in the program group, in the detailed and lively accounts of the talking, learning, enjoyment of books and household activities in which they and the children engaged.

Family day care providers: observed outcomes

While significant differences occurred in the reported behaviours of the care providers in the two groups, their observed behaviours, as expressed in group means, did not change over the period of the program. Put another way, each group – program and control – maintained (though with wide individual variations) its generally positive levels of responsiveness, control and involvement with the children.

In addition, situational variables or chance occurrences over which the program had no control came into play. There was a disproportionate increase in the program group in the numbers of children in care, and in particular the numbers of babies: both factors seen in the literature (Fosburg, 1982; Lewis and Feiring, 1982) as drawing provider attention away from the target children.

Given that these situational variables in fact disadvantaged the program group while advantaging the control group, the maintenance of positive levels of behaviour by the former and the failure of the latter to raise them may be interpreted as a likely achievement of the program.

Family day care children: observed outcomes

While reports, among the family day care group undertaking the program, were of greater responsiveness, effective guidance and involvement, we need to remember that both groups of providers (program and control groups) demonstrated generally positive characteristics throughout. In attitude as well as action, these relatively confident providers started from a high threshold. It is not surprising, then, to find that the behaviours of both groups of children – program and control – indicated that, in general, their lives in family day care were enhancing their personal, social and intellectual development.

While details will be given in later chapters, it may be said here that, in both groups, children spent much time in 'effortful engagement' (Ruff *et al.*, 1990), in reciprocal interaction, and in active monitoring of the environment. Within these general outlines, the range of individual behaviours recorded was very wide, as was that reported by White *et al.* (1979) in the Harvard Pre-school Project. Nevertheless, the overall picture of children's activity, like that of the providers in general, was a positive one.

There were, however, two significant differences in behavioural patterns which, at the end of the program, distinguished the children associated with the program group providers from those in control group homes: the former were interacting for a greater proportion of their time with providers rather than with peers and were addressing a greater proportion of their utterances to providers rather than peers.

While all developmentalists would hold that interaction with peers is important to very young children, the evidence is overwhelming that contingent, reciprocal interaction between child and adult – especially verbal interaction (Carew, 1980; McCartney, 1984) – plays a major part in facilitating young children's development. Contingent, reciprocal interaction builds up turntaking expectancies that encourage further responses in young children. It is this contingent, reciprocal interaction between children and providers that the program appears to have supported.

The heightened ratios of interaction and utterances directed by the program group children to the provider may perhaps best be explained as responses of children in this group to the enhanced responsiveness of their caregivers towards them. This was the kind of responsiveness expressed by one caregiver who, at the end of the program, described what she enjoyed doing most with the children:

> Joining in their games, whatever they're doing, which I'm very much better at now. I used to feel silly. Now, if we're doing something that calls for a song, I sing out loud – I don't think, 'What do the neighbours think?' I'm not frightened any more.

Summary of careprovider–child outcomes

The outcomes of the family day care program may be visualised in terms of Schaefer's (1982) model. Just as the enhanced parental behaviours described in the Inala program appeared (though with reservation because of the absence of a control group) to be reflected in enhanced child behaviours (Figure 3.3), so the same thing can now be far more surely said of the professionals and young children described in this section. As the dimensions of family day care behaviour reported by providers became more positive, so did the behaviour of the children in their care.

More refined measures and the existence of a control group allow us to assert, with some confidence, the effect of the arrow linking the family day care professionals to the children in their care (Figure 3.4). But it is possible to do more than assert this effect. As the key to Figure 3.4 notes, we can now elucidate it. What the outcomes of the program have shown is that the care providers' gains in attitudes, understandings and reported behaviours in the dimensions of responsiveness, control and involvement have been accompanied by children's gains in trust (responsive interaction) and initiative (utterances).

Let us turn now to the question of how these changes occurred: the question of program processes.

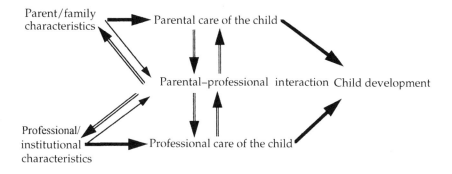

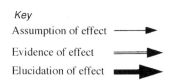

Figure 3.4 A model for parent and professional care and interaction:
modification 4
Source: adapted from Schaefer, 1982

THE FAMILY DAY CARE PROGRAM:
PROCESSES OF CHANGE AND CONTINUITY

How might we account for the continuities and changes in this program – little change in providers' observed behaviours, marked change in their attitudes, understandings and reported behaviours, some change in the behaviour of the children?

As noted earlier, there were in this program some special problems (changes in the size and age mix of child care groups) which may have impinged on the observed behaviour of the providers as they were being videotaped. In the following discussion, however, we deal with the clear-cut differences between the reported behaviours of the two groups of adults and the observed differences in the children.

A few years ago, Powell (1989) called for research which would clarify such processes. He was writing of the importance of research in elucidating family/parent change, but his call applies equally to the project we are investigating. Powell wrote:

> The need for research on family support and education programs cannot be overstated . . . How do parents deal with information that conflicts with their understandings of child development and perception of their child? . . . What program practices enhance parents' receptivity to innovative ideas and enable parents to change their belief systems and behaviours?
>
> (Powell 1989: 120)

To begin answering these questions, as they apply both to parents and to professionals, is precisely the purpose of this book, and an excellent starting point is to consider four propositions which Powell (1989) himself put forward in relation to the effectiveness of parent programs. Again these propositions may be seen as applicable also to programs such as the one we are discussing for family day care providers. Powell (1989: 110–11) suggests that to be effective:

1 Programs should appropriately match the needs, characteristics and world view of participating parents.
2 Programs should be characterised by collaborative relations between parents and program staff and shared decision making.
3 Programs need to maintain a balanced focus on the needs of both parent and child.
4 Programs should devote significant time to open-ended parent discussion.

Powell's propositions may be slightly reorganised and compressed, and their relevance to the family day care program brought out, by expressing them as the following processes:

1 Drawing on and reinforcing the ideas of the participating providers (Powell's proposition 1).
2 Introducing new ideas relevant to the needs of providers and children (Powell's proposition 3).
3 Engaging in ongoing, collaborative relationships through discussion, especially discussion of follow-up activities in the family day care homes (Powell's propositions 2, 4).

These processes may best be illustrated by some excerpts expanded from entries in the logbook I kept throughout. (To bring out the immediacy of the processes, the informal style of the logbook is retained. My role is that of the 'facilitator'.) The excerpt below describes part of the first session. After introductions and an overview of the program had taken place, providers were asked what they saw as the needs of very young children.

Logbook: first session

Providers arranged themselves in small groups with large sheets of paper and felt pens and brainstormed all the needs of young children that came to mind. A very short exposé of the ideas of Erikson followed, with early behaviour seen in terms first of building up trust, then of beginning to 'do one's own thing', then of looking outward at the world and beginning to try out new ideas. Everyday phrases such as 'doing your own thing' and 'trying out new ideas' seemed more acceptable at this stage of the program than Erikson's 'autonomy' and 'initiative' (Erikson, 1950).

Providers found that all the needs they had listed in their small groups fitted into one or another of Erikson's headings written on the blackboard.

Provider views of the needs of young children

Trust	Doing own thing	New ideas
Safety	Privacy	Stimulation
Understanding	Respect	Company
Patience	Toilet training	Information
Love	Talking	Activities
Contact	Choices	for play
Cuddles	Cooperation	Language
Clothing	Assertiveness	Stories
Food	Confidence	Music
Routine	Space to make	Facilities
Consistency	mistakes	Someone to
Reassurance	Set limits	talk to

Trust contd
Comfort
Eye contact
Praise
Approval
Attention

Having talked of the needs of young children, the group were now to feel a little of what it is like to be vulnerable, to be completely in the hands of one's care provider, to have to build up trust. Providers in pairs went on a 'trust walk', one person leading the other blindfold all round the Early Childhood Centre. Then they swapped blindfolds. This is an unnerving experience: providers stumbled back to their seats in the circle and flopped down, laughing. I pressed a lump of playdough into everyone's hands and providers began to roll it thankfully. I asked: 'Why are we doing this?' 'It's soothing,' one replied, and another suggested that a playdough cult would be more effective than worrybeads. Later in the program the group would often recall, from this experience, the therapeutic quality of soothing touch.

Some providers were soon not merely enjoying the texture of their playdough but had begun to push, pull and pummel it. My question: 'Why are you doing this?' 'Well, you've got to *do* something with it.' 'Doing your own thing with it?' The group laughed and soon everyone was squeezing and pounding their lump of dough.

Then someone was making a little elephant, and others the inevitable snakes and birds' nests. Providers realised they had moved on from simply *doing* something with the playdough to *making* things with it, and that in a few minutes they, like young children, had encountered all those basic needs that Erikson calls stages – for trust, for autonomy, for initiative – and that they had encountered them *in that order*, not able to move on to the stages of doing and thinking till they felt comfortable and secure with the material. I mentioned the phrase of an old teacher friend who said of her small pupils: 'First we set them at ease, and then we set them to work.'

All of the processes adapted from Powell (1989) – building on providers' ideas, introducing new ideas, and collaborative feedback – are exemplified in this excerpt from the facilitator's logbook.

Building on participants' ideas

From the very beginning, the program attempted to build on the experience of the participating providers. The first major act of the program was to establish a needs-based approach, with the providers, not the facilitator, suggesting the needs of young children, from their own day to day experience. The comprehensive list compiled by the providers attests to the resources already existing within the group, resources not only of knowledge of children, but also of awareness and ability to analyse experience. For some of the providers, unused to the brainstorming method, it was clearly surprising and satisfying to see how many important needs the group had identified.

The suggestion by a provider that playdough would be more effective as a relaxant than worrybeads is another example of an insight from within the group, enlivening at the time and, as the excerpt makes clear, a reference point for the future, as issues of contact and security for young children recurred.

Introducing new ideas

While the providers generated, from their own experience, the comprehensive lists of needs of young children, it was the facilitator who, from a more theoretically based perspective, suggested the structuring of those lists in terms of an Eriksonian framework – or a modified Eriksonian framework, since Erikson's (1950) somewhat rigidly age-linked stages were relaxed in this program to take account of more recent findings on the multifaceted nature of children's early capacities (Chapter 2).

As well as introducing to the providers Erikson's concepts of trust, autonomy and initiative, the facilitator initiated the opportunity for providers to experience for themselves something of the meaning of these concepts via the activities described in the excerpt. Light-hearted as were these prompts or similes-in-action, the 'trust walk' and play-dough sequences were clearly both engaging and thought provoking for the providers, laying the basis for the further negotiation of concepts through a third process.

Engaging in collaborative feedback

Open-ended discussion is important to parent groups, according to Powell (1989: 112), because 'Parents are likely to process new information according to existing beliefs and constructs about . . . child development. Discussion provides an opportunity for parents to digest new insights in relation to existing ideas.'

Powell's description applies equally to the family day care providers. In the session described in the excerpt, providers put forward their own views about children's needs, then listened to the new information about those needs supplied by the facilitator from the standpoint of Eriksonian theory. Through discussion, amongst themselves and with the facilitator, they were able to mesh the new with the old and to arrive cooperatively at the three categorisations of needs given in the excerpt.

This outcome (a starting point for later sessions) would not have been possible without all three of the processes outlined here. First was the use of the providers' own examples. These had immediacy, the validity of personal knowledge and high motivational value because of the status they were accorded in discussion. In proposing examples of children's needs, providers were receiving the message: 'Your experiences are as valid as those of the experts.' Second was the introduction by the facilitator of a framework which added a series of new insights and into which the group's examples could fit. Third was the negiotiation that occurred as group members argued about whether a need such as 'talking', in the lives of young children, should go into the second category or the third. As the providers cogitated, cited examples and asked questions of one another and the facilitator, they became more familiar with and confident about the subject under discussion.

All of the processes outlined here – affirmation of existing insights, introduction of some new ones, and the sifting of both through discussion – continued to occur throughout the program. In the next chapters, we shall look at other examples, from this and other settings. At the beginning of this chapter, the aim of our odyssey was to 'progress towards a model encapsulating more productive ways (that is, ways which meet rather than violate . . . needs . . .) in which professionals and families can work together so as to promote their mutual interests and the interests of young children'.

We are close to that goal, the stages of which we have traced in this chapter by reflecting on – and so further defining – the bare outlines of Schaefer's (1982) model (Figure 2.8). In Project 1 we saw that a program of parent–teacher cooperation in arts and crafts enabled children to flower as they met their needs for trust, for autonomy, for initiative. We noted teachers and parents gaining information and support from one another and both sets of adults increasing in flexibility and power. In the record made soon after that program, the further processes whereby this occurred remained mysterious.

In Project 2, the description of an Aboriginal parent–toddler program allowed us to firm up some of the links between parents and their children, as we saw that the parents' enhanced responsiveness to their children, exercise of more consistent, explanatory control, and participation with them in stimulating activity enriched a variety of aspects of the toddlers' lives. While the effects of professional–parent interaction in this program remained unclear (for lack of a control group against which to set the results), the program did enable Schaefer's (1982) links between parents and children to be further defined (Figure 3.3) by way of an emerging model of parental caregiving behaviour with three dimensions: responsiveness, control and involvement.

In Project 3, discussion of an in-service program with family day care providers has demonstrated that these dimensions of caregiving, framed for parents and their children, are equally applicable to professionals and the children in their care. Another arrow in Schaefer's (1982) model has been defined (Figure 3.4), as professionals have been shown to enhance their reported behavioural repertoire with specific consequent changes in children's observed behaviours.

But this chapter has achieved more. Because the family day care program had a control group in which these professional–child results did not occur, it has been possible to attribute the findings to the processes occurring within the program, namely building on participants' ideas, introducing new ideas, and engaging in collaborative feedback. In a talk given on the Aboriginal parent–toddler program in 1985, I described (Henry 1986: 7) the processes occurring in that program in almost identical terms:

1 The program introduced developmental ideas.
2 The program built on parents' and children's ideas.
3 The program was modified in the light of collaborative feedback.

Yet it was not until years later, as I investigated the family day care program in terms of Powell's (1989) propositions, that I at last came to understand the relationship of these adult–adult program processes to the adult–child dimensions of caregiving: responsiveness, involvement and control. The behavioural dimensions in both cases are not merely related, they are the same:

Responsiveness
● Adults who build on other adults' ideas *are employing the same behavioural dimension as* adults who respond to children's signals.

Involvement
● Adults who introduce new ideas to other adults *are employing the same behavioural dimension as* adults who involve themselves with children in stimulating ways.

Control
● Adults who engage in collaborative feedback (mutual control) with other adults *are employing the same behavioural dimension as* adults who engage in effective guidance of children's behaviour.

Another look at the excerpt (p. 61) describing the family day care program's first meeting will help to clarify these equivalences, which extend adult–child to adult–adult interaction. In that first meeting, based on a brainstorming session, providers, like archaeologists, dug into their own home sites for artefacts of their life history with children. The examples they brought to the surface had particular, personal meanings for them and in *building on their ideas* as 'experiences [which were] as valid as those of the experts' (p. 64), the facilitator was demonstrating a warmth, a respect for and a wish to *respond to their signals*. In turn, and increasingly over time, the providers became less inhibited, more ready to respond to other participants, including the facilitator who was eager for more glimpses of their information, more treasures from the archaeological dig. Sharing these responses brought a sense of wellbeing, of relaxation. As the provider quoted earlier said: 'I'm not frightened any more.' We see here the motivational power of the responsiveness dimension.

But providers had not come to the program merely for the pleasure of displaying to interested others their own buried treasures. They wanted to acquire more. Thus, on that first evening, facilitator *involvement* consisted of *introducing new ideas*, an informational Eriksonian framework for their examples of children's needs, plus what Bruner (1985) has called 'props and hints' or scaffolding for their ideas in the form of the trust walk and the playdough game. In turn, as group members added to their knowledge, they enabled the facilitator to do the same: to discover, for example, how adults work through the stages of trust, autonomy and initiative in playing the playdough game.

Most importantly, while the control of this first session was vested in the facilitator, the *collaborative feedback* (the negotiating, arguing, cogitating, citing examples, asking questions) which occurred throughout the discussion set the scene for all the later sessions. The format was one of *mutual control* and, thus, of enriched input both for group members and facilitator. Although, on the second evening, one provider chided the facilitator for 'sitting down in the group, not standing out in front of the class telling us what to do', it seems likely that the element of *mutual control* played its part in promoting (for all members including the facilitator) a sense of relaxed purpose, as it did in helping the earlier cited provider to feel that she was not frightened any more.

The bringing together of two major interactive theories of learning, Vygotskian and empowerment theory, can, I believe, powerfully illuminate the processes operating in the program. That illumination follows in the next chapters, with a brief preliminary outline here.

Vygotsky's (1978: 86) zone of proximal development, framed in the context of childhood learning but applicable to other contexts and age-groups, represents 'the distance between the [learner's] actual developmental level as determined by independent problem solving and the level of potential development' achievable through collaboration with more capable others.

In the family day care program, helping providers to move through the zone of proximal development was the facilitator's task, carried out largely through the exercise of the involvement dimension. For the family day care providers, the zone of proximal development was the program. It was here, over the twelve successive meetings of the group, that situations (the entering beliefs of the care providers) were defined and redefined. Already in the first meeting, for example, the brainstorming sequence was an exercise in redefining children's behaviour, so that patterns in behaviour which had not previously been visible to the providers became evident to them in new ways.

While Vygotskian theory emphasises attentiveness on the part of the facilitator to the learner's situation definition with a view, as Wertsch (1984) points out, to replacing it with another, empowerment theory (Cochran, 1988) advocates attentiveness to learner experience in order to support and validate it. Such support and validation are among the outcomes of the two dimensions of responsiveness and mutual control. As Cochran (1988: 36) writes: 'The assumption here is not that there is a deficiency that needs correction, but rather that a system of functioning adequately needs protecting.' In the family day care program such validation was confirmed by provider comments, at the end of the program, that it had 'made me more aware of what I was already

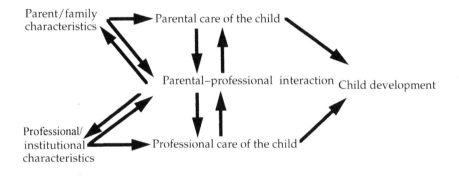

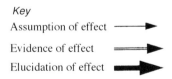

Figure 3.5 A model for parent and professional care and interaction: modification 5
Source: adapted from Schaefer, 1982

67

doing' and that the program's upshot was 'being made aware that my job was worthwhile'.

If an in-service program for caregivers (such as the family day care program) may be thought of as itself a form of caregiving, its effectiveness in fostering adult–child interactions of responsiveness, collaborative guidance and involvement may be seen as a function of the operation of like adult–adult dimensions within the program itself.

With this insight, we have reached the end of the odyssey that began with Project 1: the establishment of significant behavioural dimensions which link young children, their parents and relevant professionals and which enhance the development of all three. We are now in a position to give some substance to all the arrows in Schaefer's (1982) amended model (Figure 2.9), including those arrows indicating the relationships between parents and professionals engaged in caregiving and education (Figure 3.5).

But we have more to find out about these relationships. In Chapters 4, 5 and 6 we shall look in more detail at how, in the family day care program, the positive exercise of each of the three dimensions enhanced the development and learning of providers and facilitator, as well as that of the children in the providers' care. But we shall also, and especially, look at a variety of examples from other settings to see that it is through the positive exercise of these caregiving dimensions – responsiveness, control and involvement – that parents and professionals can facilitate not only young children's development but also that of one another.

4

RESPONSIVENESS

As shown in the responsiveness dimension in Table 3.1, the Hess variables concerning adult–child behaviours which relate to young children's need to build up trust are:

1 A warm affective relationship with the child.
2 A high regard for the child.
3 Engagement with and attentiveness to the child.

In this chapter, we shall examine the enhancement of responsiveness by looking at:

1 Some ways (beyond those already discussed) in which these behaviours came to operate between adults and children in the course of the family day care program.
2 How the same behaviours occurred among the adults (facilitator and providers) in the family day care program.
3 The operation of these behaviours in parent–professional interaction.
4 Some examples of the same behaviours occurring in other everyday interactions of young children, professionals and parents.

Before we move to sample these true stories from the real world, it is important to look more closely at the mechanisms driving the dimension of responsiveness (and in later chapters control and involvement) in the family day care program, a program whose findings are firmly underpinned by those from its control group. The better we understand the findings from this program, the better we can apply them in practice.

Statistical support for the discussion that follows can be found in Appendix 4 of this book, which summarises the results of the pre- and post-interviews. These were held, individually, with providers before the program began and again, six months later, at its end. These structured interviews (see Appendix 1) asked providers to review their relationships with the children in their care through a series of questions tapping providers' understandings, attitudes and perceived behaviours relating to the three dimensions of responsiveness, control and involvement.

THE DIMENSION OF RESPONSIVENESS IN THE FAMILY DAY CARE PROGRAM: ADULTS AND CHILDREN

The degree of responsiveness of the program group providers in their answers to the interview questions changed in some spheres but not others. A look at the areas where change did not occur helps to increase confidence in the validity of findings in the areas where it did.

No significant pre- or post-differences between program and control groups were recorded in answer to interview questions on:

- The general appeal of family day care as a job.
- Providers' warm but not over-rosy view of under-three-year olds (seen as loving, trusting, interested, but messy and constantly needing attention).
- Their assessment of the children as generally cooperative.
- The types of rules and limits set (relating to the protection of safety and property).
- The importance of talking to young children.
- Their own predominant satisfaction with their performance in the job.

These continuing responses among both program and control group providers are what would be expected, both before and after the program, of women who were described in the last chapter as having considerable motivation, who were prepared to undertake, voluntarily, a twelve-week in-service program in order to do a better job with children, and who all possessed a reasonable level of personal and material resources.

Above this quite high threshold of perceived competence and confidence, however, a variety of changes emerged in the interview responses of the program group of providers, as compared with the members of the control group. These changes encompassed: a difference in the number of aspects reported; an increase in positive aspects noted; and greater articulateness.

Number of aspects

The question 'What do you most enjoy doing with the children?' (Item 6, Appendix 1) taps into Hess's variables (Table 3.1) of high regard for child and engagement/attentiveness to child. Control group answers to this question varied little in quality from one interview to the other. On each occasion they resembled the program group's initial responses. However, the program group's responses at the second interview showed marked changes in terms of the number of aspects of interaction with the children which they saw as enjoyable. In Table 4.1 compare the typical

Table 4.1 Examples of pre- and post-program responses from program group providers to the question 'What do you most enjoy doing with the children?'

Example	Response	
	Before program	*After program*
1	'Being with them – especially playing hidings.'	'I like having them in the kitchen with me – especially helping me make cakes. They always tell me what I'm doing wrong! We act the clown, muck about. We always have a joke together.'
2	'I enjoy being with them when they're all playing happily. I *should* participate with them, I suppose.'	'I enjoy being with them when they're painting. Or in the sandpit, they'll be making sand castles, or digging. We might make cakes or ice creams. We enjoy doing the washing up together – even the real littlies can do it with plastic cups and saucers. Sometimes we use the pool to wash up in.'
3	'I get involved with them *less* now they're bigger. I do like reading them stories.'	'Joining in their games, whatever they're doing, which I'm very much better at now. I used to feel silly. Now, if we're doing something that calls for a song, I sing out loud – I don't think 'What do the neighbours think?' I'm not frightened any more.'
4	'Sitting together with them – on my lap. I treat them just the same as my own.'	'Playing games that I join in, like ring a rosy. Painting too, and stories. I enjoy them too, that's probably why they enjoy them. The more you can do *with* them, the happier they are. It makes *your* day happier too.'
5	'Music: dancing and clapping together.'	'We have fun with housework. The one without language will just point at the vacuum so we get going. They love to dust with the rag. They're thrilled to see the shine. I'm more conscious of letting them help now. I'm *slowing down* so they can.'

pre- and post-responses from program group providers to the question 'What do you most enjoy doing with the children?'

Positive aspects

No less striking than the increase in the number of aspects of enjoyment mentioned by the care providers in Table 4.1 is the increase in the number of positive phrases leaping from their second responses. Consider Example 5. As she recalls the activity engaged in round the house, this provider's rush of active verbs convey enthusiastic participation, both hers and the children's, in an enjoyable experience: 'We have fun', 'we get going', 'they love to' 'they're thrilled to', 'I'm more conscious', 'letting them help', 'so they can'. Even the emphatic 'I'm *slowing down*' indicates a conscious impulse on the part of this provider to work, as Ainsworth and her colleagues (1974: 107) write, 'with the grain of [the young child's] repertoire, rather than against it'.

Articulateness

What is significantly demonstrated in general in the later responses of the program group, but not in those of the control group, is a qualitative shift from brief and/or vague answers to articulate detail and a greater reflective awareness of the value of adult participation. One way of accounting for this change is by considering a remark made by Kelly (1955: 9) on how people come to construct meanings. As Kelly poetically wrote: 'To construe is to hear the whisper of recurrent themes in the events that reverberate around us.' When people become conscious of specific, repeated themes reverberating in their lives (as the program providers were becoming conscious of never-before-considered characteristics of the children in their care), they are able to generate constructs based on those recurrent themes. Where there are no such themes (as in the case of the control group providers) responses are not articulated.

Strategies

In the five examples of pre- and post-program responses reproduced in Table 4.1 from provider interviews, the change from laconic to enthusiastically detailed is obvious. But not all of the changes in the number of aspects of an issue mentioned by program group providers might appear as substantial. For example, in Appendix 5 of this book, Item 12 shows that from the beginning to the end of the program the mean number of strategies suggested by program group providers to encourage independence rose from 1.6 to 3.2. Such a change seems of little importance. However, while numerically small, it may represent a major shift in understanding and operation.

In Table 4.2 compare the two initial and three later strategies advocated by one program group provider in response to the question: 'How do you think family day care providers can encourage children to try things on their own?' Here a score of 2 rose only to 3 but in the second response there is a deepened quality of understanding. While the pre-program response included the strategies of observation of child capabilites as well as the essentially reactive, hands-off policy ('You don't give in when the child wants you to do it') also found in the post-response, the latter included a far more proactive and considered deployment of

Table 4.2 Strategies advocated by one program group provider in response to the question 'How do you think family day care providers can encourage children to try things on their own?'

No.	Strategy	
	Before program	After program
1	'Just be alert to what they can do.	'You've got to give them time to *try*.
2	You don't give in when the child wants you to do it for them.'	You don't do it for them.
3		I find if I get one child to do something, the others will follow.'

resources: resources of time (seen as necessary for the child's expenditure of effort) and other children (seen as motivating models).

Attentiveness/engagement

A major component of the responsiveness dimension, as suggested in Table 3.1, is the adult's attentiveness to and engagement with the child. Such growing attentiveness was demonstrated among the program group providers in their responses to some questions on the age at which they saw the start of various capabilities in young children. There were four such questions in the interview. They concerned the onset of independence (Appendix 5, Item 11), pleasure in accomplishment (Appendix 6, Item 13), receptive language (Item 16), and expressive communication (Item 17). Thus providers were asked how old they thought children were when they were able to start:

• Trying to do things for themselves.
• Being pleased that they could do something really well.
• Understanding grown-ups' explanations.
• Taking part in a conversation with grown-ups.

The differences between the two groups of providers were fascinating. In all four areas the expectations of the program group providers, initially similar to those of the control group, shifted to earlier ages, while the control group providers maintained their original expectations (see Appendices 5 and 6). Program group providers, by the end of the program, were reporting children starting to try to do things for themselves at a mean age of 4 months instead of the 17 months they had nominated earlier, starting to feel pleasure in accomplishment at 6 months instead of 16, starting to understand adult explanations at 10 months instead of 19, and starting to play some part in conversations at 12 months instead of 20.

In addition to the program group providers' growing attentiveness to the 'never-before-considered' capacities of young children, their nomination of a lowered age of onset of these capacities appeared to be a function of the increasing 'numbers of aspects of a given area articulated'. Commenting on the children's capacities, providers across the groups invariably used illustrations from their own experience. But, in addition, providers from the program group (but not the control group) appeared in their later comments to be setting these illustrations against a widened frame of reference (Kemper, 1968). Thus, for example, indications of a striving for autonomy in even their youngest charges, formerly unnoticed, were now apparent to them. It was as though, to these providers, the children had acquired added significance as members of a wider group (Table 4.3).

Table 4.3 Examples of pre- and post-program responses from program group providers to the question 'How old do you think children are when they start trying to do things for themselves?'

Example	Response	
	Before program	*After program*
1	'Too early! The minute she was sitting up in a high chair – that was about nine months – my little one was grabbing the spoon.'	'From the minute they're born – you see them trying to lift their heads.'
2		'If people hand them things, you'll see them trying to grab them from a couple of months old.'

While such a shift towards the more generalised developmental viewpoint was evident in most program group responses, many more control group responses remained bound by particular cases: 'Well, John's just starting to pull his own pants on now, and he's 16 months – I'd say about 16 months.' How the widened frame of reference of the program group might be accounted for will be discussed in the next section.

Providers were asked, not just about the specific changes just discussed, but about changes in general that they had noted in the children. Not only did the program group's responses more than double (from a mean of nearly 3 to 6, while the control group remained at 3; Appendix 4, Item 4) but many of them possessed a quality of empathic appreciation of the children (even of their more discomfiting changes) which was less evident in the control group:

You can see Jack's got the *feeling* of growing up: 'Not put nappy on me!' And then he feels to see if he's wet the bed. He's so pleased when he hasn't.

(Program group)

'Francie's more confident now – but she's become very bombastic.

(Control group)

The examples presented so far have demonstrated some clear differences between a group of family day care providers who undertook an in-service program and a control group who did not. Warmth (the first of Hess's facilitative adult behaviours in Table 3.1) did not constitute one of those differences. At the end of the twelve weeks, both groups of providers felt equal warmth for the children in their care – this was why they were doing the job – and it was a characteristic that remained constant in both groups from beginning to end of the project. But the program group had acquired greater empathy with the children and had increased their understanding of their very early capacities. In other words, they had gained in their regard for the children (Hess's second variable). Further, they were now attending to and (as seen in the 'fun with housework' example) engaged with the children in patterns of behaviour which, 'formerly unnoticed, were now apparent to them'. In sum, with the enhancement of Hess's third facilitative variable, they had become more responsive.

Children's behaviour

A reciprocal pattern of trust in their adult caregivers emerged in the behaviour of the target 0–3 year olds in the homes of the program group providers. As mentioned on p. 58, by the end of the program these children, compared with those in the control group, were interacting for a significantly greater proportion of their time with their care providers than they were with peers ($X2 = 8.05$, $p < 0.005$). This is shown in graph form in Figure 4.1. Here it can be seen that, at the beginning of the program, 83 per cent of the interactions of both sets of children were with their caregivers. By the end of the program, the proportion of child–adult responsive interaction had fallen to 68 per cent for the control group children, while it was maintained at 84 per cent for the program group. A high level of contingent, reciprocal *child–adult* interaction is seen as particularly important in very young children's development.

THE DIMENSION OF RESPONSIVENESS IN THE FAMILY DAY CARE PROGRAM: THE ADULTS

Related to young children's need to build up trust, adult–child responsiveness means much more, as we have just seen, than warm adult acceptance of children. It means adult regard for, attention to and engagement with the signals that children emit.

Similarly, adult–adult reponsiveness means that, besides evincing

75

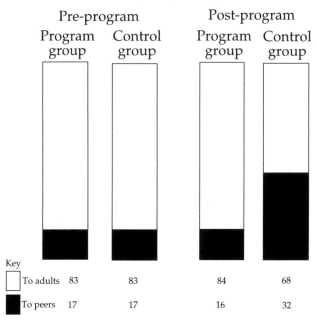

Figure 4.1 Percentage proportions of total child interactions

warmth, each adult has respect for, understands and engages with the cues of the other. Extending the dimensions of caregiving behaviour from adult–child to adult–adult interaction implies that it is by such respect, understanding and engagement that adults help one another to affirm a sense of trust in the world, in themselves and in others. As noted on p. 25, meeting the need for trust remains a fundamental challenge for adults, as well as children.

Some of the cues to which adults can be alert in one another may be needs, others strengths. As has been discussed in Chapter 3, the principle of being attentive to and engaged with adult (as well as child) cues underpinned the family day care project, based as it was on the *expressed* needs of the family day care providers. Not only was the curriculum as a whole planned to respond to these needs (to understand better children's behaviour, be able to guide it more effectively, and have more fun around the house), but also each segment of the program aimed to 'build on participants' ideas'. The brainstorming session on the first evening was an example of this procedure. Here is another, in which the group, in 'building on participants' ideas', was addressing both the needs and strengths of its members. Five weeks after the start of the program the following exchange was recorded involving Jess, a provider who had missed two sessions through family illness.

Logbook: mutual responsiveness

The group was discussing the problems of handling new babies who were upset at separation from mother. Jess told of the baby who came at 6 months and who needed, said Jess, 'firm limits' – she went on crying for two months. 'In the end I told her to "shut up or ship out" ', and she finally stopped. Both Sandra and Jean made the point that the baby might have needed her *trust* to be built up. They asked what happened when Jess held her? Jess: 'She stopped crying then.' Heads nodded around the group, and Sandra went on to talk about the effectiveness of the Papua New Guinea *lap lap* that she'd become familiar with when she lived there – a metre wide strip of material tied at the waist, going round both front and back. Baby can be carried close to mother wherever most suitable – just placed in a fold of material. Sandra had tried this with upset new babies and found it worked very well. The researcher reinforced the point: most mothers round the world keep their babies with them, give them close feelings of warmth and touch. Joan joined in, made the point that she'd found it can take quite a while to build up a sense of security – you can't force it. 'You might have done that over those two months, Jess. She might have been ready to stop.' Jess: 'You might have a point there.'

This incident gives a picture of a crash course being provided for a group member who, through absence, had missed some of the intervening steps and needed to catch up. By this fifth week the group was reaching the second major topic area. This concerned the guidance of children's behaviour as they move into the wider world from the secure base discussed in the first sessions. The group had by this time established its own secure base. It had built up a considerable sense of trust, both trust among group members and trust in the meaningfulness of program concepts, which participants had had a chance to discuss and test against their own experiences at home. As Jess, absent from these earlier sessions, introduced points which the group had already canvassed, members were eager to review them with her, suggesting other perspectives from their own situations. Apart from adding to members' own sense of self-esteem as contributors of valuable knowledge, such a welling up from within the group of information which the facilitator was able to reinforce may well have carried more conviction to the recipient than would the facilitator's more 'academic' suggestions alone. The facilitator, too, acquired new information from the group, helping to meet her needs. For all participants, then, the exchange was conducted with warm interest, respect, and attentiveness to one another's views (situation definitions), contributing to a broadened frame of reference.

By encouraging responsiveness within the group in these ways, the program was able to focus on, and help to address, the real needs of its members. This does not always happen in parent–professional programs. Discussing research in day care personnel preparation, Peters and Kostelnik (1981) have drawn attention to the propensity of many of those developing and implementing both pre- and in-service programs to proceed on the basis of participants' *inferred* rather than *expressed* needs. In particular, they see many caregiver in-service programs focusing on areas of child development, nutrition, health and safety, whereas, they suggest, 'when day care personnel are permitted to express their own needs' (p. 36) these are likely to centre initially on concerns related to themselves and their own abilities (Fuller, 1969; Katz, 1972), for example problems with the management of misbehaviour. It is only later, Peters and Kostelnik believe, that 'the caregiver turns outward and expresses concerns for the pupils' (p. 37).

While, in the family day care project, problems of management were certainly a foremost concern of the providers, these relatively experienced participants, able to look outward as well as inward, also expressed the more distal need for greater understanding of young children's behaviour and development. A further need was for more ideas for stimulating activities for children. As we have seen, all three needs of providers, reflecting the three caregiving dimensions of responsiveness, control and involvement, were taken into account from the beginning. Futhermore, the continuing process of anchoring all program topics firmly to the experience and examples provided by the group would seem to have been a major factor in the avoidance of the problem identified by Peters and Kostelnik: namely the imposition of irrelevant and ineffective material on the basis of inferred rather than expressed needs. In this program needs were both expressed and addressed.

The same may be said of participants' strengths. Devoting significant time to open-ended discussion has been elevated by Powell (1989: 112) into an important program process related to effectiveness, because of the processing of ideas such discussion allows and the reciprocity of relationships it fosters.

Open-ended group discussion is seen as an empowering activity by Vanderslice (1984: 4) because it 'draws on and validates participants' experiences and knowledge so they can begin to see themselves as valuable, knowledgeable members of a group' and it 'encourages participants to listen to, respect and learn from one another so they see themselves and each other as accomplishing a collective task'.

The affirmation that 'all families have *some* strengths [and] that much of the most valid and useful knowledge about the rearing of children is lodged among the people . . . rather than in the heads of college professors' (Cochran, 1987: 13) has a corollary: that a program based on such an affirmation enables facilitators as well as other members of the group to engage in learning. According to Vanderslice (1984: 4) such a program 'contributes to facilitator empowerment by decreasing the facilitator's responsibility for providing all the input and expertise and by providing him or her with more knowledge than would otherwise be available'.

Summary

Summarising this section, it might be said that, in adult–adult as well as adult–child interaction, exercise of the three Hess variables making up responsiveness (Table 3.1) – warmth, high regard and attentiveness/ engagement – can motivate adults to begin to widen their frame of reference and so to consider other points of view. As adults become open to evaluating one set of situation definitions against another, these definitions may begin to change. Thus Jess, because of her interaction with her peers, began to consider, alongside her own definition of a six-month old baby's needs as simply 'firm limits', the possibility of a broader need: 'a sense of security'.

The exercise of responsiveness, deriving from a warm, respectful attention to our expressed signals, does not change our thinking or behaving in specific ways. Other inputs are necessary for that (see Chapters 6 and 7). But responsiveness is fundamental to a motivational disposition to change. It helps us adults to say, like Jess, 'You might have a point there.'

THE DIMENSION OF RESPONSIVENESS: PROFESSIONAL–PARENT INTERACTIONS

Since compulsory schooling, often highly authoritarian, was introduced more than a century ago, large numbers of parents who were once children in teachers' classes have maintained their childhood feelings of fear and dread of teachers, and those feelings have often been roundly reciprocated (Berger, 1995).

With the recent explosion of child care placements, the antipathies of many of those who perceive themselves with power (the members of staff) and those who perceive themselves without (the parents) have often been extended from schools to child care centres, where there are the additional problems of role conflict concerning the care of the very young as outlined in Chapter 1 (p. 4).

For some dozen years, I have been working, along with a number of colleagues, in a tertiary institution that educates future and current professionals, attempting to leaven what is often a heavy loaf of indigestible professional–parent antipathy or, at times, a very thin mixture of minimal contact between them.

The students I work with are training to be early childhood professionals – in schools or child care settings – or are already practising teachers completing their degree courses in the evening or externally. Not all of these practising professionals are early childhood personnel. They also include late primary and secondary teachers and, sometimes, tertiary lecturers intrigued by the name of a subject called: 'Working with Parents and Community'.

The subject occupies a semester, and during those four months each student completes two assignments, both reporting on a practical self-devised project in which the student has interacted, on the one occasion, with one parent and child and, on the other, with a group of parents. While the early childhood students generally take these requirements in their stride, the practising teachers of older pupils often begin by making very heavy weather of them. Despite the rapidly increasing number of documents from central authorities requiring more contact with parents (School Development Plans, etc.), many of these practising teachers continue to assert that they seldom see a parent (except on a formal committee), and that the parents whom they do see are often uncommunicative and appear uninterested.

The view of many teachers that parents are 'uninterested' in participating in any way in their children's education has been around for a long time, as have several explanations of this, from parents themselves. In 1968, the British Schools Council *Enquiry into Young School Leavers* identified three major factors underlying many parents' alienation from schools:

> The answers from these parents themselves suggest that this apparent lack of interest is not so much an absence of concern about their child's progress as the result of three attitudes. First, the delegation of all responsibility for education to the school.
>
> Secondly, a very generally held view that they would be interfering if they went to school uninvited – it was clear that for many this needs to be a very specifically personal invitation indeed.
>
> Third, on the part of many parents there was a lack of confidence in being able to have a satisfactory discussion with the teachers if they went to the school.
>
> (Schools Council, 1968)

As noted in a slightly later source, many parents

> were afraid that anything they did would be different from what was done at school and so would confuse and hinder their children. This point emerged constantly.
>
> (Smith, 1975: 140).

These considerations are not applicable only to less well educated or low income parents. At a Brisbane in-service seminar, kindergarten teachers heard, perhaps with some surprise, one competent, well educated middle class parent reveal her feelings of uncertainty and her need for understanding:

I would like to discuss with you what it feels like as a parent in this system of kindergarten/pre-school education. Being a parent is the most responsible and can be the most rewarding job I could ever find. It is up to me to look for and provide the best education for my child in the home and in the education system. As a mother of three children ages 2–11 years, I have been involved in the various stages of education for many years now. As a parent we approach this environment full of high expectations and hoping we have made the right choice to bring out the best in our child and to be well prepared for school.

Although as people we are confident in our occupation or profession, parents can often feel unsure of what to do or who to ask about child raising. You may look at me and think, 'She's an experienced Mum – three children, she knows what she's doing', whereas I think, 'There's our pre-school teacher with lots of training in early childhood education, I shouldn't question what she does because she's so qualified' – so where are we?

Often pre-school teachers aren't mothers and, until they are, find it difficult to understand the incredible feelings of sensitivity, protection and pride a mother has for her child. Barriers can immediately be set up by a teacher's insensitive approach to a problem, such as 'Look, your child has some problems. Is something happening in his home situation which could be disturbing him?' Immediately the defences are up, as the home situation is under a microscope and the feelings of guilt and concern that flow are overwhelming. Under these conditions teachers should not be put off by a mother's reactions and in most cases a parent would appreciate an approach such as: 'Your child seems to be having some problems in this area. Why don't we approach it together like this?'

As most parents are so vitally interested in their child, they need to be made feel very welcome in the centre. Let it be known when it is the best time to speak to you and not just wait for each other to make the first move. As many parents are shy or hesitant and prefer to stand back, I feel it is your responsibility to speak quietly to that parent about his child – *often*.

We would expect you to be able to recall weekly or monthly developments in our children and to be prepared to discuss them willingly.

As many parents don't always read newsletters etc., it must be continually spelt out to us how we can speak to you anytime and that you do want to work with us on the child's development and problems that arise.

Parents need to see notices up about what is happening this week and what is going to be discussed in the program so that we can extend it into the home situation. Please talk to us in a language we can understand, *not* phrases like 'fine motor skills', as many parents wouldn't know what you are talking about and are too shy to ask. Also it may be difficult virtually to greet each child by his name and to have some follow-up personal comment but it would reassure us of your special interest in that child.

So let's work together, to improve that standard of communication and to open up all channels to help these precious children take the first steps towards being our outstanding adults of tomorrow.

(Anderson, 1984)

In reviewing the perceptions that some professionals have of parents – 'uncommunicative and uninterested' – and some parents have of professionals – people with an 'insensitive approach to a problem' who 'wait for [the] other to make the first move' – we can see that the professional–parent relationship is more complex than Wolfendale's straighforward analysis of what has held back collaboration between the two groups of adults (p. 40). It is not simply that teachers have held a 'client' view of parents as inferior people who need to be set right. Rather, many parents and professionals lack trust in the other and, because they are distrustful, keep as much distance between themselves and the other as possible. 'No parents past this point' used to be the slogan painted on the asphalt near the front of many schools. At issue here is the failure of responsiveness on both sides but, since professionals are the ones with the power and the 'turf', it is for them, as Anderson (1984) pleads, to 'Let it be known when it is the best time to speak . . . and not just wait for each other to make the first move'.

Teachers who do make the first move in responsiveness, in terms of Hess's (1971) variables, by displaying some warmth, some regard and some attentiveness to parents, have been surprised at the results. From countless of examples over a dozen years, let me cite three from those teachers of older pupils mentioned earlier.

- A Year 4 primary teacher who felt her life was being made miserable by an Aboriginal pupil, a girl whom she described as uncooperative and sulky, decided, under the impetus of peer pressure from her class at the university, to see what a home visit would accomplish. She walked home with the child, taking some of the little girl's best work to show the family whom she had never met or heard from. The next week she told us in class that the visit had been a resounding success, that she and the child's mother, who turned out to be a single parent like herself, had found a number of common features in their lives, and that the mother had expressed a wish to come to the school to help her with reading groups. Over the semester this arrangement was successfully established and the child's behaviour was transformed. At the end of the semester the teacher was investigating the possibility of school funding for a home visiting scheme.

- A secondary school music teacher asserted many times to her university classmates that 'Working with Parents' was a foolish subject for her to have chosen since she would never see the parents of her teenage students. Parents, she maintained, were the last people her students wanted more contact with. Contact, nevertheless, was essential for the subject, so she concocted a warm letter inviting the parents to come to – and participate in – a concert she and her students were arranging. To her astonishment, parents rolled up, her students were welcoming, parents not only enjoyed but many also made music with their teenagers, further dates were convened and she and a number of the parents arranged to produce an ongoing newsletter about music in the school.

- An Asian language teacher in the upper primary classes of a rural school was mystified by the idea of working with parents (most of whom she had not met). Why would they want to be involved in their children's learning of a foreign language? With some telephoned encouragement, this teacher invited parents to meet with her, leaving the location for them to decide. Parents chose an evening meeting at school, attended in force, and so much enjoyed the night – coming up with major reasons to learn another language, becoming aware of how many words English has appropriated from other languages, examining resources such as activity books and big books – that further evenings followed. Parents helped their children to reinforce their language learning at home, and were gratified at the employment possibilities opening to their children. Several helped the teacher to organise a Cultural Open Day.

We see in these three examples of unexpected (on the part of the teachers) parent–professional communication the power of responsiveness to evoke an answering chord of like behaviours. In each case the teacher, an unknown formless symbol of authority to the parents, has suddenly materialised as a flesh and blood human being demonstrating warmth, respect for their interest in their own child, and engagement with their ongoing concerns (the Aboriginal mother's awareness of the importance of reading; parents' love of music and its promulgation; parents' growing realisation, through their children, of the manifold uses of language learning). Though the teachers were astonished at the parents' reaction, is it really surprising that parents should reciprocate their positive initiatives? These, after all, are the elements of the human encounter.

McLean (1991a), in her book entitled *The Human Encounter* has taken the components that she sees making up what Buber (1965) has called 'the fundamental fact of human existence' and has applied these elements to the interactions between pre-school teachers and children. Buber has written that: 'The fundamental fact of human existence is neither the individual as such nor the aggregate as such . . . the fundamental fact of human existence is man with man.' McLean (1991a: 194), discussing what she calls this 'pinnacle of human contact', the moment when each participant is open to the other, notes that when teachers transform an 'I–It' relationship to an 'I–Thou' relationship, the persons involved are characterised by equality, mutuality and a sense of 'being there'. The teacher's respect for the other is accompanied by some confirmation of the other's actions (a condition lowered, McLean notes, when teachers are subjected to ongoing stress). In these significant moments of encounter, teachers are closely 'tuned in' to what the child is doing: 'In each setting, the teachers often "blatantly listened" (McLean, 1986) to children, showing through their body posture and verbal responses, that they were attending to the child's communication and treating it in a serious manner' (McLean, 1991a: 196).

When McLean draws out from the global concept of 'the human encounter' the elements of equality, mutuality and availability, she is using other words to describe Hess's (1971) first variable in Table 3.1: a 'warm affective relationship'. When she talks of respect and confirmation of the child, she is identifying the notion of 'high regard' (Hess's variable 2). And the picture of teachers 'blatantly listening' to children delightfully summarises Hess's variable 3: one partner's serious 'attentiveness to and engagement with the other'. For McLean, as for much of this book, those partners are teachers and children. But the purpose of the present chapter is to show that these variables also encompass adult–adult interactions, so that 'the human encounter' is seen to be of relevance across the whole spread of humanity.

Summary

This section on adult–adult responsiveness began with a somewhat gloomy look at the lack of exercise of this dimension. Parents and professionals frequently keep their distance because of uncertainty and fear arising from unpleasant past experiences. Professionals who have courageously taken a leap into the unknown and attempted to exercise responsiveness towards parents have often been startled at something that is not really surprising: the success of their genuine effort to meet parents in a 'human encounter'.

As was noted at the end of the last section, this encounter (the exercise of responsiveness) is only the first step in ongoing collaboration between partners. For that collaboration to persist, the partners, I am suggesting, must also engage in other behaviours drawn from the positive poles of the dimensions of control and involvement. But responsiveness is an *essential* first step.

In the next section, and in Chapters 5 and 6, a number of illustrations demonstrate the working of these three caregiving dimensions of responsiveness, control and involvement in interactions among young children, parents and professionals across early childhood settings (home, child care, pre-school, school and community). The illustrations chosen are drawn (with permission) from my students' work and provide practical suggestions for a variety of professionals interested in enhancing both their own relationships with families and the outcomes for young children. We begin with three stories illustrating the dimension of responsiveness.

THE DIMENSION OF RESPONSIVENESS: YOUNG CHILDREN, PARENTS AND PROFESSIONALS

Story 1 The notebook

Joanne, a Year 3 teacher in a country town, was upset at the distress of the mother of one of her pupils. The time was approaching for Renata to take her seven-year old daughter Kimberley for their quarterly trip to the doctors in the city. Kimberley had severe physical problems and needed regular checks and advice from several metropolitan sources.

Joanne and Renata got on well together, Joanne was able to assist the mother with Kimberley's exercise program at school, and the child was making good progress in the classroom. But Joanne noted that each time Kimberley returned from her visit to the city with her mother, the child seemed disturbed, the mother flustered. As the time for the third trip of the year approached, Renata confessed to Joanne that she dreaded the round of visits to the doctors because she often felt confused at the various specialists' information and inadequate when she could not remember all their different suggestions for Kimberley. Many phone calls were often necessary after coming home to sort out the problems.

'I feel such a fool,' said Renata.

'I've always felt a fool going to the doctor,' said Joanne, 'and that's just one doctor, not a whole lot, like you've got to see. I found I could never remember exactly what he told me, but I've solved it now. I take a bit of paper and write down what he says.'

'I could take a notebook! What a marvellous idea! I won't write it myself though. I'll ask the *doctors* to write down what they want.'

The return of the travellers was a delightful occasion not only for them, but also for Joanne.

'The notebook was perfect,' said Renata. 'Thanks so much for the idea.'

'I only had half the idea. *You* thought of the notebook. How did it go? Did they do what you wanted?

'It was perfect. They all wanted to write their comments and suggestions and they said what a good idea it was. A couple of them said they're going to start using this method as a general rule. The best part of all was that each one could read what the others said and tie their suggestions in. We've got a better organized program for Kim than we've ever had. And I didn't feel a fool once.'

Story 2 Parking stations

Miranda, an Aboriginal student, was coming to the end of her early childhood degree course, and as part of her 'Working with Parents' subject decided to have a talk with members of her family who had young children.

Miranda's family lived in a country town. During one of her home visits, conversation with two of her older sisters turned to the troubles they were having with the local school. Jocelyn had had a note asking her to go up to school because her six-year old daughter was having difficulties. She had no wish to go. She told her sisters how uncomfortable she felt, how she could not relate to the teachers, and how little she could do to help her children whom she wanted to do well at school.

'I don't know what to do, Miranda. You ought to have some ideas.'

There was no time to talk further that day, but the sisters agreed to get together again at the weekend. Jocelyn suggested meeting in the nearby park where the adults could sit and talk and keep an eye on all their children as they played on the park equipment. Park barbecue facilities would make a picnic lunch easy too. Miranda said that she would look out some materials she was using in her course which her family might like to see.

At the weekend a couple of cousins joined the party, one bringing a non-Aboriginal friend. After lunch under the trees, the children ran off to the swings, and the toddlers scrabbled in the sand near their mothers' feet. The discussion took off and lasted for almost two hours.

Jocelyn had been to school to see the teacher, but the interview had only deepened negative feelings. 'I don't know,' she told the group. 'She wants me to help Jacquie with her maths at home. How can I do that? I never finished primary, her father's the same. I've never heard those teachers say one good word about my kids.'

Round the concrete table heads nodded. Most of the mothers had only bad news from school – including tales of racism (name-calling) from other children, which both they and now their children had experienced. Going to see the teacher made them feel, as sister Natalie said, 'just not wanted'. What surprised these Aboriginal mothers was that Joan, the non-Aboriginal friend of cousin Lynne, said that she had felt exactly the same way when she had been called up recently to see the teacher about her children's difficulties. 'Well, maybe we've all got the same trouble with those teachers,' said Natalie.

'They're not all bad,' said cousin Lynne. 'Greg's teacher's lovely. She came round to see me at home and showed me some ways I can help him with his maths – games to play like snakes and ladders – and she wants me to come up to the school and tell the kids some of our stories. I might too.'

'What do you mean, games like snakes and ladders?' said Jocelyn. This was Miranda's chance to show the group the articles she had got from the Education Department's Aboriginal and Islander Section on ways of helping young children with schoolwork at home. Everyone wanted copies. Miranda also suggested getting in touch with the local Community Education Counsellor, an education resource person from the Aboriginal and Islander community. No-one in the family group knew about this position but Natalie said that she would make enquiries and invite the counsellor to their next meeting.

'Another meeting?' said Jocelyn.

'Of course,' said Natalie. 'We've got some ideas now.'

It was suggested that other relatives and friends might be interested in coming, and so the group broke up with some hope and with a date fixed for their next meeting in the park.

Story 3 The sofa under the sea

Prudence, the director of a pre-school, had thought for some time that Christine, the mother of four-year old Bella, was perhaps a non-reader. Prudence had sensed this from a number of clues over the months – Christine's non-collection of notes to be taken home, her questioning of other parents about information in newsletters. In the course of the year Christine had told Prudence a good deal about her past life, one of frightening abuse from parents and boyfriends, and about her ongoing difficulties as a single mother with five young children, who was now living for the first time a fairly stable life in a housing commission house.

Bella tended to be shunned by her classmates. She was a tough little nut like her mother, with whom she shared a staccato relationship.

Usually their only talk was to quarrel. This mirrored Christine's relationships with the older children in the family, whose competencies – especially in language – were low. Christine's life seemed wrapped up in her children, but she could not communicate with them. Prudence reflected that Christine had probably never had a positive role model. Prudence thought about the power of modelling and awaited her opportunity.

In the pre-school, the children had turned the book corner into an undersea cavern. Crêpe paper seaweed, painted fish and octopi adorned the walls around the book shelves, and the folds of a net, draped high over all, enclosed an opening that ushered the reader into a grottoed world of mystery. An old sofa, one family's gift to the pre-school, had been lugged into the corner, and served either as a couch to curl up on with a book or as an underwater ledge to laze on.

'Look at our sofa under the sea, Mum,' called Bella to her mother, pulling her inside the grotto. Bella had worked hard on this hideaway, and pride made her more positive than usual with her mother. They sat down on the sofa and Christine looked round admiringly. Prudence arrived, sat down with them and pulled out a book from the shelves next to the sofa. 'This is just a lovely place to read now,' she said. 'Like a story, Bella?'

Christine looked at the book in astonishment. 'But it's got no words,' she said.

'Quite a lot of our pre-school books haven't any words, just pictures,' said Prudence. 'It's good – we can make up our own stories,' and she began to do so, asking Bella questions about the cover, the pictures, and the story as it took shape. Christine looked amazed at first, but soon was joining in, taking her cue from Prudence, asking Bella questions, building on her responses, while Bella snuggled up beside her, and soon several other children as well. Prudence excused herself to see what was happening outside, offering Christine another wordless book as she went. Christine and the children stayed with the books for quite a long time.

Since then, Christine, Bella and others have enjoyed more story sessions on the sofa under the sea. Christine has a way of making her stories come to life that the children love. Prudence has been able to talk freely to Christine about the importance of chatting with children and snuggling up together with a book. Many more of the kind with no or few words have gone home with Bella from the library. Bella told Prudence that Mum loves reading to the kids in bed, and that now even Jake, the eldest, snuggles in to listen too.

These three stories, all true, concern pivotal moments of change in the lives of young children, parents and professionals. In the last chapter we examined some changes occurring among the members of pairs of these people – parent and child, professional and child, parent and professional. Here, on the other hand, it is useful to adopt a systems method and see how changes occurring in one or more members of the combinations affect the other members. Changes occur, in these stories, in all the aspects of caregiving behaviour – responsiveness, control and involvement. In this chapter, the dimension under focus is responsiveness. (Changes in the other dimensions remain as challenges for you to think about.)

In all of these stories, a positive outcome occurs in respect of a problem involving young children's progress, or at least a step is taken towards a positive outcome. The question to be determined in this chapter is whether this positive step has been associated with the exercise of responsiveness by players in these stories. Since responsiveness has already been shown to be associated with the development of trust (pp. 21 and 66), a further question is whether the need for trust and confidence has been met, to some degree, in both children and adults in these stories, through the exercise of responsiveness by other players. Rather than looking at responsiveness as a broad general term, we examine its operationalised component behaviours as suggested in Table 3.1: warmth, regard and attentiveness/engagement.

BUILDING CHILDREN'S TRUST THROUGH ADULT WARMTH, REGARD AND ATTENTIVENESS/ENGAGEMENT

In Story 1, Kimberley, formerly disturbed and uncertain of her exercise instructions, has come home from the city with a better organised program than ever before. In Story 2 the Aboriginal children who are performing poorly and are negatively regarded by their teachers and some classmates, have received helpful information through their student aunt. In Story 3, Bella, something of a quarrelsome outsider in the pre-school, has acquired some pride, status and a new, useful capacity to 'snuggle' and take in information.

In all of these cases, before the stories began, at least some adults had already exercised the behaviour of warmth in relation to these children, but that adult warmth was not enough to mend their situations. Their problems remained. What appears from these stories to have been essential was an extension of warmth to other behaviours. Warmth from an adult appeared necessary but not sufficient to motivate change in behaviour. Like warmth from the sun, it created the climate for other factors to stir into life, laying the dispositional basis for behavioural change.

One of the factors was certainly high regard. The sense that these children all had capabilities which they were not yet reaching, but could reach, appears to have been a strong motivational force impelling the adults to take a further measure to help. Just as important appears to have been the factor of attentiveness/engagement. There are indications that this was in operation before the stories began. The three teachers, Joanne, Miranda and Prudence, all had the situations of the children (and their parents) in mind at the start of the action, impelling Joanne to think about another way of approaching a series of doctors, causing Miranda to look out some appropriate printed materials to take on her visit home, and raising thoughts of role modelling in Prudence.

Similarly, the three sets of parents all held their children in high enough esteem to want to take a good deal of trouble for them – organising a notebook message system, wanting to read printed materials and locate a Community Education Counsellor, spending time and energy on books at school and at home. Again, these ongoing actions by each of the three sets of parents bespoke their lasting engagement and attentiveness to the children. These are aspects of engagement worth remembering by teachers who dismiss parents such as Christine (Story 3), and Jocelyn and Natalie (Story 2) as being 'uninterested'. These mothers' feelings of commitment and regard were, in turn, boosted by the reciprocal commitment and regard demonstrated in their children by professionals. In each story, one or more adults helped to enhance not only each child's sense of trust, but also that of the reciprocating adult/s.

BUILDING TRUST IN ADULTS THROUGH WARMTH, REGARD AND ATTENTIVENESS/ENGAGEMENT

As Joanne and Renata built on each other's ideas to concoct the notebook scheme, and later congratulated each other on the role each had played in its success, their mutual responsiveness reinforced their own feeling of confidence, not only in the other, but in themselves. As Renata said, 'I didn't feel a fool once.'

The mutual picking up and attentiveness to each other's cues by Prudence and Christine on the sofa under the sea (Prudence seizing the moment when Christine showed interest in the wordless book to demonstrate its use, to be followed by Christine's increasingly confident role modelling) is another example of the establishment of trust: the teacher in her procedure, the parent in her own abilities, Bella in her sense of ease as she snuggled in beside the adults. It was the enhanced sense of trust on the part of each member of the trio that laid the foundation for later talks about the importance of literacy and ways to achieve it. Such conversations would have been unthinkable between the two adults without the positive effects of the earlier incident of mutual responsiveness.

Perhaps the most telling example of the significance for adults of meeting the need for trust comes from the story of the Aboriginal family, with their desperate wish and inability to help their children's school-work. Here one finds examples of two opposing professional approaches. Some of the teachers in the school appear to have opted for the reverse of responsiveness. They demonstrated authoritarian coldness by sending notes summoning parents to the school, low regard for child or parent ('I've never heard those teachers say one good word about my kids'), and in asking parents 'to help the child with maths at home' showed no attentiveness to parental needs for guidance in doing so. As a trust-building exercise, their approach left parents feeling 'just not wanted'.

On the other hand, one teacher in the school employed every element of responsiveness. Instead of summoning the parent, Lynne, to the school, the teacher made a home visit. There is a myth among some teachers about home visits. They have been called 'intrusive' and indeed they can be, but conducted with sensitivity (e.g. having an initial meeting with the householder on the front verandah instead of bursting into the house) they are clearly a warmer and more respectful form of approach than calling a parent up to the school like a miscreant to the office. By venturing on to the householder's 'turf' the visitor can be seen as evincing a wish to offer the hand of friendship. On this home visit, not only has the teacher associated with Lynne engaged with her by bringing some games which parent and child can play to help maths skills, she has also stayed (further engagement) to show Lynne how they can be used. Finally, she has demonstrated high regard for Lynne by asking if she would contribute some Aboriginal stories to the classroom program. The result? 'Greg's teacher's lovely,' says Lynne. Because her trust in herself and her capabilities has been reinforced by the teacher, she is playing the maths games with Greg, she may go up to school to tell some stories, and her child will benefit. So will the teacher, who has earned the collaboration, rather than the alienation, of a parent, and in addition has acquired significant storytelling resources for her program.

Some of the ways in which Miranda, the student home on a visit, demonstrated her warmth, regard and commitment to her older sisters have already been discussed. A further comment about her status is in order. Because Miranda is not yet a teacher, not yet a figure of authority, her family feel able to communicate freely with her, call on her for support and ideas. The undergraduate students whom I ask to make contact with parents in their early childhood course find this constantly happening to them. They are valued resource persons who have not yet put on the dreaded mask of authority. Parents tell them how upset they have been by some professionals' bossy or distant behaviour. They beg the students, when they graduate, not to become like 'them'.

Over the years, however, I have seen many examples of 'them' turning into 'us': teachers who would have been seen as authoritarian by parents becoming colleagues with parents (like the three teachers of older students mentioned on p. 83). The experiences of these teachers strongly suggest that the exercise of responsiveness can be consciously attempted and can be successful in laying the dispositional basis for behavioural change.

In laying this basis, these teachers' experience suggests that – of the responsiveness variables listed in Table 3.1, warmth, high regard and attentiveness/engagement – the key variable for professionals to practise is that of attentiveness/engagement. High regard will be discussed in the next section, and some warmth is essential, but, as noted earlier, and in Stories 1, 2 and 3, warmth is not enough. Further, warmth is not an attribute readily practised. What can be practised is active attentiveness to where the parent is coming from. This may not be where the professional thinks the parent is coming from. It may be necessary to ask the parent some questions, and to listen to the answers. In this way professionals can tune in to the 'situation definitions' (Wertsch, 1984) that parents are bringing with them.

ATTENTIVENESS TO SITUATION DEFINITIONS AS NEEDS

To say that a parent and a professional may have different views of the world, a child, or a particular event is a truism. But the implications of this truism are profound, since young children's development is influenced by those most significant to them, and parents are likely to be far more significant than professionals. It is in the professional's interest, then, to find out about the parent's views, and, if possible, to explore ways of bringing parent views and professional views into some synchrony – that is , to 'bring the two halves of the child's world together' (Bronfenbrenner, 1974).

The views that parents bring with them to their association with a professional are the parent's situation definitions. A situation definition, according to Vygotskian theorist Wertsch (1984: 9), consists of a 'representation of objects' and the 'action patterns for operating on those objects'. We shall discuss these elements further in Chapter 6. Here it is worth noting that a parent's situation definition, which gives rise to a signal or cue from the parent, may often be expressed as a need.

In Story 1, 'The notebook', the parent's situation definition was that making medical rounds in the city with her daughter caused her to feel 'confused and inadequate'. Here Renata's 'representation of objects' was the making of medical visits, her 'action pattern' was to feel confused and inadequate.

The key significance of professional attentiveness to Renata's need is evident in the result of the differing behaviour of two sets of professionals. The doctors were attentive to the medical needs of Renata's daughter Kimberley, but inattentive to the mother's organisational needs. Thus the success of the visits was prejudiced. By contrast, Joanne, Renata's teacher friend, was attentive to these needs and made an appropriate suggestion based on her own related experience. Meeting Renata's basic need to get some order into the input from the doctors allowed the flowering of some of her organisational strengths as she built upon Joanne's suggestion.

It is important to note that several sets of needs were satisfied here. As well as the needs of the mother, Renata, other needs to be met were those of the doctors, through the medium of the notebook. The doctors were able to dovetail their instructions with those of other colleagues, and, as Renata pointed out, were 'going to start using this method as a general rule'. Joanne, the teacher, met her needs for a smoothly progressing program for her pupil, Kimberley, whose needs, central to the entire operation, were well satisfied.

There is a message here for professionals who are attempting to exercise attentiveness to parents' needs. Needs interlock, and pro fessionals must be equally attentive to their own. Whether we are professionals or parents, subjugating our own interests is no way to promote the interests of others, as proponents of assertiveness training point out (Adler *et al.*, 1983). One object of the professional's attentiveness and engagement must be the satisfaction of as comprehensive a balance of needs as is realistic to attempt. (For helpful models of this process, see a'Beckett, 1988, and Nedler and McAfee, 1979). Such a balance encompasses the needs of all participants. In Story 1, for example, these participants, all with needs related to 'the notebook', included a teacher, a parent, several doctors and other health professionals, and a child.

In this less than best of all possible worlds, the satisfaction of as comprehensive a balance of needs as possible may mean that not all needs can be completely, or immediately, satisfied. This was the case in Story 2. Miranda was able to satisfy her own needs:

- To find out more about the problems of Aboriginal families such as her own.
- To build up her own repertoire of collaborative skills.
- To offer her relatives some information and support.

Thus the needs of these family members to know how to help their children were at least partially satisfied. But the step taken by Miranda was incomplete and temporary. The needs of the teachers at the school to find effective ways of communicating with families of non-performing pupils remained totally unsatisfied, an ongoing source of poisoned relationships. Some hope for the future lay in the possible support of the parents by the Community Education Counsellor, the ongoing support (at a distance) of Miranda, and the parent–teacher partnership of Lynne and her child's teacher. The ripples from these partnerships might spread further through the participants.

Again, in Story 3, the book reading incident on the sofa under the sea may have laid foundations for some meeting of the needs of all participants (teacher, parent, child) for more positive, collaborative relationships. But a fundamental need of the mother actually to read remained unfulfilled, and would take many further steps to achieve.

Thus it is important to recognise that needs may take time to satisfy, and that only some needs may be susceptible of satisfaction in a given time. It is of great help to professionals to draw up a table to see what and whose needs are likely to be satisfied from a given set of actions (see the section on Questions at the end of the book).

Determining needs

It is enormously important that co-participants be invited to *express* their needs. As Peters and Kostelnik (1981) have noted about needs, inferred conclusions may be inferior conclusions.

In the family day care program (Chapter 3), it was possible to proceed with confidence in organising a curriculum founded on needs because the program participants had expressed those needs. In Story 1 in this chapter, teacher Joanne and mother Renata framed a program – 'the notebook' – based on the needs which they had openly discussed with each other. In Story 2, Miranda assembled materials and information to offer her sisters based entirely on the needs that they had shared with her.

Asking parents what their needs and interests are is foreign to many teachers. As hundreds of my students have told me, doing so can spark enormous parent interest. It can be done in discussion, in informal chat, where teachers listen carefully to note whether their questions and suggestions are eliciting real interest, or just polite nods. A collaborative partnership will not run on mere politeness. It will quickly fade away as parents vote with their feet. Professionals must be alert for the genuine reaction. In Story 1, for example, Joanne's recounting of her own needs brought forth an immediate answering response from Renata.

Professionals can also make contact with parents in writing (though here they must also be alert for adult literacy needs). At the Parent/Toddler Centre at my university, groups of parents enrolling with their children have been asked to fill in a questionnaire (Table 4.4). In response to the heading, 'Personal concerns of parents', the mother who wrote: 'How to fit it all together and keep one's sanity' was expressing, very directly, a need from the heart.

Table 4.4 Questionnaire for parents enrolling at Parent/Toddler Centre

We would like to make our Toddler Group mornings as interesting and helpful as possible for you and your family.

Your answers to the questions below will help us do that. We have also left space for you to write in other topics you would be interested in that we may not have considered.

Please indicate how important for our discussion sessions you consider each of the following:

	Very important	*Fairly important*	*Not very important at this stage*

Concerns of parents in relation to children
  Developing self-confidence
  Developing independence
  Developing creativity
  Other ....

  Getting on well with others
  Building trust
  Sharing and caring for others
  Other ....

  Speaking skills
  Listening skills
  Thinking skills
  Other ....

  Toys
  Books and stories
  Television
  Other ....

  Health
  Nutrition
  Safety
  Other ....

  Large muscle skills
  Finger dexterity
  Balance and coordination
  Other ....

Areas where parents influence children's behaviour
  Toilet training
  Temper tantrums
  Not eating
  Fighting with others
  Biting
  Jealousy
  Crying
  Fearfulness
  Taking others' things
  Not doing what parents want
  Other ....

Personal concerns of parents
  Choosing child care
  Having a life of one's own
  Managing the household
  Other ....

Any other topic you would like to discuss? ....

Questionnaires are not, of course, the only form of written communication with parents. A letter or a notice may serve. A staff member of a child care centre, for her practical project, wanted to find two parents who would permit her to make some home visits. On the board inside the front door of the centre she posted an attractive notice reading:

Parents

Have you any particular interests or concerns about your children and how we can work together to help them to grow and learn?

I am available to discuss these ideas with you at home, where there is more time to talk than at the Centre.

If you would like me to come and visit you at home, please write your name below.

She then signed her own name. At the end of the first day two mothers had written their names, and two more names appeared the next day. Since the staff member could accommodate only two sets of home visits, she speedily took down the notice.

Often parents are only waiting for a sympathetic approach.

Summary

Whether professionals go about indentifying parental needs in a more or less direct fashion, it is important that:

1 Professionals should not impose on parents their own preconceptions of what their needs are, but instead should elicit those needs from the parents themselves.
2 Professionals should consider how these parental needs intermesh with the needs of the children and their own needs as professionals.

ATTENTIVENESS TO SITUATION DEFINITIONS AS STRENGTHS

As was seen previously in discussing the family day care program, both parents and professionals who enter an association bring with them strengths as well as needs. All members of the group described on p. 77, including the professional, were able to learn from the shared experience flowing from one to another around the group. In that case, the experience concerned a number of ways of strengthening babies' trust (through cuddling, touching, and holding, for example in a New Guinea style *lap lap*), which formed the subject of shared discussion. Attentiveness by all members to one another's accounts allowed these strengths to emerge and, like one light sparking another, to multiply.

As Cochran (1987: 13) has noted: 'all families have some strengths [and] much of the most valid and useful knowledge about the rearing of children is lodged among the people . . . rather than in the heads of college professors'. In Stories 1, 2 and 3 a variety of family strengths are evident. Mention has already been made of Renata's ability to perfect a partially thought out suggestion of Joanne's, Aboriginal parents' capacity to use resources for self-help meetings and to share their own resources (storytelling) with mainstream children, and Christine's newly discovered capability to entertain children and her preparedness to come to grips with literacy problems. Several of these parental strengths, noted in the section (p. 90) concerning the building of adult trust through responsiveness, are counterparts of the increased teacher strengths also mentioned in that section. Through *the mutual attentiveness* evident in some parent–teacher dyads in Stories 1, 2 and 3, teachers as well as parents had needs for trust and confidence fulfilled, and were able, like the parents, to display still further strengths.

Perhaps the greatest strength that most parents possess is their determination to do their best for their children. While parents have powerful needs for both information and support in this endeavour, their underlying capacity to persist with what is often the inconvenient and demanding task of rearing children is an enormous parental strength. Both the needs and the strength are evident among all the parents in Stories 1, 2 and 3.

Professionals who, in their association with parents, are attentive to this strength, can acknowledge it and thus help to reinforce it. In particular, professionals can attend to parents' everyday interactions with their children and, in conversing with parents, confirm to them the great developmental value of the behaviours many parents practise intuitively. These are the behaviours listed as Hess's interactional variables in Table 3.1 and recapitulated in the family day care handout (Table 3.4). They are the behaviours displayed to children as warmth, high regard, attentiveness/engagement, consistent, explanatory guidance, encouragement of independence and achievement, by-the-way teaching, talking with (rather than to), and having interesting things around for children. These are the 'situation definitions' of many parents in regard to their children, and, because they are so commonly seen, the world generally takes them for granted.

By taking note of these behaviours and by reassuring parents of their value, professionals can move beyond attentiveness and engagement to high regard and warmth. By commenting favourably on these parental behaviours, professionals can help to reinforce and enhance them, to the enormous benefit of children. This is why responsiveness is above all an empowerment dimension.

5

CONTROL

Though it sounds a paradox, the control dimension may also be one of empowerment. This dimension, which concerns influences on behaviour, is the dimension which relates to the development of autonomy. In adult–child interaction, the facilitative pole of the control dimension involves adult guidance of children's behaviour in ways which foster the growth of the child's self-control and sense of autonomy. Similarly, in adult–adult interaction, the facilitative exercise of control allows both (or all) of the participating adults the opportunity to exert control over the situation. For parents and professionals, this means the exercise of mutual control in their interactions.

The adult–child behaviours identified by Hess (1971) which I have related to the dimension of control in Table 3.1 are:

1 Consistency of regulatory strategies.
2 Explanatory rather than arbitrary regulatory strategies.
3 Encouragement of independence.

In this chapter, we examine how the sense of autonomy, both of children and adults, is enhanced through the exercise of these behaviours. As in the discussion of responsiveness in Chapter 4, we look at:

1 Some ways (beyond those already touched on in Chapter 3) in which these behaviours came to operate between adults and children in the course of the family day care program.
2 How the same behaviours occurred among the adults (facilitator and providers) in the family day care program.
3 The operation of these behaviours among young children, parents and professionals in other real-life interactions.

THE DIMENSION OF CONTROL IN THE FAMILY DAY CARE PROGRAM: ADULTS AND CHILDREN

In Chapter 4, analysis of the growing responsiveness of family day care providers in the program group suggested that a major product of greater reponsiveness was a more positive attitude to the children. As program group providers became more attentive to (and thus aware of) the capabilities of young children, the positive attitude associated with this increased awareness carried through into their reports of guidance of children's behaviour. A marked change occurred in the program group in the ratio of positive to negative guidance strategies, as evidenced in pre- and post-program answers to interview questions (Appendix 5).

Before the program, providers in both the program and the control groups maintained that managing or guiding children's behaviour requires both positive and negative strategies. At the beginning of the program, the reported employment of both kinds of strategies by the two groups was quite similar. At the end, it differed significantly (Appendix 5). Figures 5.1 and 5.2 graph the differences.

In Figure 5.1 we see the changes over the course of the program in the methods that providers reported using to manage the children's behaviour. What distinguishes the groups is the difference, over the course of the program, in their reporting of negative strategies. At Time 1 the two groups reported using similar numbers of such strategies but by Time 2 (the end of the program) there was a sharp decline in the program group's reporting of negative strategies. By contrast, reports of such

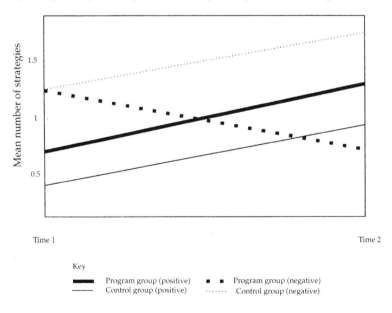

Figure 5.1 Providers' reported control strategies

99

strategies from the control group continued to rise (F[1,40] = 8.20, p< 0.001).

In Figure 5.2, graphing providers' reported use of strategies encouraging children's cooperation, emphasis is on the positive rather than the negative. Again, initial reports from the two groups showed them at the same level. By the end of the program, however, a marked increase had taken place in the program group's reported use of positive strategies. The control group remained virtually constant at the lower level (F[1,40] = 23.07, p< 0.001).

In conjunction with the program group's decrease in negative and increase in positive control strategies reported, it is instructive to look at some examples of these strategies (Table 5.1). That the management of young children should be attempted at times through coercive forms such as smacking and 'biting back' is by no means surprising. Though legally forbidden in family day care, such methods remain widely accepted in Queensland's social climate (Ferguson and Solomon, 1984), especially as children move into assertive and often non-compliant toddlerhood (Schneider-Rosen and Wenz-Goss, 1990). The decrease in the mention of such arbitrary punishments by the program group is the more noteworthy.

In combination, the marked increase in positive guidance reported by

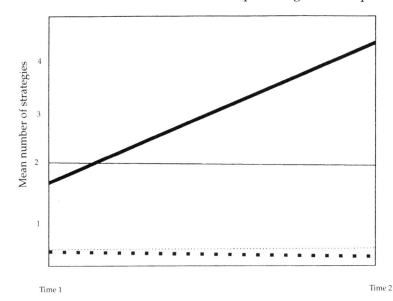

Figure 5.2 Providers' reported cooperation strategies

Table 5.1 Negative and positive control strategies reported by both program group and control group providers in the family day care program

Negative or punitive strategies	Positive strategies

Physical punishment:
e.g. smacks
    washing mouth out
    'going after them with the flyswat'
    'biting back'
 	
Deprivation:
    of attention
    of toys
    of television
 	
'Time out'
 	
Reporting misdemeanour to parent
	Setting up situations so problems do not arise:
	e.g. ensuring plenty of materials
	    ensuring enough food
	    ensuring enough rest
	    ensuring a secure routine
	
	Being firm and consistent:
	    'you have to know what you want'
	
	Positive reinforcement:
	    'lots of hugs and cuddles'
	    'I tell them how good they are'
	
	Explaining and modelling what to do:
	    'I don't tell them what not to do, I *show* them what to do'
	    'you have to really teach them reasonable manners'
	
	Offering other choices:
	    'they're very distractable';
	
	Encouraging empathy:
	    'I get A to take M's hands and show him things'
	    'I explain my feelings to the children and I point out *their* feelings too';
	
	Being involved:
	    'you've got to play *with* them'
	    'just being there'.

program group providers and their detailing (in the list above) of the methods used provide clear illustration of two of Hess's facilitative control variables (Table 3.1). These are *consistency of style* – in this case an authoritative style (Baumrind, 1971) as program group providers increasingly combined warmth with firmness – and *explanatory rather than arbitrary strategies*.

Turning to Hess's third control variable, the *encouragement of children's independence*, this was also strongly evident in the program group's responses on the strategies used (Appendix 5). Providers in the program (but not the control) group reported an increasing variety of means to 'encourage children to try things on their own' (Table 5.2).

In doubling the mean number of strategies selected from this pot-pourri of options (Appendix 5), providers in the program group were recognising the links, previously invisible to them, between the independence of

Table 5.2 Examples of the program group providers' strategies to encourage children's independence

Strategy	Comment
Being aware of the child's capabilities:	'Find their motive to do something – *then* you can encourage them.'
Noticing what the child is doing:	'Give them time and attention.'
Allowing children to try (not doing it for them):	'Let the child try – let them have a go.'
Helping enough to avoid frustration:	'I help when they're in trouble.'
Direct teaching, modelling:	'By example – mine or one of the children.'
	'You can teach them how.'
Demonstrating physical and verbal encouragement:	'I give lots of praise and cuddles.'
Getting one child to help another:	'I get one to help me teach another.'
Making materials and opportunities available:	'Give them things to try out – big bright things in the cot.'
	'Make things accessible.'

the children and their own caregiving behaviours. These behaviours included giving the children 'floor freedom' (Stayton *et al.*, 1971) and providing stimulating opportunities for play (Bradley and Caldwell, 1984). Above all, like Ainsworth *et al.* (1974) and Long *et al.* (1985), these providers were confirming the links between contingent reciprocity and independence in young children (see p. 21).

Children's behaviour

While the providers in the program group enhanced their sense of effective management, this gain did not translate into significant differences in behaviours related to autonomy or self-control among the children in the family day care homes. One explanation for this was that the overall picture of children's personal outgoingness that emerged from videotaped observations was a very positive one, in both the program and the control group homes.

Across groups and observations (Appendix 7), children spent 5–7 per cent of their time in *self-initiated locomotion*, moving about homes and yards towards goals such as sandpits, wheeled toys, blocks, construction sets, playdough and painting equipment or towards the care provider herself, as she engaged in pursuits susceptible of child assistance such as pegging out clothes or assembling a snack. Once the children's goals had been reached, a mean percentage of some 40 per cent of their time was spent in *mastery activity* (constructing or exploring), alone or with others. Aimless behaviours (*procuring objects*: picking things up and putting them down, *large muscle activity* without apparent purpose, and *non-involved* or desultory wandering) occupied relatively little of the children's time: no more than a mean of 4 per cent for any of these behaviours.

Across both program and control groups throughout the program, children's collaboration with others was generally high. Chapter 4 (Figure 4.1) has shown us that children in the program group maintained their interaction both with care providers and peers, while control group children turned increasingly to their age-mates. Across the groups, children's total time spent in reciprocal interaction (some 20–30 per cent with providers and 5–10 per cent with peers) compared favourably with the percentages reported by Fosburg (1982) in the US National Day Care Home Study (approximately 15 per cent with providers, 2 per cent with peers). Negative interaction (no more than two to three instances of resistance or aggression in an observation) was a rare occurrence.

Thus the children's lives in family day care, as seen in the videotaped observations, were purposeful, active and relatively harmonious. Other than the differing ratios of interaction (and utterances, Chapter 6) with care providers and peers, no significant differences were recorded between the program and the control groups of children. Yet the enhanced pleasure of the program group providers in their increasingly effective guidance strategies described at the second interview would suggest an ongoing benefit for the children in their care. If there were such a benefit occurring across a broad sweep of experience, it may have been inaccessible to the videotaped observations.

An instance is the contrast in one program group provider's responses to the question of how a family day care provider might help children to get along together (Table 5.3). At the beginning of the program, 'just

Table 5.3 An example of pre- and post-program responses from one program group provider to the question 'How can a family day care provider help children to get along together?'

Response before program	Response after program
'Just being there – sitting down with them.'	'Sometimes when T starts to push a bit – she's fascinated with people her own size and she wants to hug them – I'll talk about it as I see her going up to one of them: "We can handle your feelings about cuddling without disturbing this other person – let's pat her gently." It works! And then you can put them in situations together – in the water, in the sandpit – where it's big enough and there's interesting things for everybody. We go shopping together too – they love carrying the bags together.'

being there' summed up this provider's approach to helping children get on well together. By the program's end, a whole series of strategies came to mind as she talked of what worked well. In developmental terms, these included consistency of guidance, encouragement of articulation of feelings, fostering of empathy through modelling, ensuring sufficient materials for all and providing opportunities for prosocial behaviour.

A response such as this, which ranges over times and settings, both in and out of the home, represents an increase in reported behavioural options which half-hour observational sequences cannot match, since at any one moment only one option can be realised.

What processes operating within the family day care program might have been responsible for these changes in behaviour of the care providers?

THE DIMENSION OF CONTROL IN THE FAMILY DAY CARE PROGRAM: THE ADULTS

It is possible to postulate a social desirability explanation for the positive results reported here. It is not uncommon for interviewees to give responses designed to please (de Vaus, 1985). In relation to control strategies in general, program group providers may have divined the facilitator's attitudes to coercive punishment and responded accordingly at the second interview. Little mention, however, favourable or unfavourable, was made of coercion as a strategy during the program, the facilitator preferring to sidestep a contentious issue in favour of discussion of positive strategies on which more agreement was likely (Halpern and Larner, 1988).

The possibility of a social desirability effect must also be considered in accounting for the program group's marked increase in enunciation of positive strategies for fostering cooperation. What the responses suggest, however, is not that program group providers replaced negative with positive reports in order to please the facilitator, but that an expansion took place in their repertoire of positive options.

How might this have happened?

On p. 66 it was noted that two interactive theories of learning, Vygotskian and empowerment theories, were found useful in analysing the changes taking place among the adults in the family day care program. Both come into play in explaining how program providers expanded their repertoire of positive options in guiding behaviour.

In the Vygotskian model of teaching/learning, learners move through the zone of proximal development: 'the distance between the [learner's] actual developmental level . . . and the level of potential development' achievable through collaboration with more capable others (Vygotsky, 1978: 86). The family day care program was the zone of proximal development for the providers. Here they recast situation definitions in the light of new insights introduced by various 'capable others'.

In the Vygotskian approach, the situation definition that eventually comes to be adopted by the learner is that of the facilitator or teacher. Among the 'new insights' introduced by the facilitator was the notion of the beneficent rather than vicious cycle of relationships with children that may be set up by 'accentuating the positive'. During the first of four sessions on guiding behaviour, the facilitator told the group about the simple but highly effective mechanism established by a paediatric service dealing with child management problems (Schroeder, 1979) in which, as described by Schaefer (1982: 13): 'instructing mothers to count the number of times they attended to positive behavior of their children resulted in increases in attention to positive behavior, increases in the child's positive behavior, and decreases in inappropriate behavior of the child'.

The program provided the opportunity to follow Schaefer's call, in relation to these findings, for 'the professsional to direct parent attention to the identification, reinforcement and development of positive behaviours rather than focusing entirely upon identification of symptoms, deficiencies and deviations in the child's behavior and development' (Schaefer, 1982: 13). The suggestion was made that providers make a mental note each week, for sharing within the group, of some examples of how they had been 'accentuating the positive': 'catching a child being good' and commenting positively to the child. Subsequent sessions began with an exchange of examples of positive reinforcement noted by providers during their previous week's experience. These examples stimulated much discussion in the group. One session began with the following cascade of examples:

Logbook: examples from Brenda, Sandra, Hetty and Lois

Two of the children were fighting over a post box. Brenda successfully distracted the child who had tried to grab the box towards another toy. Later, the children did briefly share, and she complimented them: 'That's lovely of you to share.' Shortly after, one of the children offered the toy to the other.

Three-year old was bouncing on the sofa (not allowed) but, seeing Sandra, stopped bouncing and sat quietly. Instead of scolding him (as she said she would usually have done), she said: 'Oh, you are being a nice grown-up boy.' Nothing happened at the time, and she thought the child had not 'registered', but hours later when his father came he ran to him and said: 'I've been a nice grown-up boy.'

One child never helps to tidy up though he is always being admonished to. When Hetty started to tidy up and the other children

105

helped a bit, she made a point of saying: 'Oh, you *are* helping me such a lot. That's lovely.' At which the recalcitrant child at once ran over and started to help.

It's not just the little ones. My 12-year old daughter tidied her room up like it's never been done before. It was after she did the washing up and I said how well she'd done it. I never make a fuss of her usually. It really works.

In these examples, the facilitator's introduction of a new insight about positive reinforcement has enabled providers to move, in Schaefer's (1982: 13) words, to 'the identification, reinforcement and development of positive behaviours rather than focusing entirely upon the identification of symptoms, deficiencies and deviations in the child's development'. In Wertsch's (1984: 11) terms, providers have begun to redefine both the 'representation of objects and the representation of action patterns for operating on those objects'.

At the same time, these extracts from the program logbook show something else going on. As providers tell their own stories, reinforcing and extending one another's repertoires, they have moved beyond a Vygotskian perspective, in which the facilitator's definition is the one finally adopted by the learner (Wertsch, 1984), to an empowerment approach, in which learner experience is attended to, supported and validated (Cochran, 1988). It is the combination and intermeshing of these two approaches that makes the discussion group so potentially effective a format for ongoing mutual control by adults.

On p. 78, open-ended group discussion was proposed as an empowering activity by Vanderslice (1984: 4) because it 'draws on and validates participants' experiences and knowledge so they can begin to see themselves as valuable, knowledgeable members of a group' and it 'encourages participants to listen to, respect and learn from one another so they see themselves and each other as accomplishing a collective task'. These quotations point up two essential features of the effective discussion group. First, such a group 'draws on and validates participants' experiences and knowledge' if it has been based on the responsive eliciting of participants' entering situation definitions (reviewed in Chapter 4). If this has occurred, it is posssible to maintain the process of 'anchoring all program topics firmly to the experience and examples provided by the group', providing support and, in many cases, validation. Second, the group itself needs to be comparatively small.

Group size and the control dimension

In the family day care program there were twenty-one participants, but the decision was made long before the sessions started to split this number in two and create two groups of ten and eleven, to allow 'more congenial small-group discussion'. There is, after all, good biblical precedent for a twelve-person discussion group, but we live in an age when latter day economic messiahs, who abound in education as elsewhere, have attempted economies of scale through approaches to learning that place the major emphasis either on 'autonomous' (i.e. largely solitary) study or on very large groups of learners. It is useful, therefore, to restate some of the reasons why 'smallish is beautiful'. In particular, smallish is beautiful in relation to the dimension of control, that is, to how one affects, or is affected by, a situation.

In these terms, studying alone is partially effective. As we read a book or operate a computer program, we may get feedback that guides our behaviour, but we cannot simultaneously give feedback that influences the behaviour of the writer of the book or program. (We may change the options the program offers us, but not the program writer's basic mindset.) Small groups, however, invite such two-way feedback. Vygotskian theory with its stress on 'the social formation of mind' (Wertsch and Stone, 1985) has added to 'the considerable evidence that making decisions in groups integrates complex information more effectively than when individuals work alone' (Johnson and Johnson, 1985: 5).

Thus, for example, family day care providers in the small group discussion format were able to recast their definitions of such concepts as 'helping' and 'sharing' so as to apply these terms and their own related behavioural options to a wider range of practical situations than formerly. In the examples of 'accentuating the positive' given above, they did this by negotiating definitions with other participants (including the facilitator) within the zone of proximal development (the program), trying out their amended definitions in particular situations in the field (the family day care homes), and subsequently returning to the zone for further negotiation. The smallish size of the group, where all definitions were able to be tapped and negotiated, was an integral part of this process.

In relation to large groups of learners, Campbell (1995) has well summarised the obverse of the argument that large units provide more resources and so are more powerful in their effects. Drawing on the clear-cut, but currently unfashionable, findings from both his own research (Campbell, 1990) and that of Barker and Gump (1964), Campbell (1995) writes of large and small schools and classes, but the principle may be seen to hold for discussion groups:

> From the outside, large schools look rich in resources, powerful and impressive, but, to the students within them, it is the small schools which are more stimulating. Good resources are translated into good experiences only if they are accessible. This conclusion is reflected in

the established findings relating to the effects of school size which can be summarised as follows. In comparison with students in small schools, those in large will:

(a) experience weaker pressures towards participation in activities, and less warmth and support within them;

(b) participate in fewer activities, a smaller number of operational roles, and less varied activities;

(c) display weaker attachments to the school, weaker senses of responsibility for the maintenance of school activities, and lower concern for persons.

. . . As a group, the graduates of the small schools display greater and earlier maturity, increased senses of responsibility, and greater capacity for leadership.

(Campbell, 1995: 5)

Campbell (1995) goes on to write of the growth, in small groups (schools), of participants' self-concept and sense of control, qualities of particular concern in a discussion of the dimension of control.

If the size of a group has significant effect on the self-concept and sense of control of its participants, so too does the way in which group programs are structured.

Program structure and the control dimension

How programs are structured – highly structured, semistructured or unstructured – reveals how they are controlled. A structured program is tightly planned by the leader or facilitator, who keeps firm control of its aims, content, resources and direction. Facilitators of semistructured programs have an overall plan of the program and its content and some resources they believe essential. They also believe that other members of the program have their own content and resources to contribute, and make room for these contributions while keeping watch that overall aims and direction are fulfilled. In an unstructured program, aspects of planning, direction, content and resources are left open as far as possible, to be negotiated by the members as the program proceeds. Such a program has the advantages and disadvantages of all *laissez-faire* regimes. It can quickly get 'out of control'.

A direction of the family day care program was to 'anchor program topics to the experiences provided by the group'. On a Vygotskian view, this direction should be most effectively met within a structured program. On the other hand, the amalgamation of Vygotskian and empowerment viewpoints would lead, rather, to the kind of semistructured format exemplified in the family day care program. Let us consider these alternatives.

From a Vygotskian perspective, it is within the zone of proximal development (in this case the family day care program) that situation definitions (the 'experiences provided by the group') are defined, negotiated and redefined. It is through this process that participants acquire new situation definitions, qualitatively different from those they originally held. These new definitions are either those of the facilitator or else intermediate definitions assisting participants to move to an eventual acceptance of the 'correct' definitions. A step-by-step progress towards the goal(s) known to the facilitator, that is, a structured approach, would appear the most effective format for such a program.

On the other hand, adding an empowerment to a Vygotskian perspective enables existing situation definitions to be conceptualised in some cases as needs, in others as strengths. A model of learning in the zone of proximal development which combines elements of the Vygotskian approach with an empowerment perspective allows for the preservation of these strengths, affirming that 'much of the most useful knowledge about the rearing of children is to be found among the people actually engaged in the undertaking' (Cochran, 1988: 72). The examples given earlier from the family day care program, in which providers demonstrated how they 'accentuated the positive', showed how these strengths were reinforced within the program group.

Where contributions from both participants and facilitator are negotiated within the zone of proximal development, results should include the strengthening of some existing definitions of participants, their adoption of some new ones and, at times, the modification of the facilitator's definitions. The flexibility called for in such an approach would lead appropriately to a semistructured program, operating through mutual control.

In the home visiting program involving Aboriginal mothers and their young children (Watts and Henry, 1978), in which the mothers were encouraged to see themselves playing an important role in their children's development, a semistructured approach meant that:

> the mothers would have distinctive contributions of their own to make and that the program would be open to modification. Indeed the sessions became more interesting as the Parent Educator learnt as much from the mothers as she gave to them, and the roles of initiator and respondent were often interchanged.
>
> . . . In line with the aim of sharing responsibility for initiation and response, the Brisbane program did not adopt the approach of programs such as those of Levenstein (1970) and Karnes (1969) in which tightly pre-structured activities were introduced by the program staff. . . . While in the Brisbane program materials and activities were introduced by the Parent Educators, and indeed

pre-planned at weekly planning meetings, those activities were always designed with a potential for modification as seemed appropriate to the children, the mothers or the occasion. And some activities were mother initiated.

(Watts and Henry, 1978: 159)

Semistructure, again, was the hallmark of the Inala Aboriginal parent program overviewed in Chapter 3, in which Karen Martin described how program visitors:

offer me advice concerning different and new methods of play or sometimes we exchange methods of play and communication . . . In general, we discuss and experiment with suggestions and ideas, and we get the chance to show off our creativity in the making of an item of play for our sons and daughters.

(Martin, 1979)

The semistructured rather than structured approach should, then, contribute both to the internalisation of new ideas (Wertsch, 1984) – to be discussed further in the next chapter – and to the encouragement and protection of existing facilitative functioning (Cochran, 1988). That such functioning, helpful to children's development, also enhances adult self-esteem and sense of internal control is evident from some further outcomes from the family day care program. These are the findings concerned with presage variables.

PRESAGE VARIABLES

A glance back at Table 3.1 shows high self-esteem and a sense of internal control as the presage (pre-existing) characteristics of parents who are most helpful to young children's development.

In Appendix 8, the results are given of provider responses to questions asked about these variables. At the beginning and the end of the program, providers were asked whether working in family day care had been what they hoped it would be, whether the things they had done as family day care mothers had measured up to their expectations, and whether they felt they were on top of things or if things were getting on top of them. Responses to the last of these questions showed changes taking place in providers' sense of internal control by the end of the program. At this time, a significant difference emerged between program and control groups, with the mention of negative factors (those reducing the sense of being 'on top of things') decreasing for the program group, increasing for the control group (Appendix 8, Item 23).

In responding to these items, it was fascinating to note that providers universally framed their comments in terms of their sources of support or stress. They used precisely the same categories of support or stress as those identified by Belsky (1984) in describing factors that influence parenting, namely:

- Their own *personal* characeristics and strategies.
- *Children's* characteristics.
- *Network* characteristics (other family members, family day care parents, coordinators).

Of these three sources of satisfaction/dissatisfaction, the providers' perceptions of only one changed sufficiently to make a significant difference between the program and control groups. By the end of the program, members of the providers' network (scheme coordinators, members of children's families, and other providers) were mentioned more often by the program group as sources of support (a mean of 0.7 increasing to 1.3), less often by control group providers (1.1 decreasing to 0.6; $F[1,40] = 5.93$, $p< 0.02$).

Thus, as the program helped its participants to behave more positively towards the children in their care, it also enabled them to see the behaviour of the adults around them in a more positive light. These network members came to be perceived less as sources of stress, more as sources of support, offering providers opportunities to exert more control of their situations.

Evident here may be a somewhat similar process to that revealed in a study by Oliver (1992) of the changes in self-perceptions of parents as they engaged in a Management of Young Children Program. In this program, parents learned to have more control over their relationships with their out-of-control young children. At the beginning of the program, parents had very low self-esteem. This rose significantly as they began to feel more competent as managers of their children. At the time of the study it had not, however, reached the level of a comparison group. There were also differences between the MYCP and comparison groups in their degree of contact with neighbours and community (MYCP group little, comparison group significantly more). Noting the link between self-esteem and network contact, Oliver (1992: 80) suggests that the 'increase in program parent self-esteem could possibly help a parent over time to engage in or "own" more of these community network contacts'.

Cochran (1987), too, has drawn attention to the sequence observed among participants in the Family Matters program as they began, psychologically as well as physically, to 'move outwards' towards the community:

a trust-building process conducted within the security of their own homes was required before some parents would seriously consider

venturing out into neighbourhood oriented cluster group activities
. . .

Thus there appeared to be several different aspects of empowerment, beginning with an individual's view of herself and progressing through relations with nearby others to interactions with more
distant organizations and institutions.

(Cochran, 1987: 23)

For the family day care providers, who at the beginning of the family
day care program were women of quite high self-esteeem and sense of
control, it was clearly not necessary for relationships with the program
to be built up 'within the security of their own homes'. But it appears
that some of the features of the sequence described by both Cochran
(1987) and Oliver (1992) were operating and are worthy of further study.

Summary

So far this chapter has focused on the dimension of control in relation to
the family day care program. It appears that a program which
encourages adults to be more effective in helping young children's
growth of self-control and autonomy also helps those adults to develop
the same qualities in relation to one another.

Does this apply, too, in the everyday interactions of young children,
parents and professionals?

THE DIMENSION OF CONTROL: YOUNG CHILDREN, PARENTS AND PROFESSIONALS

Story 4 Only connect

Marilyn, group leader at the child care centre, pondered over several
questions. Did the Chinese parents want their three and four year olds to
be integrated with (i.e. to play with) the Australian born children? Or
did they want their children to withdraw and keep to themselves – as at
present they certainly did? Did the Australian parents want their children to build more or fewer connections with the newcomers? What did
her fellow staff members think? And what did the weekly staff visitor, a
Chinese member of the Children's Community Council whose personnel
dropped in to help at all ethnically diverse child care centres, think about
this issue of integration?

Marilyn loved the changing look of the suburb where the child care
centre was located. She liked the interesting groups of new faces from
overseas that she saw in the streets. But she wondered whether the child
care centre was doing much to make the Chinese newcomers feel at

home. She decided to ask the parents, both Australian and Chinese, for their views and produced a handout with some simple questions such as 'What should our Centre's goals be for your child?' and 'Would you like your child to mix with the children from other countries at our Centre?' No Mandarin speaker herself, she asked the Community Council helper to translate the questions for the Chinese parents. She also had informal chats in the staff room with her colleagues and found that they were sympathetic to the difficulties they believed Chinese families must have in settling in to a new country. On the other hand her colleagues were aggrieved at the perception they had that they themselves were regarded as lowly child-minders by these parents.

Just over a quarter of the child care centre families – both Australian and Chinese – handed in replies to Marilyn's questions. Responses from both sets of families revealed the wish for a caring and stimulating environment, and an appreciation of what the Centre was doing for their children (one Chinese family comparing the quality of care which would affect the personality of their child with the fertilizer and water which would produce a fine, mature tree). Further, both sets of responses (from Australian and Chinese families) indicated a strong wish for all the children to play and learn with and from each other.

Staff members derived great encouragement from these parental responses. They realised that the problems they had perceived between Chinese parents and themselves had more to do with difficulties in communication than with condescension. When the Community Council member was present to translate, they began to make overtures to the Chinese parents at pick-up time, explaining what their children had done that day. These parents began to spend up to twenty minutes longer in the afternoons at the Centre, and Australian parents were observed also beginning to communicate with the Chinese parents, attempting to share incidents observed among their children.

Staff members interacted more readily, too, with the Community Council worker, asking her for more information that would help them to communicate better (e.g. finding out the proper pronunciation of children's names). Above all, staff members reciprocated the parents' encouragement in the questionnaires by making more inclusive their program for the children, introducing more Chinese objects, such as silk dress-up garments, woks, bowls, Mandarin illustrated books and pictures, which all the children, Chinese and Australian, began to use. The Community Council visitor helped the Chinese children to learn the English names of some of the materials, and when she introduced songs in Mandarin all the children listened and tried to join in.

A 27 per cent questionnaire response rate is low, but it had a dramatic effect in this Centre. That effect, instigated by Marilyn, might be called one of diffusion. Bronfenbrenner (1994) has written of the power of

113

diffusion in enabling an intervention program to enhance the development, not only of the 'target' child, but also of other siblings in the family. We might say the same thing of this Centre 'family': not only the children, but the parents, the staff, and the Community Council helper benefited when parents were enabled to voice their opinions.

Story 5 Good ideas

Jan was a kindergarten director who believed passionately in child-directed play and exploration, Mary was a strong-minded parent who did not. On each roster visit to the kindergarten, Mary would bring materials with her to make some highly structured object such as a folded paper basket. The children, full of admiration, would clamour to follow suit. 'See,' Mary would say to Jan, 'these children just need more direction. They could be learning really useful things, far more than you've got them doing here.' Despite Jan's attempts to explain the importance of children's trying out their own ideas, Mary remained scornful and distressed at the 'mess' in the kindergarten.

One day Jan mentioned to Mary that she had decided to hold a parents' evening meeting about Children's Play, and asked Mary – whose craft skills she recognised and admired – if she would help her by making a poster to advertise the meeting. The mother readily agreed and there was a good turn-out in response. Explaining that at this meeting action would precede talk, the teacher introduced two sets of activities for parents to try out. One was 'The Butterfly', a large stencil which parents were to colour in, the second was a collection of bits and pieces which they could use in any way they wanted.

After considerable enthusiastic activity, the teacher asked which task parents had enjoyed most. Some had preferred colouring in the butterfly: 'I need to know what I'm supposed to do'; ' I like to have clear directions.' Some said they liked letting their heads go with the free construction. Among these, Mary, the mother whose paper basket had started it all, had been highly inventive in putting together a kind of train with complex rails made of straws. 'That was fun,' she said. 'I've never done anything like that before. I really enjoyed working out how to do it.'

The teacher took the opportunity to pass on to the group some recent research findings linking creativity, parents' self-directing values and children's high achievement at school. Parents discussed, from their own experience, the importance of this at a time when people have to be flexible in changing jobs and acquiring new skills.

On her next roster visit some days after the meeting, Mary was heard to say to another parent: 'You know, these children have some really good ideas here.'

Story 6 Pause, prompt, praise

As a primary school remedial teacher, Thomas was sometimes asked to talk in the evenings to quite large parent groups about ways in which they could help the children to read at home. Thomas favoured the 'pause, prompt, praise' method, and would explain to parents how children with reading difficulties needed:

- Time to pause and consider.
- Some hints (prompts) to help to decipher meaning from context.
- Some encouragement (praise) for an effortful try.

After one such meeting Yvonne Kelly, the mother of one of Thomas's remedial pupils, eight-year old Ben, intercepted Thomas as he was leaving. She wanted to express her disquiet at Ben's refusal to let her help with any reading practice at home, even of the interesting books Thomas supplied for the purpose. Yvonne looked very worried. 'He says it's better for him to read them on his own,' (Thomas knew that it was not) 'and if I pressure him, he says he just hates school' (Thomas knew that he did).

Thomas decided to take a new tack and asked Yvonne about Ben's leisure time activities. 'He loves riding his bike. And he likes playing games like snakes and ladders and monopoly. He just loves winning.' Thomas asked Yvonne if he could come and see them at home, bringing a new game that might appeal to Ben and help his reading too. Yvonne looked amazed – and appreciative.

Thomas turned up at the Kellys' armed with a lotto board with numbered spaces, counters, dice, and some reading material. The rules of the game, he explained to Yvonne and Ben, were that when you landed on a numbered square, you had to read that number of sentences before proceeding. Reading with minimal prompting allowed you to move on an extra place.

Ben loved the game. He had trouble with some words, but his mother, who played the part of prompter, did her job with plenty of attention to pausing and praising. Ben was delighted with the reward of moving an extra space. Occasionally when it was Yvonne's turn to read, she, too, made a mistake, and had to correct herself. Thomas congratulated her. She said, 'I thought, "that sounds wrong", so I read to the end of the sentence and saw what the word must be.' Ben looked pleased as he saw his mother making the reading method work.

At school over the next few weeks, Thomas noticed a steady improvement in Ben's reading, especially comprehension, in the remedial sessions. Ben told Thomas that he had invented a new rule for the game – moving forward not just one extra space but as many spaces as the number of sentences read correctly. 'What a good rule,' said Thomas.

On a follow-up visit to the Kellys', Thomas found that Yvonne had devised some new games, for example, incorporating the reading of labels on the packets of breakfast cereal on the table, and that other members of the family were playing as well. Yvonne had taught them, too, to pause, prompt and praise. Thomas asked Yvonne whether the books he was sending home with Ben were still suitable. She told him, with pleasure, that while she and Ben would often start reading with the aid of a game, they now sometimes continued without it, because 'the books he's chosen are so interesting'. At school, Ben's classroom teacher said to Thomas: 'You've really switched Ben on to reading now.'

In these three true stories, we find elements of the dimension of control that enable adults to help children, and other adults, to exercise more autonomy, or personal outgoingness, or engagement with the environment. First we look at adults helping children.

THE DIMENSION OF CONTROL: ADULTS AND CHILDREN

In Chapter 2, adult help in fostering children's fulfilment of the need for autonomy (versus shame and doubt, Erikson, 1950) was teased out into a number of strands. Examples were given of adult help that consisted of 'encouraging self-help', 'mediating conflict', 'promoting confidence and competence' (p. 22). In Stories 4, 5 and 6 we see all these mechanisms at work.

Encouraging self-help

Encouragement of self-help was linked, in Chapter 2, to the degree to which adults made available to young children 'many small choices that were genuinely theirs to make'. In all three stories in the present chapter, the alliance between the sets of adults (that is to say, the *mutual control* exercised by professionals and parents) has led to an increase in the number of real choices available to the children concerned.

At the beginning of Story 4, Chinese and Australian children are spending their time in a state of withdrawal into two separate groups with little communication: a state of non-choice in relation to one another. The putting into practice of the motif of novelist E. M. Forster, 'only connect' (that is, making connections among the adults, group leader, parents, staff and Community Council visitor), begins to bring about a range of opportunities for decision making for all of the children. For example, in their play children begin to make choices in their mutual use of the 'silk dress-up garments, woks, bowls, Mandarin illustrated books and pictures' introduced by the adults.

The theme in Story 5 is in fact the opening up of choice. Instead of the

116

children following the lead of the strong-minded mother who always shows them how to make tightly structured objects (with no room for choice), we hear, in the final scene, the mother announcing that: 'these children have some good ideas'. In other words, they have interesting intellectual choices that they are allowed to make. This remarkable change has occurred because, on her roster days, this mother, through her enhanced communication with the teacher and other parents, is now encouraging the children's choices.

Because of the collaboration of a teacher and a mother, Ben in Story 6 moves from a state where, like the children in Story 4, he is frozen into reading withdrawal and non-choice, into energetic decision-making. His decisions involve not only the reading games he is now playing with his family – and for which he is helping to devise new rules – but also the choice of books to bring home to read, a choice made in partnership with his teacher.

Many of the increased choices made by the children in these stories are likely to have been influenced by social referencing. Social referencing, in which young children look to the emotional reactions of significant others to appraise an uncertain situation (Berk, 1994), has been demonstrated in a variety of studies of, for example, babies gauging an adult's facial expression before venturing to play with an unfamiliar toy or deciding to cross a visual cliff. To young children, parents are far more significant others than are teachers (Watts and Henry, 1978). The physical presence and positive, encouraging looks and words of their parents are highly likely to have played a major role in children's choices to attempt the metaphysical cliffs of new experience as Chinese and Australian children began to approach one another, as kindergarten children saw that it was now permissible for them have their own 'good ideas', and as Ben made a courageous guess at an unfamiliar word.

Mediating conflict

As we saw in Chapter 2 and in the first section of this chapter, adults spend much of their time dealing with conflict in young children (conflict against 'the rules' and against one another). In Stories 4, 5 and 6, is there evidence that the mutual control exercised by the respective interacting adults has made their exercise of guidance more effective?

Readers of Stories 4, 5 and 6 will have noted that the stories contain little mention of overt conflict behaviour among the children. Children are not depicted as fighting with their peers or with adults. But, as depicted in the Schedule of Child Behaviour (Appendix 3), non-collaborative behaviour (or conflict) may involve more than fighting or aggression. In the Child Behaviour Schedule two codes were used to categorise the non-responsive moves of children. These codes were *aggress* and *resist*, the latter consisting of a portmanteau of codes:

> Resist: To resist domination, to assert self: To oppose any intrusion on one's personal domain including both (a) resistance to demands, orders, or any trampling underfoot, and (b) protection of property. Also includes rejecting overtures by adults or children (physical or verbal).
>
> (White *et al.*, 1979: 96)

Of the three stories presented in this chapter, two (Stories 4 and 6) are underpinned at their outset by examples of resistance, manifested as withdrawal, by the children concerned. In Story 4 it is because both Chinese and Australian groups of children resist playing with each other that group leader Marilyn decides that a circuit breaker is needed and approaches parents for their opinions. This is a pivotal moment in Marilyn's anti-bias curriculum (Derman-Sparks, 1989).

Young children who keep their distance from (i.e. resist) one another, and whose withdrawal is reinforced by disaffected adult group members, can mature into the Montague–Capulet (or European–Aboriginal or US–Soviet or Christian–Jew) groups of adults whose misunderstandings, each of the other, are exploited by the powerful to carry out their conflicts. Interesting differences between people become, in the eyes of the other group, signs of subhumanity, commonalities across groups are swept aside, and resist balloons into aggress.

We see this metamorphosis occurring in Story 6. The story begins with Ben's mother making an anxious plea to his teacher, Thomas, for advice about Ben's *resistance* and *withdrawal* from the school's remedial home reading program. But other feelings than resistance are involved, she reveals. Under pressure from her to read, Ben has started to say that he 'just hates school'.

By the end of both stories, the communicative action of professionals and parents has converted these examples of resistance/aggression to collaboration. Chinese and Australian children are playing, talking and singing with one another. Ben is both playing and reading with his parents, and reading more with his teachers at school.

As Kean (1994) has demonstrated in a range of early childhood classrooms and associated homes, when adults give attention to supporting children's emotional development, children learn better because they are less anxious and less angry. Kean's studies reported on parents and teachers acting independently of one another. The stories presented in this chapter demonstrate the increased power of the benefit that accrues to children when professionals and parents exercise *mutual control* (i.e. work together).

Promoting competence and confidence

Among the young children in our society there are large differences in both competence and confidence. How do parents and professionals approach these differences? One approach is as follows: 'Unto every one that hath shall be given and he shall have abundance; but from him that hath not shall be taken away even that which he hath' (St Matthew, 25: 29). Though this manifestly unfair 'social injustice' policy frequently obtains in the real world (the rich get richer, the poor poorer), the social justice policy of democracies attempts to make the balance fairer. Sebastian-Nickell and Milne (1992) express this approach and tie it to an early childhood philosophy:

> The central strategy is that more should be given to those who have less, that is, people with fewer resources, less power or greater need should have a greater share of public resources. By this strategy the government seeks to redress existing injustices.
>
> Early childhood educators must be professionally active in redressing inequalities in parents' access to services, and disadvantages for young children arising from social injustice. This is firmly embedded in the history of the early childhood movement.
>
> (Sebastian-Nickell and Milne, 1992: 116)

In this chapter's discussion of *mutual control*, we may find a path through the confusion of these two clashing policy statements, a path that can illuminate both the 'real' and the 'fair' aspects of each. The child who 'hath not' may be helped, through the input of significant others (parents and professionals), to contribute his or her own activity to the sum of mutual input, and by adding to what little he or she in fact already 'hath', may gradually build an abundance on what was there. This is what has happened with the children in Stories 4, 5 and 6.

Each of the children in these stories has become, during the course of events, 'one that hath'. In each story, the factor that has moved the children from a negative situation (one 'that hath not') to a positive one has been the impulse towards collaboration of professionals and parents. In each case, the behavioural steps leading from this collaborative control have converted a potentially vicious cycle of child behaviour into a beneficent one. Withdrawal from others (Story 4), tightly prestructured adult directions (Story 5) and coercive adult discipline or 'pressure' (Story 6) all lead to a narrowed set of experiences for young children. In the course of these stories, what the adults have done is to broaden the range of experience of the children by making room for the children's input as well as their own. The children, by adding their own input to that of the adults, have acquired, as we leave them, more confidence and more competence: competence in communicating (Story 4), in creativity (Story 5), in reading (Story 6).

A program (at home or in centre/school) in which children actively interpret their experiences and make sense of them *in collaboration with others* may be called a contructivist program (De Vries and Kohlberg, 1990), since knowledge and relationships are constructed by the learners rather than being simply transmitted to them by parents or professionals. Such programs have been shown (Perry, 1994) to demonstrate more cooperation and richer interpersonal strategies among the children than programs emphasising direct instruction. In their explanation, DeVries *et al.* (1991) bring out the significance of the *mutual control* of *all* participants:

> When children experience on a regular basis an environment in which the teacher is predominantly unilateral and in which social interaction is discouraged, children's developing ability to enact a higher level of interpersonal understanding is more limited than when the children experience a cooperative environment in which they are interpersonally active.
>
> (DeVries *et al.*, 1991: 508)

Such interpersonal activity on the part of children is enhanced, this section has suggested, when teachers and other professionals are also interpersonally active with parents.

THE DIMENSION OF CONTROL: PARENTS, PROFESSIONALS AND CHILDREN

Summarising the adult behaviours in the control dimension which have helped to guide the children described in Stories 4, 5 and 6 to more interesting and constructive paths of action (i.e. to increase their own autonomy), we can see that in each case the adult schemes of guidance incorporate the three interactional variables (Hess, 1971) associated with the control dimension in Table 3.1.

Consistency of regulatory strategies

In promoting basic confidence and building on the competence children already have, the approaches of the two sets of adults (professionals and parents) in each story have drawn closer to each other. This is an important manifestation of Hess's principle of consistency. We have seen in Chapter 2 and again in discussing responsiveness in Chapter 4, that consistency – that is, predictability, the repetition of the familiar – is a key factor in building young children's trust, the foundation for later learning.

Writing of the *dis*continuity, the *in*consistency that is often found between parents and professionals in schools (and more recently in child care centres), Watts and Henry (1978) have noted that:

> This has perhaps had minimum adverse effects on some young children, but the adverse effects on many children have been extreme. These are the children from homes and sub-communities whose values and styles of life differ in some ways from the values of the school which is essentialy a mainstream culture institution.

Obviously there are some areas of overlap between home and school for most children; there is probably rarely complete overlap, even in the case of mainstream middle-class children. For these latter, the situation might be seen as:

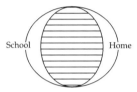

For many culturally different children the area of overlap is much slighter:

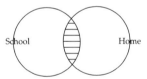

> While the magnitude of the overlap is of importance, the most significant issue is the content of the areas where there is no overlap. Some incongruities betweeen the home and the school experiences of the child are probably of little import; all children can (and need to) tolerate a degree of dissonance, a degree of conflict. But there are some areas of the child's life situation where dissonance between home and school experience has a major debilitating effect on his educational and personal development and fulfilment.
>
> (Watts and Henry, 1978: 5)

Among the children described in this chapter, how were damaging dissonances between parents and professionals decreased, consonances and consistency increased? The answer might be framed in terms of two hypotheses of Bronfenbrenner (1979):

1 The developmental potential of a setting is increased as a function of the number of supportive links existing between that setting and other settings.
2 The developmental potential of a setting is enhanced when the supportive links consist of others with whom the developing person has developed a primary dyad . . . and who engage in joint activity and primary dyads with members of the new setting.
(Bronfenbrenner, 1979: 215)

In this chapter we have seen precisely these processes occurring among the adults in Stories 4, 5 and 6. By primary dyads, Bronfenbrenner means that each of the two persons involved has formed a significant, not a merely casual, relationship with the other. As was noted in discussing attachment and social referencing, a child and a parent are likely to have such a relationship, but not necessarily a child and a teacher.

At the beginning of all three stories, we know more about the gulfs than the links between the characters. In Story 4 there are gulfs between Chinese and Australian children, Chinese and Australian parents, Chinese parents and Australian staff members, and considerable gulfs between all these characters and the Chinese Community Council helper. In Story 5 there is a gulf between Mary, kindergarten parent, and Jan, kindergarten teacher. In Story 6 there are gulfs between Ben and his remedial teacher and Ben's mother and the teacher.

At the point at which we leave these stories, the responsiveness of one or another adult in each case has established a number of links: that is, primary dyads. Significant and ongoing relationships have been created between all the sets of characters just mentioned, who have all engaged in joint activity, helping to create a consistency of approach between home and centre and thus to enhance the developmental impact of the educational setting. Particular aspects of joint activity will be discussed in the next chapter on involvement. However, we might briefly fore-shadow that chapter here.

In Story 4, Chinese parents and staff members communicate about the program in which, as it increasingly recognises their culture, Chinese children feel more at home; Chinese and Australian children engage in mutual play; and Chinese and Australian parents communicate about play; the Community Council member provides interpretive links for all these persons. In Story 5, the communication of Jan, Mary and other parents leads to greater agreement on the value of creative ideas, to be discussed further in the next section. In Story 6, Ben, his mother Yvonne and teacher Thomas all form not only a group but also three significant dyadic relationships (primary dyads, Bronfenbrenner, 1979) as they communicate both at home and at school. All extract more meaning from reading and reading methods, and all contribute to enriching those methods through games and additions to games. Other members of the family also gain from the added communication.

Engaging in joint activity, as foreshadowed by Bronfenbrenner's (1979) second hypothesis, will be discussed further, in terms of Vygotskian theory, in the next chapter on involvement.

Explanatory rather than Arbitrary Control

Explanatory strategies (Hess, 1971) were seen as one of the effective strategies increasingly reported by providers in the family day care program, and in Stories 4, 5 and 6, children have moved from a negative (narrowed) course of action out into broader landscapes in part because adults have explained or modelled (explanation in action) new ways rather than adopting punitive coercion.

Examples of explanation or modelling being used by staff members provide a key to children's participation in the enlarged, more inclusive play program (Story 4) as children tried out new equipment such as woks and silk dress-up clothes. In Story 5 the children themselves had the opportunity to explain (and hence to discover more about) their own creative ideas in paint, collage and construction to a mother who had begun to appreciate such ideas; and in Story 6 non-reading Ben was enabled to improve this skills as reading explanations were subsumed within an explanation with more immediate appeal: how to win at a boardgame.

In these stories, the explanations between adults and children were essential elements in the gains made by the children. But just as essential were the explanations between the adult participants. Professionals who have spent years refining their understanding of their field need to remember that many parents do not understand their (professional) explanations. Story 5 contains a striking example, applicable to many teacher–parent contacts like those of Jan and Mary. Early childhood teachers who have spent four years of pre-service education unpacking the possibilities of learning through play often find it intolerable that some parents refuse to believe that play is the perfect medium for young children's learning. Such parents return to the explanations they grew up with, that hard work and rote memorising under adult direction are what constitutes learning. In Story 5, Jan arranged a situation where her explanation to Mary and the other parents (supported by well assembled research findings) carried weight because it occurred in the context of unthreatening shared experience (that is, mutual control). Play was modelled, and then explained, a powerful learning mode.

Parents also have important explanations to offer the professionals.

Ben's step forward into a new regime of reading enjoyment (Story 6) occurred only because Yvonne, his mother, explained to Thomas, the teacher, that the 'pause, prompt, praise' method was not working at home. Thomas was able to build creatively on this explanation. In Story 4, the whole climate in the child care centre changed when Marilyn elicited from a number of parents explanations of their views and wishes for their children in the centre, explanations previously unsuspected by the staff.

The need to take others into our confidence and explain what we are doing and why is something that all of us often overlook. We feel our explanations are too obvious. But as Crowe (1973: 176) has noted: 'the greatest lesson to be learnt about the gaps between what children know, what parents think children know, and what teachers think parents know about children is that everyone concerned assumes too much.' As Anderson (1984), the competent pre-school mother who longed for more explanations, remarked (on p. 81): 'it must be continually spelt out to us how we can speak to you anytime and that you do want to work with us on the child's development and problems that arise.'

Among the problems that continually arise in adult–adult educational relationships are those concerned with clashes in values.

Value orientations

Value orientations have been defined by Watts (1970: 100) as 'patterned principles, combining cognitive, affective and directive elements, which influence human behaviour'. Story 5 contains a clear example of such patterned principles concerning 'good' practice in the kindergarten. For parent Mary, tightly prestructured ideas emanating from an authority figure are 'good'. On the other hand, teacher Jan sees 'goodness' residing in the uninhibited creations of individuals (including individual children. This is a clash between two powerful value orientations (Kluckhohn and Strodtbeck, 1961): lineality (where group continuity is maintained by strictly ordered leadership figures) and individualism (where the individual has autonomy). Clashes between the two approaches can be painful and severe.

Yet, by the end of this true story, some resolution of the underlying conflict between Mary and Jan has been reached, largely through a third approach to decision making: the support of participants (including Mary and Jan) towards one another in the group as they pool findings and experiences about the uses of flexibility in uncertain times. This is the value orientation of collaterality, where the goals of the laterally extended group carry weight (Kluckhohn and Strodtbeck, 1961).

How has such a resolution been possible? Partly it is because of Jan's continuing responsiveness to the situation definitions brought to the group by Mary and the other parents. However, it is largely because of Jan's skill and courage in setting up a parents' evening at which the issues can be aired (explained, both in words and action) in an unthreatening (indeed enjoyable) way, and with mutual control. In the course of that meeting, Mary (and probably others) have begun to change position. Jan too has made a shift, gaining in her understanding of the parent group.

Both as parents and professionals we need to look for the adaptive strengths in the values of those from groups or cultures other than our own, in order to see past the blinkers of our own prejudices. At the same time, another form of prejudice is to take for granted that all members of a given cultural or social group hold certain values assumed to be typical of that group. We need to steer a course between the Scylla of ignorance of other value systems than our own and the Charybdis of stereotyping. In Story 5, Jan has steered such a course by setting up the group meeting with its built-in activities leading to both the airing and the possible shifting of values. While values are adaptive for the groups and societies in which they exist (that is, they help to preserve the group's existence), it is also true that, as social conditions change, and as groups of people come into contact with others, values shift both between and within groups and individuals.

The title of this section, 'Explanatory rather than arbitrary control', is another way of describing the airing of views and the shifting of values (and therefore behaviour) that may follow. Our behaviour may willingly change *as others have the opportunity to explain* to us previously uncomprehended concepts. This may be especially necessary in contacts between members of different cultural groups. In Story 4, the questions asked of the Chinese parents by group leader Marilyn revealed strong similarities rather than differences among the Chinese and Australian parents' wishes for their children. These were similarities on which she was able to build. But this does not always occur. Tizard *et al.* (1983) discuss the need, when cultural values differ in early childhood settings, to ensure that all parties have the chance to be heard:

> We do not underestimate the difficulty of explaining modern teaching aims and methods to parents from a very different culture. Nor do we suggest that teachers should – or indeed would – accede to parental wishes which were totally at variance with their own approach. But unless schools are prepared to discuss such issues with parents, explain their approach, listen to parents' points of view, and go some way towards meeting them, they cannot hope to enlist parental support for their work. Teachers might think it worth considering whether, because of their intimate knowledge of a child and his environment, his parents' opinions about his educational

needs should be taken seriously. For instance, if parents are worried because 'modern maths' seem to have superseded mental arithmetic, a teacher might consider supplementing her mathematics curriculum with arithmetic, or showing parents how they can help their child to learn it at home.

The objections of parents to sand and water play may disappear if they receive an adequate explanation of why the teacher considers the materials important, especially if the children are provided with suitable protective clothing – like hats for sand play and waterproof overalls for water play. Alternatively, the teacher may decide in the face of entrenched parental objections that sand and water play are not educational essentials. If parents are concerned that their children are not being taught English systematically at school, the staff may have a fresh look at what is known about second language teaching for young children, and the comparative effectiveness of different methods.

It is not, of course, likely that one meeting or discussion with parents will be very effective in improving mutual understanding. This is only likely to develop over a period of time, in which teachers have shown in a variety of ways that they respect the parents' culture, want to listen to their opinions, and are willing to take their points of view seriously.

(Tizard *et al.*, 1983: 235)

While differences between cultural groups pose particular challenges for parents and professionals, the more general importance of bringing values issues into the open for mutual consideration is emphasised by Massey (1995):

Where there may be differences in values, I suggest it is important to be tolerant of values that are different from one's own – tolerant, that is, in a strong sense which involves welcoming the other (Isaacs, 1995: 11) – and, perhaps more importantly, to seek to engage with others with different values so that one allows for the possibility of a fusion of ethical horizons. Such fusions do occur, and it is on this basis that we can live and work together in relations and communities with shared values, shared purposes and shared commitments. When a member of such a community, however, comes to question some of those shared values, it is important that they are not pilloried, forced to obey or coerced into conformity. This, it seems to me, represents a challenge not only for all of us in our myriad communities but also for schools, teachers and others engaged in ethical education.

(Massey, 1995: 6)

We return to this question in the next chapter.

Encouragement of independence

According to Erikson (1950), children's move towards independence, towards autonomy, towards 'trying to do things for themselves' as the family day care provider interview phrased it (Appendix 1), is one of the great drives of early childhood. In helping children to make this move, we have seen that adults have an enormous role. In Stories 4, 5 and 6, we have seen adults combining to help children to communicate across cultural boundaries, to try out their own ideas, and to read. In 'Encouraging self-help' (p. 116), we have seen adults playing their role in helping children to take these major steps, in part by making small choices available to them. In particular, the coming together of the parents and professionals has made these choices *more consistently* available ('Consistency of regulatory strategies', p. 120), so that the children in these stories have had a firmer base of the familiar from which to step off on their new choices.

In these stories we see, too, how the adults' coming together makes interesting choices increasingly available *to the adults*, to their benefit as well as the benefit of the children. At the beginning of each of the stories the adults are in a state of inaction (lack of choice) in relation to one another. As with the caregivers in Story 4 who believed that Chinese parents were 'looking down on' them, or with Jan, the teacher in Story 5, who feared the scathing tongue of parent Mary, such inaction is often the result of a perceived rebuff. Professionals as well as parents can resemble Shakespeare's snail in *Venus and Adonis*:

> whose tender horns being hit,
> Shrinks backwards in his shelly cave with pain,
> And there, all smother'd up, in shade doth sit,
> Long after fearing to creep forth again.

Despite such rebuffs, in each story one or other adult partner in a dyad or group did creep forth. When either the parent or the professional *responded* to the challenge of meeting needs, the *mutual control* they established, as adults, opened up for them (as well as for the children) a series of valuable choices (Table 5.4).

Each item in the list of 'new choices' emerging by the end of each story represents a challenge which has become available and which has been met (rather than discarded) by one or other or all of the adult participants. (The children's acceptance of new choices has already been discussed in 'Encouraging self-help' on p. 116.)

A glance through these adult choices will show that, as with the children, the growing *consistency* of approach, as dyads or groups of parents and professionals collaborate in a consultative (*explanatory*) way, creates a base of mutual familiarity from which adults are able to 'lift off'

Table 5.4 How the coming together of adults (professionals and parents) makes interesting choices increasingly available to them

Story	At start	At end
	Professionals and parents apart – misunderstanding: lack of choice	*Mutual control by professionals and parents: new choices for adults*
4	Misunderstanding of centre goals: staff and Chinese parents	Discovery of mutual goals: staff and parents
	Underuse of Community Council helper	Expanding of centre program: staff
		Spending time in centre: Chinese parents
		Intercommunication: Chinese and Australian parents
		Expanded role: Community Council helper
		More intercultural learning: all participants
5	Values clash – parent : adult direction teacher : self-direction	Collaboration on meeting: teacher and parent
		Range of experiences, values offered: teacher
		Range of experiences sampled: parents
		Consideration of values: parents and teacher
		Shift in values: parent
6	Teacher advises parent group, parent unable to carry out advice	Approach to teacher: parent
		New method devised (game at home): teacher
		Collaboration in game: teacher, parent
		New game possibilities devised: parent, family
		School materials selected for home use: teacher

independently as choices arise. Not only does this process add to the sense of self-esteem among the participating adults, it also enhances their sense of control. Sense of self-esteem and sense of control are the presage variables associated with adult facilitation in children's development (as we saw in Table 3.1). When control is *mutual control*, it is an empowering dimension of behaviour.

6

INVOLVEMENT

While the responsiveness and control dimensions are about *how* adults behave, the involvement dimension in adult–child interaction emphasises content – *what* adults do with children. To meet children's need to build initiative through new ideas, adults offer challenges, talk with children, pass on information, make resources available. Similarly, in the adult–adult interaction of parents and professionals, the proffering of resources and the keeping in touch through ongoing exchange of feedback is essential to facilitative involvement.

In Table 3.1 the variables related to involvement, whereby adults offer and assist young children in challenges, talk with them, and provide them with information and resources, are described by Hess (1971) as:

1 Encouragement of achievement.
2 Maximisation of verbal interaction.
3 Parental teaching behaviour.
4 Diffuse intellectual stimulation.

As in Chapter 4 (Responsiveness) and Chapter 5 (Control) the first section of this chapter looks at these variables by way of the family day care program. Adult contributions to children's development of initiative in the program are discussed; then we examine the involvement variables as they applied, in the family day care program, to the interactions between the family day care providers themselves. Finally we look, as we have in the earlier chapters, at some real-life examples of these involvement variables in the interactions of other children, professionals and parents.

THE DIMENSION OF INVOLVEMENT IN THE FAMILY DAY CARE PROGRAM: ADULTS AND CHILDREN

Appendix 6 presents the findings for eight items in the family day care interview in which providers were asked how they saw young children developing intellectually, and what part they saw themselves playing in

129

this. Of these eight items, only one (Item 15: the importance of talking to young children) revealed no significant pre/post differences between the program and control groups. Almost without exception providers endorsed the importance of talking to young children.

As seen in Chapter 4, over the course of the program providers in the program group (but not the control group) became increasingly *aware of*, because increasingly *attentive to*, the capacities of very young children. As they attended more closely to the children in their care, they saw evidence at earlier ages of the children's moves towards independence, towards pleasure in accomplishment, towards understanding of adults' speech, and towards a capacity to take part in conversations.

In Chapter 5 we have already discussed the first of these care provider discoveries: children's move towards independence. Here, in considering involvement, we examine how the providers' appreciation of children's growing accomplishment, comprehension and verbal expression was associated with their own strategies towards the children.

That providers in the program group, by comparison with the controls, significantly expanded their sense of their own involvement in children's growth is evident in the change in responses to Item 14. In this item providers were invited to describe how they believed that caregivers could help young children to feel pleased at their own accomplishments. Program group providers increased from 1.7 to 3.4 the mean number of strategies cited, while control providers continued to report approximately 2.

Fascinatingly, the strategies described by the providers (Table 6.1) as

Table 6.1 Examples of the program group providers' strategies to encourage children's pleasure at their accomplishments

Strategy	Comment
Being aware of the child's capabilities	'You need to be aware of what will stimulate that child, make it go further.'
Noticing what the child is doing	'Noticing what they're doing instead of ignoring them.'
Allowing children to try (not doing it for them)	'They really appreciate what *they* can do.'
Helping enough to avoid frustration	'Give them a hand when they need it.'
Direct teaching, modelling	'You can do it together – they imitate you, then "We made this together" they say.'
Demonstrating physical and verbal encouragement	'We all join in and clap hands.'
Getting one child to help another	'Let the child show other children.'
Making materials and opportunities available	'You can put away the dangerous things so they can try things out'; 'Arrange the set-up so they can *feel* that accomplishment.'

encouraging children's accomplishment spanned precisely the same range of categories as those they reported using to encourage independence (as a glance back at Table 5.2 will demonstrate). As the providers reported these achievement examples and the strategies that led to them, they were recognising the links between their own contingent, reciprocal interactions with the children and the children's achievement.

Comments on aspects of importance in looking at books with children (Item 18) further demonstrated program group providers' enhanced perceptions of their own role in widening children's horizons. 'We bring home library books – it used to be just the older kids liked them, now the little ones love looking at the pictures with me' exemplifies the program group's post-program responses. These averaged five as against fewer than three aspects of book-sharing initially seen as important by providers in both groups. The mean score of control group providers did not increase.

Asked what they believed the children were learning in the family day care homes (Item 19), providers in both groups and on both occasions gave responses ranging across the domains of children's development: personal ('everyday living skills'), social ('learning to fit in with a group'), and cognitive ('lots of language', 'doing new things by copying the older ones'). From pre- to post-interview the mean score for the program group almost doubled (from 4.0 kinds of perceived learning experience to 7.7) while control group scores moved from 4.1 to 5.3.

The program group also came to see enhanced opportunities for children's activity round the house (Item 20). Examination of responses within this item revealed a further significant difference between the two groups of providers. This difference occurred in one reported area of children's activity, namely engagement with the caregiver in everyday household pursuits, e.g. cooking together, feeding the chickens together, gardening together. Scarcely mentioned at the beginning of the program, these occasions for informal learning with the caregiver were reported, at the end, by almost all program group providers (a mean of 0.2 rising to 1.9; while the control group mean was unchanged at 0.67); $F(1,40) = 9.07$, $p < 0.01$.

Child behaviour

How did these advances in adult functioning in the program group help to broaden children's intellectual horizons? As was seen in the discussion of children's behaviour in Chapters 4 and 5, the behavioural means of both groups of children, both before and after the program, indicated that, in personal and social terms, their lives in family day care were productive ones (Appendix 7). This applied, too, in the area of intellectual development. Across the groups and at both observations, cognitive functioning took place during the 40 per cent or more of children's time given to exploration and investigation (mastery activity) both alone and with others. A further 17–19 per cent of time was spent processing information during active observation of the environment – the 'steady staring' seen to be so valuable by White *et al.* (1979).

Over the period of the program, only one significant difference in the cognitive behaviour of the children was found. Just as the children from the program group were interacting for a greater proportion of their time with providers rather than with peers (p. 75), so they were addressing a greater proportion of their utterances to providers rather than peers. Figure 6.1 demonstrates the change. At the beginning of the program, 76 per cent and 70 per cent respectively of the utterances of the program and control group children were directed towards their care providers, the rest to their peers. By the end of the program, control group children's utterances to their care providers had fallen to 61 per cent, while the adult)directed utterances of children in the program group had risen to 85 per cent (X2 = 49.70; p < 0.001).

How might these proportions be accounted for? One would expect maturational factors to have played a part. The ability to sustain engagement with peers has been shown to increase significantly between two and two and a half years (Brownell, 1990; McGraw, 1987), and this factor may have been coming into play for children in the control group as they turned increasingly to one another, less to the provider. By contrast,

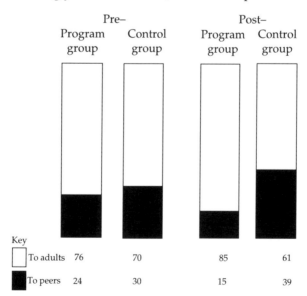

Figure 6.1 Percentage proportions of total child utterances

children in the program group continued to interact and vocalise proportionately more with the provider than with peers. This was despite the onset of situational variables – increased group size, increased number of babies in care – which might have been expected to make it harder for the target children to achieve contact with their providers (Fosburg, 1982). Notwithstanding, by supporting adult responsiveness, it appears that the program was also supporting the exchange of language (or pre-language) between these adults and the young children in their care, a major factor in intellectual development.

THE DIMENSION OF INVOLVEMENT IN THE FAMILY DAY CARE PROGRAM: THE ADULTS

At the beginning of this chapter it was noted that children need to build initiative through new ideas. Adults, too, need new information (Chapter 2) from which to build new ideas and initiative.

As the family day care program was ending, one of the providers, Stephanie, sent me a letter that included the following paragraph:

> Thank you for thinking about us, for the more one *understands* about what is happening the better job one can do and the easier it is to cope when we don't feel well, or have an overactive or stressed child, or we have a new addition, and many other things that can get us down.

The kind of understanding Stephanie was talking about here was not so much the greater appreciation of her charges that came from a closer warmth and attentiveness to them (responsiveness). Nor was it the affirmation she and her colleagues in the group received from their shared input into the lively stories of their procedures in the family day care homes (mutual control). Rather it was the understanding that came from being able to make greater sense of these elements as new insights, new frameworks emanated from within the discussion group. This is the understanding that derives from the involvement dimension.

Involvement with other people makes possible the exchange of feedback from the environment. Some of that feedback (as seen in the chapters on the responsiveness and control dimensions) validates existing behaviour (or situation definitions). But some feedback consists of new information. Implied in Stephanie's acknowledgement of the facilitator's role is the provision of such information. As she noted, an impetus towards 'doing a better job' (Hess's encouragement of achievement, variable 7, Table 3.1) is the acquisition of more understanding of 'what is happening', and part of that understanding comes from new information through involvement with other people.

In Chapter 3 the involvement dimension was described, in adult–child terms, as the behavioural area where adults do things in company with children that broaden their intellectual horizons: keeping them on track, talking *with* them, teaching them, bringing resources to their notice. In the last section of this chapter we have seen that the family day care providers in the program group significantly enhanced their reported performance (in comparison with the control group) in all these areas: they helped the children in desired accomplishments (variable 7), they talked more with them (variable 8), felt the children were learning more from them (variable 9), and instanced more resources with which the children occupied themselves (variable 10), in particular the resources of everyday activities.

What evidence is there of these variables being enhanced among the program providers themselves? How did the program itself enhance their achievement, their talking, their teaching, their provision of resources?

Encouragement of achievement

Stephanie's acknowledgment that the program had made it 'easier to cope' and to 'do a better job' suggests that providers did develop a sense of accomplishment. The fact that the children interacted more with them and vocalised more to them confirmed the reality of this. Why did it happen? My own hunch is that their homework task played a major part in this accomplishment. Though it contained no written requirement, the task of 'accentuating the positive', noting what happened each time and reporting back to the group week by week, was just as taxing as written homework. It was also enjoyable because, as we saw on p. 106, it was not only the children who were positively reinforced but also the providers such as Lois:

> It's not just the little ones. My 12-year old daughter tidied her room up like it's never been done before. It was after she did the washing up and I said how well she'd done it. I never make a fuss of her usually. It really works.

One of the tricks, discussed in the group, of managing positive reinforcement is to find out *which* reinforcement is satisfying to the individual being reinforced (Berger, 1988). Otherwise the method will of course not work. The group had a chance to see how this trick can be accomplished as we followed a problem of provider Kate over a number of weeks.

Logbook: Kate's problem

Quite early in the program Kate raised the problem of how to handle two year old Danny's 'mucking up' – attacking her own child,

134

kicking and jumping on the sofa – when carried in and later picked up by mother. Kate felt very angry and aggrieved. The group had been considering the importance of expressing feelings and helping children to express theirs. Some providers thought Kate should make her feelings known to the mother – 'Tell her that kind of behaviour won't be tolerated.' Kate thought this might be a good idea. Other points made in discussion concerned:

- The possible role of attachment issues (such as separation anxiety) in the situation.
- The importance of determining Danny's needs at this point and whether they were being met.
- The need to put a stop to aggression, so it was not seen as licensed.
- The possibility of positive reinforcement (a major current theme of the program) – finding strengths of both Danny and his mother and approving them, since advances often come not from addressing the problem directly but from more approval (building up trust) in other areas.
- The usefulness of looking for small gains in behaviour rather than big dramatic advances.

Kate decided that Danny's needs were for more independence. She was going to ask his mother to walk him in, instead of carrying him; this would also remove Danny's position of dominance over her own child. 'He could carry his own little bag,' suggested a colleague.

. . . Next session Kate reported that her strategy had not worked at all. The mother had complied with her request, but Danny was more aggressive than ever at drop-off and pick-up time and Kate was feeling an anxious failure. The researcher reviewed with Kate and the group the other earlier suggestions, all relevant to topics under general consideration, as well as particular to Kate's situation.

. . . The following week Kate reported that she thought she had solved the problem – 'I evaded it!' She had not confronted the mother further, and had not continued to try to make Danny more independent, having decided he might still have unmet security needs. She was now looking for – and finding, she said – more occasions for hugs and cuddles during the day, occasions, as the group now called it, to 'accentuate the positive'. She had eliminated the trigger for Danny's morning aggression by getting her husband to keep her son happily occupied till after Danny's arrival. 'Hey presto,' she said, 'no more problem!' A couple of providers were sorry. Like Jess with the baby who should know its 'firm limits', they felt that the child should have been made to give in. Others took up the suggestion, made two weeks earlier, that an indirect approach may sometimes achieve more. Kate remarked how glad she had been to have the group to talk things over with.

In the final interview, when asked, 'Do you feel you're on top of things – or do you feel things are getting on top of you?', Kate recalled the feeling of accomplishment, of heightened self-esteem, that she had received as she worked over the weeks to find the key to meeting Danny's need for trust, rather than placing so much, perhaps premature, emphasis on independence. She believed that this had contributed to the mother's sense of self-esteem, as well:

> *Now* I feel on top of things. The course really helped there. I think I've become more caring but a little bit more detached – I can stand back, and not feel upset. Now I can give Danny a kiss to send him on his way instead of being so upset inside when he plays up when mum comes. And that makes her feel better too, that I can give him a kiss and a cuddle, even when he's being a little rotter. She knows I'm really saying, 'He's a good kid.' And you can see it, the way she walks out, she feels it's all right too. It's just how the kids are with divided authority. It's helped her too.

A reading of these extracts helps to bring out the associations between the providers' discovery of the reinforcements satisfying to the children in their care (in this case more security), the reinforcements satisfying to themselves (solving distressing problems), and the reinforcements satisfying to the parents (sharing the solution). It also brings out the association between providers' acquisition of a sense of accomplishment and the rise in their positive relationships with their social networks, including parents.

Adult teaching behaviour

In considering how participants in the family day care program acquired new ideas and initiative, it is useful to reflect further on some Vygotskian terms that shed light on the processes of involvement in the program. Within Vygotsky's (1978: 86) zone of proximal development, the concepts of situation definition, intersubjectivity and semiotic mediation, referred to in earlier chapters, are of particular relevance here:

Situation definitions
- The beliefs and experiences that learners bring with them as they enter the learning situation (zone of proximal development). Learners, in interaction with facilitators, change their situation definitions, both their 'representation of objects' and the 'action patterns for operating on those objects' (Wertsch, 1984: 9), a change that is qualitative rather than quantitative (p. 11).

Intersubjectivity
- Being on the same wave length as another and knowing it. The mutual awareness that exists 'between two interlocutors in a task setting when they share the same situation definition and know they share the same situation definition' (Wertsch, 1984: 12).

Semiotic mediation
- The use of signs and signals (often linguistic) to convey meaning. The use of facilitative language to negotiate intersubjective situation definitions (Wertsch, 1984: 14).

It has been noted earlier that, for the family day care providers, the program was the zone of proximal development where, over the successive meetings of the twelve-week course, their situations were defined and redefined. In addition, new situation definitions were introduced, since it became clear that these providers, who were making the weekly trip to class after a day that for some had begun when the first child arrived at 6.30 a.m., were there for more than an exchange of their own ideas.

Logbook: information exchange

In the session on the uses of language, Phyllis had been telling how the carpenters next door had asked her to stop the children talking incessantly, and how she had told them that children *have* to talk. Later, summarising the evening, the facilitator noted that we'd learnt that we were doing something very important when we talked to little children. Donna: 'That's what we seem to be doing all the time, though – finding out what we're doing already, not learning *new* things!' Anna agreed: 'Yes, we mightn't have given them [the stages of trust, autonomy, initiative] fancy names like that, but we certainly were doing those things. But,' she added thoughtfully, 'it gives you a firm base for what you know.' Others joined in. Ellen said she'd learnt a lot of new things. Even Donna, the critic, told the group she'd given the mother of one of her day care children the hand-out on tantrums and feelings and they'd had a long talk about it – 'It certainly gave that mum some new ideas.' Most group members, however, seemed to agree with Valda that what they wanted was 'definite guidelines – just what to expect and just when'.

The facilitator explained why she was wary of 'definite guidelines' and discussed with the group the idea of individual differences. But after the session (which ended with Harriet confessing over supper that she was feeling 'a bit let down because I thought you'd be standing out the front of the class, giving us a lecture'), the facilitator decided to add to the group's resources the guidelines (flexible rather than 'definite') from *Learningames for the First Three Years* (Sparling and Lewis, 1979), in which broad developmental norms are sensitively meshed with caregiving suggestions. They turned out to be just what the providers wanted, as ongoing points of reference.

This excerpt makes evident the tension, noted in the adult education area (Halpern and Larner, 1988), between the need to acquire new knowledge from the 'expert' and the need to assert one's own knowledge in the face of the expert. That this tension was successfully negotiated in the present program was confirmed by the readiness with which group members amalgamated both sources of information – their own and that emanating from the professionals – as the program progressed.

Such shared understanding (intersubjectivity) may appear difficult to attain when situation definitions of learners and facilitators are far apart. A case in point, in the family day care program, was the initial difference in attitudes to child management. While the facilitator favoured positive and explanatory strategies, some providers included in their repertoire highly negative and arbitrary ones (Table 5.1). In considering how intersubjectivity within the program was achieved, a curious Vygotskian controversy concerning what actually happens in the zone of proximal development is illuminating.

Writing of the processes occurring in the zone of proximal development, most Vygotskian theorists (e.g. Rogoff and Gardner, 1984) have drawn attention to the motivational as well as the cognitive importance of facilitators' establishing intersubjectivity by attending to the other's cues and building on the familiar. In other words, teachers do well to 'start from where the student is'. But not all Vygotskian theorists take this approach. Zeuli (1986), for example, has suggested that, at least where higher mental processes are concerned, Vygotskian principles would lead teachers to promote discontinuity, not continuity, with former learning. Zeuli points to the resistance of students to relinquishing faulty notions based on their everyday experience (p. 13). He emphasises 'assistance as the student tries to understand the relationship between concepts – not how connections are made to the student's everyday concepts' (p. 11). Oddly, in the same passage Zeuli cites the Socratic method as an example of this process. Yet one of the striking features of the dialogues of Socrates, the quintessential self-styled 'supportive gadfly', is the philosopher's skill in identifying familiar – and common – ground to his student partner before impelling the novice on to unfamiliar territory.

What may resolve the contradiction betweeen Zeuli's views and those of writers such as Rogoff and Gardner (1984) is closer attention to the issue of intersubjectivity. Zeuli specifically casts doubt on the 'relevance of transferring information from the familiar setting to the novel one' (p. 13). But what appears to be needed is not to create discontinuity in the interests of guarding against the 'transfer' of students' irrelevant concepts, but a preliminary identification of relevant and shared student/teacher concepts from which to make the intersubjective leap to a new situation definition. In this way, student 'resistance' need not occur.

Within the family day care program, an example of this focus on relevant, shared concepts was the bypassing, to a large degree, of discussion of providers' negative control strategies and the concentration, instead, on the positive strategies of which many had a common understanding, both with one another and with the researcher. As indicated in earlier sections, this pooling of shared understandings appeared to increase the providers' repertoire of positive guidance strategies, without setting up the resistance, identified in Zeuli's example, which might well have resulted from an intrusive imposition of the researcher's situation definition. Instead, intersubjectivity between providers and facilitator was maintained.

Some examples from other programs illustrate further the importance of maintaining intersubjectivity by attending to 'where the participants are coming from' and thus establishing shared relevant situation definitions.

- In a home-visiting program involving Aboriginal mothers and toddlers in which, as in the present program, an increase in mothers' positive engagement was recorded (Henry, 1980), a somewhat similar situation, handled in a similar way, was recorded in the researcher's logbook. One mother had been deploring her toddler's 'getting into mischief' round the house and her own resort to smacking as a punishment. The logbook records the program personnel both sympathising with the mother's dilemma and discussing the possibility of putting breakables out of reach.

  'If he can keep on exploring as many things as you can let him have, safely, that's how he learns, that's how he goes on being interested in things.' Mother: 'But he's got to learn to do what he's told.'
  The problem is not resolved: it will surely come up again. It is no part of our business to denigrate a mother's pattern of childrearing. What we can do is to offer a further perspective which may extend rather than conflict with her present one, and which she may care to consider . . . At the suggestion of raising the problem of managing children at a forthcoming Mothers' Meeting, the mother smiles with evident relief.

  (Henry, 1980: 20)

- In the effective Child Survival/Fair Start project (Halpern and Larner, 1988), some Mexican–American mothers are described as having traditional magical beliefs concerning children's illness which are at variance with the program goals. The authors discuss the sidestepping of the issue and the finding of common ground:

  > The home visitor's work is not to convince the mother that a neighbour's stare cannot cause fever, but to discuss other possible causes, help the mother learn to use a thermometer, take steps to reduce the fever, and suggest that temperatures above a certain level require medical attention.
  >
  > (Halpern and Larner, 1988: 199)

- The Parent Education Follow Through program (Olmsted, personal communication) offers a further example of participants, initially hostile to the program's situation definition, being enabled to move into the zone of proximal development through sensitivity on the part of program staff to the possibility of finding common ground and achieving intersubjectivity. In this program, the asking of questions (on the part of both parents and children) is seen as a particularly desirable mechanism whereby learning is advanced (Gordon, 1977). When resistance was sensed on the part of the Spanish–American parents to the notion of children questioning their parents, program staff were able to point out that what was at issue here was not the undermining of parental authority (an important traditional value, Kluckhohn and Strodtbeck, 1961) but the help that parents, by anwering questions, could give children with their learning, an objective shared by both program and parents.

In all of these cases program staff and participants moved forward together to new, broadened situation definitions because, as Rogoff *et al.* (1984: 36) put it in the context of adult–infant interaction, the facilitator was not 'intrusive, uninvolved or oblivious to . . . cues'. Rather, attentiveness to cues allowed a shared understanding to be preserved and enlarged.

Maximisation of verbal interaction: 'talking together with'

'Please talk to us in a language we can understand, not phrases like 'fine motor skills' etc. as many parents wouldn't know what you are talking about and are too shy to ask.

(Anderson, 1984)

Anderson, the mother of kindergarten children whom we met in Chapter 4, is drawing attention to an all-too-common occasion for misunderstanding. The issue was raised in the last chapter, in discussing the mutual control of explanations. In the present chapter on the content of involvement, we look more closely at the actual language used in information exchange.

Among professionals, who have spent years building up their expertise about children's development and learning, professional language is an essential means to easy communication. For professionals, the phrase 'fine motor skills', like a well-constructed portmanteau, embraces a complex set of concepts packed into a small purpose-built container. But for many parents, the container hides the concepts.

A small role-play on the situation mentioned by Anderson has helped my students to appreciate the professional–parent misunderstandings that may occur:

TEACHER   [to Mother, arriving at pre-school to pick up her son Jason] Jason's spent a lot of time on the climbing frame today. It's very good for his gross motor skills.

MOTHER   [thinks] What on earth are his gross motor skills? He can't drive a car. And boy, she's rude! How dare she call him gross?

TEACHER   His *fine* motor skills need a bit of developing, though.

MOTHER   [thinks] She's mad! Why do they need developing if they're fine?

What Anderson (1984) was begging teachers for was intersubjectivity: the mutual awareness 'that exists between two interlocutors in a task setting when they share the same situation definition and know they share the same situation definition' (Wertsch, 1984: 14). Wertsch has described the negotiating of intersubjective situation definitions as occurring through semiotic mediation: in particular the use of language. In the family day care program, the use of language in group discussion reflected the degree of intersubjectivity attained. Thus, for example, the pooling of participants' experiences of 'accentuating the positive' in daily life with children became an important part of the program as group members came increasingly to apply the concepts involved in a catchy phrase familiar to all of them.

As Wertsch (1984: 14) notes: 'Speech can create, rather than merely reflect, an intersubjective definition.' The very use of phrases such as 'accentuating the positive', or 'doing one's own thing' and 'new ideas' (in place of Erikson's 'autonomy' and 'initiative'), made it possible to express key concepts in ways accessible to the whole group. As providers came to use these terms freely, and relate them to their own observations and actions, Erikson's concepts were also introduced, prompting the remark by one provider that 'We mightn't have given them those fancy names but we certainly were doing those things'.

Such a discussion about the meaning of words and their relation to

141

action could occur because providers and facilitator were able to achieve initial intersubjectivity concerning the reference function of terms such as 'accentuating the positive'. But as Wertsch and Stone (1985: 169) point out in relation to children's learning, agreement on the reference function of words is merely a beginning, 'easily mistaken for agreement on meaning'.

It is agreement on meaning, achieved through the use of language in social interaction, that marks the achievement of internalisation of a concept (Wertsch and Stone, 1985: 171). In the family day care program, such agreement on the meaning of concepts was a gradual process, taking place over the weeks, as terms took on the rich accretion of experiences shared through discussion.

The gradual creation of further shared understandings through mutually accessible language is one of the processes in parent–professional programs in need of further study, as is the degree to which understanding is inhibited by the absence of such language. Powell and Stremmel (1987) have described the problems in communication that many early childhood teachers and parents appear to have, problems expressed in Australia in Anderson's cry to 'talk to us in a language we can understand'.

Within a program in which the language used is accessible to all participants, the discussion group format produces a wider range of shared understandings than is likely to occur in communication within a dyad. Within the family day care group, a detailed example of the cognitive as well as motivational processes in operation is the account (p. 77) of the group's encouragement to one of its members to consider a new definition of the 'crying baby' situation. Other providers' 'hints and props' (Bruner, 1985: 27), in the form of questions and examples from their own experience, allowed this provider to move from a definition predicated solely on the baby's need for firm limits to one that included the need for trust. Peer guidance, it was noted, 'may well have carried more conviction to the recipient than would the facilitator's more "academic" suggestions alone'.

Overall comments made by providers about the usefulness of the program – 'not feeling so alone', 'solving problems through discussion', 'more understanding of children's needs and growth patterns', 'new ideas on how to handle situations' – underline both the motivational power of the discussion process (Braun et al., 1984; Powell, 1989) and its ability to help participants to arrive at new, intersubjective situation definitions.

Diffuse intellectual stimulation

What Hess (1971) meant by 'diffuse intellectual stimulation' for young children was, as the hand-out for program group providers (Table 3.4) put it, to 'have interesting things around for children', that is, interesting resources which might broaden children's horizons.

To encourage new ideas and initiative among adults, interesting resources are equally important. In addition to the guests who contributed to the family day care program, audiovisual and other resources added much to its liveliness. Films, videotapes, kits available for borrowing, puppets, and original role-plays and hand-outs all helped to create the fertile ground where discussion flourished.

Why was the ground fertile? One reason was that the resources related to the well ploughed, well harrowed soil that already belonged to the providers, mixed with the fertiliser of new ideas. Thus resources were selected for their appropriateness to where the providers were coming from. They were links between providers' existing positions (situation definitions) and new situation definitions being introduced by the facilitator. As the Open University (1979: 176) notes of resources for young children: 'The most helpful toys for your child are those that are matched to her interests and learning needs of the moment . . . [and offer] a little bit of a challenge to get her interested and make her want to try.'

It is this combination of familiarity and novelty that creates the learning climate, as Bruner (1985: 32) notes: 'it is a matter of using whatever one has learned before to get to higher ground. What is obvious . . . is that there must needs be . . . a support system that helps learners get there.' For this support system (resources) to be effective, Bruner concludes (p. 32), 'tutors' must be 'partners in advancement'. That is to say, they must be *involved* with the learners. Here is an example of resources (both people and books) combining the essential elements of familiarity and novelty with close involvement:

Logbook: stories, rhymes and books

Before the visiting lecturer arrived, the researcher suggested that as we'd been talking about little children's needs for trust, for 'doing their own thing' and for new ideas, we might see how the stories, rhymes and books she was going to introduce helped with all these needs . . . The lecturer's vibrant performance had the group recalling the nursery rhymes they knew, joining in unfamiliar ones (like the nappy changing rhyme, 'Leg over leg over/Dog went to Dover/ When he came to the stile/Oops, he went over!'), and following the sequences in *One Woolly Wombat* and *Bananas in Pyjamas*. During the lecturer's reading of some old favourites from *Mother Goose*, lecturer and researcher both drew attention to examples of familiarity and trust being created through repetition, of autonomy being promoted through mastery themes, and of new ideas in the simplest nursery rhymes. As the group wandered later among the lecturer's display of books, there was further opportunity to discuss these issues. Providers noted themes of familiarity (trust), of things being lost and then found in *Where is Spot?*, of homely occasions in *Pete's Chair*; they observed the hero being powerful (autonomy) in *Giant John*; and they and the professionals talked about the many new ideas for toddlers in books like *The Very Hungry Caterpillar*.

After the session Harriet said, 'That was very interesting. I'll have to try harder with my stories.' Next session, Wendy and Jan reported recommending *Once Upon a Potty* to scheme coordinators so other providers could build up 'toilet training trust', and Valda commented on some of the trust themes (such as cosy underground homes) in her day care children's favourite books. Ellen said that she had been analysing her reading since last session – something she had not done before.

THE DIMENSION OF INVOLVEMENT: YOUNG CHILDREN, PARENTS AND PROFESSIONALS

On p. 122 two potent hypotheses of Bronfenbrenner (1979: 215) were introduced:

1 The developmental potential of a setting is increased as a function of the number of supportive links existing between that setting and other settings.
2 The developmental potential of a setting is enhanced when the supportive links consist of others with whom the developing person has developed a primary dyad . . . and who engage in joint activity and primary dyads with members of the new setting.

In Chapter 5, the emphasis was on the developmental impact of Bronfenbrenner's 'primary dyads' and other smallish groups of adults and children, and adults and adults. In the remainder of the present chapter, we look at how the processes of 'joint activity' in which adults are involved with young children apply in settings beyond the family day care program. Here are three more examples from the real world of young children, parents and professionals.

Story 7 Duty of care

In Story 4, 'Only connect', we saw that even if only 27 per cent of parents in a child care centre express their opinion, they may create ongoing change in centre operation. We have called the process one of diffusion. In another centre, staff and 87 per cent of parents of under-two year olds got together over one day and effected major positive change – not so much diffusion as putting the ingredients together in a jar and shaking them. This story illustrates that although parents of children in child care are not available during employment hours to participate in the centre – their absence at work is precisely why their children are in care – many such parents can *and want to* play a role in the direction of the centre *if* the staff make this initiative possible.

The director of the centre, Katrina, in consultation with her staff, drew up a questionnaire which was sent to all parents of 0–2 year olds to determine how satisfied or dissatisfied they were with centre services. From personal and telephoned comments it became clear that parents did not 'feel ownership' of the goals and objectives staff had set out for this age group. Katrina decided that the differing parent and staff goals needed to be further discussed. A staff meeting resolved to hold talks with the parents so that staff could clearly understand parents' concerns. A notice placed in the signing-in area brought recommendations from parents for a Saturday meeting at the centre, with lunch included. Staff members were organised to supervise the babies and toddlers and one or more adults from 13 of the 15 relevant families arrived. All told, there were 24 parents and staff.

Parents' reactions to the questionnaire had raised several major concerns, such as: 'How does the program emphasise the development of my child?', 'How can I ensure the opportunity to discuss with staff how my child is progressing, not only day to day but over longer periods of time?', 'Will the number of staff and children in the nursery allow for one-to-one interaction with my child as well as interaction in a group setting?' The staff–parent group first held a plenary session to discuss these questions generally. Then staff suggested breaking up into four-person groups to discuss issues in more depth. Both this procedure and the accompanying lunch allowed members to feel more at ease with one another.

After lunch an intensive consultation occurred as first pairs, then small groups, then larger groups, then the whole group reworked the issues, creating, as Katrina noted approvingly, a prioritised list of the aims of the 0–2 year babies group which all parents and staff had actively helped to design.

Enthusiastic parents were now talking of making posters to acquaint the community, the local Council, and the Parents and Citizens Association with these ideas. In addition, they decided to circularise all centre parents with the list of aims, accompanied by an Action column where parents who had not been present might suggest further strategies for achieving the aims. Another lunch was planned, as well as ways in which parents and staff could keep in regular touch by using notes, questionnaires, phone conversations and chats at drop-off and pick-up times.

As the day ended, Katrina bade farewell to her staff, the children and the group of parents, strangers who had now become friends. She reflected that, although our increasingly mobile society has separated many parents from their traditional support networks, child care centres can offer some of that support, and not only to young children. By sharing in these parents' child-rearing concerns, her centre was becoming, for them, a kind of extended family.

Story 8 Many hands

There had been a rural recession, and in the country town many of the parents who used to come and help as volunteers in the primary school classrooms had left to go into part-time work. The three Year 1 teachers, Beth, Susan and Nikki, missed the parents who had played a part in their classroom programs, and they believed the children missed them too. The school, they felt, was in a bit of a trough. The three young women wondered how they could reinvigorate their programs by getting parents back despite their part-time work schedules. 'If we had a lot of parents doing a little bit, instead of a few parents doing a lot, they'd be able to manage that and their work as well,' said Beth. 'How can we possibly get a lot of parents when right now we see hardly any?' scoffed Susan. 'I know,' said Nikki. 'A wish list – from the children.'

All of the children in the Year 1 classes told their teachers what they would love to do at school if they could have their wish. These wishes were reproduced on a sheet of paper on which a thought bubble emanating from the heads of a dreaming boy and girl carried the message 'Wish we could . . . ' to a host of balloons, each bearing a child's wish: 'Sew', 'Dress up', 'Make hats', 'Learn tricks and magic', 'Make play houses', 'Climb things', 'Make a band', and so on. The back of the sheet depicted two grown-ups looking at the balloons floating down. Some of the descending balloons had labels: 'Cook', 'Sew', 'Cut', 'Dance', 'Paint'. From the mouths of the pictured grown-ups, the message 'I'd like to give these a try' headed a blank space for parental responses to the children's Wish List.

Having duplicated the sheets, and keeping the supply in reserve, the Year 1 teachers sent parents an invitation to a short meeting about some changes in the Year 1 program. The timing was made especially convenient, 5.30 p.m., to fit in with mothers' and fathers' work schedules. At the appointed time, the turn-out at the school was large.

The three Year 1 teachers announced some minor changes to take place in the Year 1 program and then, with hearts in mouths, they revealed the major change they were proposing: the children's Wish List. The sheets were distributed and details divulged. Friday mornings, from 10 to 12.30, would be the time for group activities. Teachers would be there to coordinate, assist and help with resources, parents would be in charge

146

of activities and could nominate how often and for how long they could come. The Parent Room would be open for morning tea and relaxed chats with other parents and teachers.

The hearts of Beth, Susan and Nikki did not remain long in their mouths but began to beat enthusiastically as parents filled in their reactions to the Wish List and it was clear the response was high. The teachers' interest and excitement had rubbed off. Six parents volunteered immediately for the start of the program on the following Friday. These six subsequently organised themselves into an advisory/liaison group with the teachers. Over the next months approximately two-thirds of the almost seventy families in Year 1 were involved in the program.

What created such a level of ongoing cooperation and engagement? The most basic answer is that the program met its participants' needs. At its heart were the children who wanted these activities, chosen by themselves, and nagged their parents to help provide them. The teachers called the children their 'publicity agents' and highly effective agents they were, never losing the messages or newsletters sent home about the program. Meeting their parents in small groups with their friends to make kites or create dress-up clothes gave the children a new feeling of respect and pride in these familiar adults. The children of participating parents had first choice of activities, adding to their sense of achievement.

Parents' needs, too, were able to be stated and acted upon. Not all parents were able to come on Fridays and the advisory group organised some evening sessions of the program, doubling as social get-togethers. Support and flexibility were the watchwords. Parents were in charge of the activity they elected, but those who needed help in choosing an activity suited to their skills, those whose work schedule was changed and who needed to alter their commitment, those who had problems with babysitting, transport or materials had immediate support figures available in the advisory group or the Year 1 teaching trio. The flexibility of the program derived, as Beth had foreshadowed, from 'a lot of parents doing a little bit, instead of a few doing a lot'. It was not unduly demanding of anyone, and parents could choose ahead their own dates and times.

For the teachers, the program met their need for more help and more excitement in their teaching program. They have all found it challenging, satisfying and not too difficult to coordinate their large team, only occasionally having to double, in an emergency, as a reserve for one of the parents. Their principal job of coordination they have accomplished in three main ways. The first is by keeping in close touch with the advisory group who have liaised effectively between teachers and individual parents needing to get or give information. Secondly, they have communicated constantly with parents, always using paper with the program logo, to organise schedules and reminders in language free from jargon. Thirdly, they have encouraged parents to come early on their activity day so they can relax beforehand, chat to the teachers and be introduced to other parents in the Parent Room. Here, on Friday mornings, teachers prepare morning tea and share it with the parents. Teachers and parents are increasingly at ease now, on a first name basis, amd problems and concerns are often sorted out over a cuppa in the Parent Room.

At this stage of a well-oiled program, teachers are noting some differences among parents. While some are content – as are their child groups – to enjoy everyday activities such as simple cooking and gardening, other parents, more highly educated and career directed, are eager to try more complex mathematical and science-type activities, but worried lest they fail. Said Susan to Beth and Nikki: 'I can feel another parent group meeting coming up. We need to talk together about *all* these activities being part of early education. Including the everyday ones.'

Story 9 Quite contrary

Geraldine's seven year old son Michael was in trouble in Year 2 because he hated writing. As Geraldine called for Michael at school one day, his teacher informed her of Michael's problem and suggested that she might 'like to do some writing with him at home'. The teacher gave no other suggestions, and when Geraldine sat down with Michael and asked him to write her a story, he simply muttered 'I hate writing' amd stamped off into his favourite place, the garden.

Geraldine made another attempt, another day, with similar results. She felt as angry and upset as Michael. 'I just don't know what to do,' she told her friend Louise. 'Would you have any ideas?' Louise, a primary teacher, did have ideas, but did not want them to overwhelm her friend's own initiative in the matter. She said: ' I think it's really hard to just sit down and write a story. I couldn't do it. You need to have some *reason* for writing. What's something that Michael's really interested in that he might like to write about? What does he really like doing?'

'Gardening,' said Geraldine. 'We both love our vegetable bed – we've just been planting lettuce.'

'Well, how about planting something else – what's a quick grower? – bean seeds? And Michael could keep a diary of what happens. Or better still, a scrapbook that you could help him with. And I could be the photographer. I'll bring over my instamatic.'

'I could ask Michael's teacher if he could take the scrapbook to "Show and Tell".' Geraldine was quite excited. 'And maybe he'd write a letter with copies of the photos to Nan and Poppa in America.'

'Terrific,' said Louise.

Michael was keen to go with his mother and Louise to the shops to buy the packet of seeds and the scrapbook. On the way home Louise raised the possiblity of borrowing some gardening books from the library to add to their information.

The planting was a time of great excitement. A photographer snapping key moments (Michael following his mother in loosening the soil, measuring the distance between seeds, popping the seed in the hole), a photographer, moreover, who asked Michael many questions about what he was doing and why, added to the sense of occasion. Geraldine, too, took her cue from Louise and chimed in with her questions and conversation. 'Maybe you should hose the bed first, Michael. It's dried out since the rain. . . . Do you think this hole's deep enough?'

When they came inside, the first thing they needed was afternoon tea. Then the scrapbook came out and Michael began to look intimidated, but brightened as he said, 'I'll get a piece of paper for a rough copy. That's what we do at school.' 'Good idea,' said Louise, and went on to ask Michael to remind them of all the important things they had done. The questions she and Geraldine had asked and he had answered in the garden figured clearly in his memory.

'So how would you start the story?' asked Louise. 'Mum and I planted some beans,' said Michael. 'That's a great opening sentence,' said Louise, and away went Michael. As he came to unfamiliar words, Louise asked him to sound them out, modelling for Geraldine ways of giving encouragement, and helping when necessary by writing in words that were very difficult. A few sentences later, Geraldine had taken over the helper role from her model and she and Michael were getting on as well together as they had in the garden. When they heard the front door open, Michael was off with his rough copy to read out his story to Dad and share his triumph.

This was only the first of many triumphs. From that afternoon burgeoned a series of satisfactions, unfolding like the beanplants in the garden: praise from Michael's teacher, the pleasure of reading the story and showing the photos to the class, grandparents' delight and a long letter back from across the seas, new books from the library, and – Geraldine's idea – a dictionary of plant and gardening terms to which the whole class was contributing.

Not only Michael was developing self-esteem and initiative. Geraldine, too, had a new confidence in her voice, as she rang Louise to communicate the latest progress. Louise, likewise, had acquired new insights from this experience with her friends. She thought of the times when she, like Michael's teacher, had given parents very brief, possibly inept, advice at the classroom door and had left it at that, and she contrasted those occasions with the flowering that followed this episode when parent, teacher and child had collaborated, over time and in context.

In only the last of these three stories is the young child presented as a major member of the cast of players. In the other two the children are discussed rather than appearing as individual actors. Consequently, in the following section the children appear as part of the whole system of children, parents and professionals, as they relate to the Hess behavioural variables associated with the involvement dimension (Table 3.1).

Encouraging accomplishment: young children, parents and professionals

At the beginning of Stories 7, 8 and 9, all of the adults in these stories have goals for children, goals for themselves and goals for one another. By the end of the stories, the horizons of all the participants, not only the children, have been broadened (that is, the goals have been at least partially fulfilled) and new horizons (new goals) have emerged.

In Story 7, staff members have goals for the development of babies and toddlers. Parents, too, have goals for their children. The task is to bring these goals together and to arrive at a set of agreed goals. At the end of the story, this has been accomplished through parental involvement with staff, and a further mutual task is set: to share their understandings with the local community.

In Story 8, primary teachers have the goal of revitalising their classroom programs and call on the involvement of parents in order to do it. Largely because of children's involvement (nagging!), parents and teachers are brought into contact, and teachers find a variety of ways of staying closely involved with parents. As the perspectives of all players broaden, new goals arise to be addressed in the future conduct of the parent–child groups.

In Story 9, Michael is quite contrary about the writing goals his parent and teacher have for him. Yet he launches forth on a series of writing projects because of the involvement, with him and with each other, of his mother and a professional friend of hers. They achieve *their* goal of giving Michael 'some *reason* for writing' by demonstrating its relationship to his real goal, gardening. The reciprocal feedback of the adults brings both of them a heightened feeling of self-worth and some valuable insights for future action.

The goals in all three stories require, for their fulfilment, the mutual involvement of all the participants. Because this involvement has, in every story, been consciously built into the planning of the sequence (along with responsiveness and mutual control), the result is in each case 'mission accomplished'.

These stories indicate that *accomplishment* is *encouraged* (Hess variable 7, Table 3.1) when participants (stakeholders) formulate some goals and collaborate with other stakeholders in working towards them. That this is no truism has been demonstrated in the drama of *Hamlet*. The hero of the world's greatest play came to ultimate grief because he could neither decide what he really wanted nor collaborate with others long term to get it.

Involvement is not, however, concerned only with knowing where we and others want to go. It is also about the means of geting there. The last three of Hess's ten variables concern these means.

Communication: young children, parents and professionals

In addition to the propositions about the value of supportive links between settings, Bronfenbrenner (1979: 216) has proposed that: 'The developmental potential of participation in multiple settings will vary directly with the ease and extent of two-way communication between those settings.' In this chapter on involvement, we look at what the participants actually *do* to promote ease and extent of communication.

An important foundation for what they do is to eat, drink and be, if not merry, at least mellow. The essence of social relationships is *social* relationships. In Story 7, ease and extent of communication grow as parents, their babies and staff members have lunch together while the adults continue to chat over their agenda. In Story 8, problems and concerns are often sorted out over a cup of tea, prepared by the teachers, in the Parent Room. And in Story 9, the three protagonists go shopping and do some gardening, both social activities, followed by well-earned afternoon tea to set up the fortitude (physical and psychological) for cerebral work.

As Midwinter (1973) years ago remarked, from a long experience of bringing schools and their communities together, these social relationships are quite fundamental to parent-teacher collaboration and indeed are a pre-requisite: 'all would be well advised to follow the path of natural evolution from informal and indirect communion, via social interrelation, to participation.' Such informal social occasions as those instanced in Stories 7, 8 and 9 (and the barbecues, fashion parades and sausage sizzles held in many early childhood settings) not only allow professionals and parents to get acquainted but also, in the conduct of parent groups, fulfil the need for parents to get to know one another. Teachers have often mentioned to me how surprised they have been, late in the year, to find that parents whom they have got to know quite well are often still shy and unacquainted with one another. Name tags at social functions are a must. So is the introduction of one parent to another that often only the teacher (as the common link) is in a position to perform (Berger, 1995).

In a study of the formal and informal conversations taking place in parent discussion groups, Powell and Eisenstadt (1988) monitored both the timing and the content of these two forms of communication. In a well-functioning long-term parent group, the authors reported that the time spent in what the authors call 'kitchen talk' rose, over the period of a year, from 24 per cent to 39 per cent of the total session time. Such talk, the authors found, was an extremely valuable form of communication. It was purposeful, often sparked by the more formal discussions, and was more focused on individual concerns including those embracing the wider social environment. Such 'kitchen talk', an important source of information for professionals involved with parents, requires 'both adequate time and comfortable physical surroundings' (Powell, 1989: 95).

These are also requirements for the free flow of the more formal discussion periods. The advice of an Australian pioneer of parent discussion (McNamara, 1967) still stands:

> The place of meeting should be pleasant, comfortable and welcoming. This is important, especially for a group of [parents] who are often tired and need to feel that it is a pleasure as well as a duty to attend the group. Someone's home is ideal as a meeting-place, or a small hall with comfortable chairs, good ventilation and facilities for refreshments. A cup of coffee or tea works wonders in breaking the ice, easing tensions or loosening up minds and tongues.
>
> Seating arrangements should be right for discussion. Chairs should be in a rather tight circle, close enough for each member to see and hear each of the others without strain. There should be no obstacle such as a table between members of the group. If anyone wants to take notes (as when one member acts as recorder of the proceedings) the notes can be written on lap or knees.
>
> (McNamara, 1967: 6)

Communication, as so far discussed in this section, has been face-to-face conversation. In the view of Bronfenbrenner (1979: 217) this is much the most effective way to communicate: 'The developmental potential of settings is enhanced to the extent that the mode of communication between them is personal (thus in descending order: face-to-face, personal letter or note, phone, business letter, announcement).'

In Stories 7, 8 and 9 we see effective face-to-face communication among varied numbers of people. In Story 7, parents and staff members communicated in a plenary group of approximately twenty people, later in a variety of smaller groups which 'allowed members to feel more at ease with one another'. In Story 8, teachers and parents met in a large, enthusiastic group, parents and children later worked in small groups, teachers and their six-person advisory group talked to one another regularly, and teachers solved problems over cups of tea with individual parents in the Parent Room. Story 9 saw highly effective two-way (teacher–parent) and three-way (child–teacher–parent) discussion.

In all of these stories, face-to-face communication in dyads and in small and larger groups contributed to the enhancement of adults and children. But these stories also show us other examples of effective communication employing all the modes listed by Bronfenbrenner as less successful. In Story 7, the useful upshot of staff–parent understanding of and impetus towards developmental goals for babies and toddlers was achieved not only by talk but also through the inter-setting means of a school-derived parent questionnaire, telephoned responses, a notice from the centre to parents, and prioritised parent–staff compiled lists. Other inter-setting methods used in Story 8 (with the outcome of long running parent–child activity groups at school) were notices addressed to children and to parents, and frequent and regular messages carried to and fro by children. In Story 9 – whose very theme was the growth in a child's ability to communicate through writing – a variety of communication forms (creation of a scrapbook and a dictionary, photos, letter to grandparents) all played a further part in successful links between settings.

The essence of Bronfenbrenner's strictures about notes, phone messages, business letters and announcements is not that they are not delivered face-to-face, but that they are impersonal. His fundamental injunction is that the missive should sound a personal note that can resonate with each of its recipients. The communications in Stories 7, 8 and 9 did this for three reasons.

- They could 'talk to us in a language we can understand' (Anderson, 1984). The questions to be prioritised in Story 7 were couched in everyday language: 'How can I ensure the opportunity to discuss with staff how my child is progressing, not only day to day but over longer periods of time?' The messages sent home in Story 8 were scanned by the teachers to ensure they were jargon-free. Consequently they were welcomed and acted on.
- They were well presented: clear, attractive and easy to read. Letters sent home that are 'unprepossessing . . . ineffective, patronising, illegible, or incomprehensible' (Tizard *et al.*, 1981: 146) are like a slap in the face – personally rude. In Story 8, messages went home 'using always paper with the program logo'. Is this a sign of impersonality? On the contrary, it is a thoughtful recognition that a parent recipient is a busy person, and that putting the reader in touch as speedily as possible is an appreciated gesture.
- They were able, in the words of the family day care hand-out (Table 3.4), to 'talk with rather than to' the reader. Thus they allowed for a personal reaction. Examples were the Wish List in Story 8, and the list

of child care goals in Story 7, whose priorities were susceptible of change through discussion. Even the final list in Story 7, to be circularised throughout the child care centre, was to be accompanied by an Action Column, allowing for further individual responses. That is to say, even written communications can be personally responsive, can – like the spoken words from group members on p. 77 – invite the recipient to say: 'You might have a point there.'

Teaching behaviour: young children, parents and professionals

'Talking with rather than to' is another way of describing the building up of intersubjectivity through semiotic mediation. These processes, discussed in relation to the family day care program (p. 137), underlie effective teaching and learning.

Why was it important for the participants in Stories 7, 8 and 9 to talk with rather than to each other? Why did they need to build up intersubjectivity? Because intersubjectivity, getting on the same wave length, was essential to the broadening of horizons central to each story. That is to say, new situation definitions emerged through the participants' involvement with one another. At the same time, some existing situation definitions were confirmed. In Story 7, both parent and staff members wanted to understand better one another's perspectives on infant development. They achieved (at least in the short term) the remarkable feat of synchronising their perspectives. In Story 8, teachers hoped to persuade parents to help them to revitalise their program. Parents responded by unwrapping their own lifeskills and putting them at the children's disposal in the activity groups at school. In Story 9, a mother and her teacher friend wanted to unlock the world of written words for a seven year old. They succeeded, and in the process these adults, like those in the other stories, brought new insights to each other and to themselves.

What were the processes that brought about these remarkable results? We have focused on the achievement of intersubjectivity through the use of appropriate language, but within these, two highly important elements need highlighting. They are well illustrated in Story 9, a close-up view of the protagonists engaged in teaching and learning. The first of these elements is the use of questions in information exchange.

Questions

As noted earlier on p. 140, 'the asking of questions (on the part of both parents and children) is seen as a particularly desirable mechanism whereby learning is advanced (Gordon, 1977)'. This is because questions inherently lend themselves to the production of contingent response or feedback. Questions call for a response to be made to the questioner, evoking a further response, and so on; a command or directive, on the other hand, calls for a response to be directed towards some other person or object, with less likelihood of further feedback.

Tizard and Hughes (1984) have distinguished between questions asked by parents and questions asked by teachers. They suggest that:

> the kind of dialogue that seems to help the child is not that currently favoured by many teachers in which the adult poses a series of questions. It is rather one in which the adult listens to the child's questions and comments, helps to clarify her ideas, and feeds her the information she asks for.
>
> (Tizard and Hughes, 1984: 254)

It follows from this study by Tizard and Hughes of talk between children and their parents and talk between the same children and their teachers that what helps learning is not the string of 'test' questions characteristic of many teachers but a mutual adult–child dialogue in which the adult both responds and initiates, often asking questions which are prompted by genuine curiosity (exploring *with* the child). Tizard and Hughes find this use of questions more characteristic of parents than teachers.

In Story 9, of Michael laying the groundwork both for a garden and for writing prowess, we do not have to make a judgment about the relative effectiveness of these two kinds of questioning techniques. It is worth noting, however, that both techniques are there; the teacher taking photographs as she 'asked Michael many questions about what he was doing and why', while his mother 'chimed in with her questions and conversation'. In the upshot, as Michael summoned up his resources for writing, both sets of adult questions turned out to be significant motivators, as the teacher 'went on to ask Michael to remind them of all the important things they had done. The questions she and Geraldine had asked and he had answered in the garden figured clearly in his memory.' At this point, the teacher's questions were no longer 'test' questions, but an empowering method of validating what Michael already knew. At this point, too, both adults were also enjoying 'exploring *with* the child' what they could remember of their afternoon in the garden.

Questions between the adults play a similar part in stimulating new ideas while helping to affirm some existing ones. Stimulation of new ideas is highly evident at the beginning of Story 9, as parent questions teacher, teacher parent, and each question sparks ideas in the other that evoke still further ideas to help Michael. At the same time Louise's questions allow Geraldine to consolidate for herself the value of the gardening sessions she and Michael so enjoy as the basis for further activity.

Modelling

A second potent process, involving all three participants in Story 9, is that of modelling. We have seen Michael 'following his mother in loosening the soil, measuring the distance between seeds, popping the seed in the hole', while Geraldine 'took her cue from Louise and chimed in'. Later, Louise models for Geraldine some positive methods of helping the young writer, and soon Geraldine has 'taken over the helper role from her model and she and Michael were getting on as well together as they had in the garden'. In the future, it may be that Louise, the teacher, will model at school the successful methods she has seen Geraldine, the mother, using with her son in the gardening activity.

Over the years teachers have shown me hundreds of stories about their developing relationships with parents, almost all containing some element of modelling (often the teacher demonstrating and the parent following suit), and I remain astonished at the ease with which this operation occurs and at its almost universal short-term success. I suppose that the reason for this is that teachers, as skilled professionals, are modelling operations which they have set up to produce positive reinforcement. In the story of Michael, for example, Louise has set in train the capturing of the hero in a series of photographs for the scrapbook, an inbuilt guarantee of raised self-esteem for child and mother. On such a train, Geraldine is happy to jump aboard and follow her model. As Story 9 demonstrates, this does not mean that she slavishly imitates Louise. On the contrary, as Bandura (1977: 205) has suggested, modelling may well produce 'behaviour that is generative and innovative in character'.

Diffuse intellectual stimulation: young children, parents and professionals

Involvement, as defined in this book, means interaction in ways that broaden the horizons – that is, interaction with others in stimulating ways. What kind of interaction is that and how do Stories 7, 8 and 9 illustrate it?

In the family day care program hand-out (Table 3.4), the variable of 'diffuse intellectual stimulation' (Hess, 1971) was called 'hav[ing] interesting things around for children'. Professionals and parents are used to thinking of books, toys, and computers as interesting things for children, but these are narrow perspectives. To have interesting things around for young children, as Caldwell (1974) said in her film *Child's Play and the Real World*, we do not have to go on big trips to exotic places. This applies also to adults. Jean Henri Fabre, the great French naturalist, remained in his country garden observing for forty years and changed the face of entomology. Horizons can be broadened in a small garden. How did Fabre do it? He had a total involvement with his insects:

> I have made it a rule to adopt the method of ignorance in learning about the instinct of insects. I set myself stubbornly face to face with my subject until I contrive to make it speak. I know nothing. So much the better.
>
> (Doorly, 1936)

Young children also begin by knowing nothing, but they have an easier time than Fabre. From the start, they are usually surrounded by people wanting to help them learn. Rogoff (1990: 39) describes young children as 'active learners in a community of people who support, challenge and guide novices as they increasingly participate in skilled, valued socio-cultural activity'. Note that Rogoff's categories of help correspond to the three dimensions of caregiving behaviour discussed in this book: the helpers support (*responsiveness*), challenge (*involvement*) and guide (*control*) the novices. Writing further of the 'skilled, valued sociocultural activity' in which young children participate (that is, everyday activity), Rogoff has remarked that: 'We tend to overlook the numerous, implicit everyday opportunities for children to gain understanding and skills of the world around them' (p. 151).

Rogoff is writing, as a researcher, of the tendency of research to overlook these everyday opportunities in which young children learn. Like Bruner's (1957) fish, the last to know water, many researchers have to date ignored some of the most obvious, pervasive and learning-charged features of young children's lives: their close interactions (involvement) with adults within everyday activities and routines. These naturalistic contexts through which young children progress constitute 'diffuse intellectual stimulation'. By taking part with others in eating, being bathed, changing clothes, 'helping' to make the bed, 'helping' to wash up, young children build the immense stock of competence acquired long before school entry (Edgar, 1993).

A few researchers have begun to tease out the processes occurring in adult–child involvement in such everyday activities (Gahan *et al.*, 1994; Rheingold, 1982; Rogoff, 1990; Tizard and Hughes, 1984). Gahan *et al.* (1994), for example, have found that in a sample of middle-class parents and their 12-month old babies, parents often incorporate diversionary games and jingles into feeding and dressing, but not book or toy routines. Parents indicate that they see books and toys as possessing intrinsic interest for their children, but they attempt to make the caretaking activities more interesting. The resulting multi-focus opportunities were demonstrated by one 12-month old girl who sat on her mother's knee, rocking and singing 'See-saw Marjorie Daw' with her mother, while pulling on socks.

Meanwhile, the more general neglect by researchers of how involvement with adults in everyday contexts helps young children to develop trust, autonomy and initiative has been paralleled by similar neglect in much of the practical work of professionals.

In the widely used early childhood handbook, *Developmentally Appropriate Practice in Early Childhood Programs Serving Children from Birth through Age 8* (Bredekamp, 1987), the focus is almost exclusively on children's autonomous learning and play. In the examples given in the book, adults act as responsive facilitators and supporters, but hardly ever as collaborators in the 'skilled, valued sociocultural activity' (Rogoff (1990: 151), whereby children could contribute to the everyday life of the enterprise. Here is an exception:

> Adults provide opportunities for three-year olds to demonstrate and practice their newly developed self-help skills and their desire to help adults with dressing and undressing, toileting, feeding themselves (including helping with pouring milk or setting the table), brushing teeth, washing hands and helping pick up toys.
>
> (Bredekamp, 1987: 48)

As I have commented elsewhere:

> How much more comprehensive the list could have been if the focus had widened to include not only children's self-help or the simple aiding of an adult, but had embraced also the shared fun and learning potential of watering the garden together, folding the clothes together, polishing the furniture together.
>
> (Henry, 1990: 43)

Thus it is delightful to see this shared fun and learning potential being demonstrated by children and adults in at least two of the three stories in this chapter. Of Story 7 we cannot be sure, because the content of the parent–professional group discussion is undisclosed, but it would seem likely that the parents in this story, in considering how their home aims for their young children mesh with centre aims, would share with child care staff some of the everyday moments of fun and learning at home with the toddlers – for example, the pleasure of pegging out clothes on the line together.

In Story 8, 'diffuse intellectual stimulation' is at the very core of the Friday morning parent program instigated by the Year 1 teachers. Much of the stimulation in which parents and children are involved consists of everyday, family-style activity. 'Cook', 'Sew', 'Cut' said the labels on the balloons. It is interesting that at the end of the story the teachers are acknowledging aloud the value of the element of diffuseness in the parents' program. They see all its facets as educative for the children, not only the scientific and mathematical activities offered by a few of the parents. The teachers plan to reinforce this at a future parent–teacher meeting. 'We need', said Susan, 'to talk together about *all* these activities being part of early education. Including the everyday ones.'

In Story 9, we see how the 'shared fun and learning potential' of Geraldine and Michael's everyday bean planting bore remarkable results. In itself it was a learning experience. Geraldine's words, for example, 'Maybe you should hose the bed first, Michael. It's dried out since the rain . . . Do you think this hole's deep enough?', created opportunities for the growth of trust, autonomy and initiative. Trust: the recalling of earlier shared times in the garden, in the rain (planting the lettuce?). Autonomy: Michael was invited to make and carry out two decisions, whether to hose, whether the hole needed to be deeper. Initiative: both decisions required further information exchange with mother, concerning mathematical estimations, climate, rain patterns, agricultural implements, the growth habits of legumes.

Not only was this experience a true seed bed for the subsequent academic exercise of writing in the scrapbook, it also brought forth other satisfying and intellectually stimulating shoots: 'Praise from Michael's teacher, the pleasure of reading the story and showing the photos to the class, grandparents' delight and a long letter back from across the seas, new books from the library, and . . . a dictionary of plant and gardening terms to which the whole class was contributing.'

These are some of the 'learning potentials' of the diffuse intellectual simulation of everyday activities. But they arise only because children find them, as noted above, such 'shared fun'. Children love to do things around the place, together, with their significant adults. Thinking back to our own childhood, was it not so, too, for us? Rheingold (1982) has demonstrated that children as young as 18 months are determined, given the slightest opportunity, to 'help' with a variety of household tasks. Goodnow and Burns (1985) have instanced the children, back from a holiday overseas with their family, who were asked what they enjoyed most and who recalled not the exotic places of their big trip (Caldwell, 1974) but the times 'when the family sat around together working out what they would do, or stayed up late talking' (p. 148).

This is involvement, and it appears that adults, if they can see a variety of everyday experiences with children as important, enjoy it too. Close collaboration with children, in the children's interest, was, after all, what all the adults in Stories 7, 8 and 9 were wanting. This included the parents in Story 7 who, while at work, wanted to achieve this end with and through their fellow adults in the child care centre. In the family day care program, the providers' post-program responses to the question 'What do you most enjoy doing with the children?' clearly demonstrated this pleasure in involvement with the children in 'diffuse intellectual stimulation' (Table 4.1).

In many of the above examples with a family setting, adult–child interaction does more than broaden children's intellectual horizons. Because this interaction is framed around *diffuse* stimulation, it is also concerned with the accessible, the available, the odds and ends, the bits and pieces that make up life in a household: the vacuuming, the dusting (Table 4.1, Example 5). Such interaction enables even very young children 'to contribute to the everyday life of the enterprise'. Diffuse intellectual stimulation in everyday activities makes possible an amalgam of competence and prosocial behaviour in young children. This has been recognised in Amato's (1987) study of older children in which the life-skills that are helpful in a family, such as the ability to make a bed and change a light bulb, are seen as constituting a category of competence.

Thus diffuse intellectual stimulation at home is often (not always but often) about *helping* activities. Such activities provide a moral dimension in which the early childhood profession has much to learn from what parents and children do at home. Professionals might ponder the following comment by a'Beckett *et al.* (1988), framed in relation to child care, but applicable to *all* early childhood settings:

> A major feature of satisfying family life is the commitment that family members have not only to one another's well being but also to the maintenance of the family itself. A challenge for child care is to translate this impetus – despite the constraints of the environment – into the child care setting.
>
> Referring to another institutional setting, Bronfenbrenner (1979: 11) has pointed to the possibility of young people graduating from high school 'without ever having had to do a piece of work on which somebody else depended'. He has urged the adoption of a 'curriculum for caring'. There is ample evidence that very young children are responsive to such a curriculum. Given appropriate opportunities and encouragement from adults, activities such as folding nappies, tending pets and tidying up are enthusiatically embraced even by toddlers as ways of helping . . .
>
> Thus, in the centre setting, a 'curriculum for caring' would mean not only caregivers caring for children, but also children helping to care for others in an enterprise bigger than themselves.
>
> (a'Beckett *et al.*, 1988: 17)

We have seen in this book that adults from home settings (the family day care program, the Aboriginal parent program) are highly responsive to the notion that adult–child involvement through diffuse intellectual stimulation (including everyday activities) can help young children build up both their competence and their prosocial motivation. In the Aboriginal parent program (Henry, 1980), discussed in Chapter 3, parents were asked what they enjoyed most *about* (not with) their child.

Children's helping behaviours, hardly mentioned at the beginning of the program, figured, at the end, in over a third of all child activities recalled. One mother, for example, described her toddler's efforts at cooperation: 'She picks up the papers with me, chucks cups in the sink. She's trying to help – you can't go mad with her even if it breaks' (Henry, 1980: 46).

A later comment concerning this is highly pertinent here:

> What is interesting about the mothers' replies, with their stress on parent–child collaboration, is that these were answers to a question about the *child*, not a question about the *parent-and-child*. Yet these parents tended to answer as though the question did concern parent–child interaction. It may be that given support, encouragement and an understanding of children's developmental sequences and their own ability to enhance them, what parents – and other caregivers – find most rewarding is not just to stand back and admire their children, as it were, from a distance, but rather to engage actively in collaboration with them.
>
> (Henry, 1990: 40)

It appears, then, that both young children and their parents find it rewarding to be involved with one another around everyday activities. But as Stories 7, 8 and 9 show, adult–adult involvement around 'diffuse intellectual stimulation' creates a further sphere of benefits. In these stories, parents and professionals both model for and learn from one another, making available existing situation definitions and building on them to create novel outcomes.

In Story 9, for example, Louise, the professional, searches for and finds motivational cues to spark Michael's interest in a writing exercise. But this is only possible because Geraldine, the parent, proffers the cue, an area of shared familiarity and pleasure for Michael (gardening) which only the parent is in a position to make available to the professional.

In Chapter 2, we noted that both parents and professionals need information and support. In Stories 7, 8 and 9, we have seen both these elements, information exchange and the support of an 'extended family' (Story 7), being made available through parent–professional involvement.

There is a symbiotic relationship between these partners: 'Many parents are eager for reassurance that in their ordinary, daily interactions they are helping to foster their children's development. It should be one responsibility of professionals to provide such reassurance' (Henry, 1988: 10). Additionally, one of the most important messages from the stories in this chapter is that professionals can do more than reassure and applaud parents. In terms of parents' involvement with children in everyday activities, professionals can learn from them.

We might remind ourselves of the findings of Gahan *et al.* (1994) mentioned on p. 157. They decribed an example of everyday learning in the baby girl who sang 'See-saw Marjorie Daw' with her mother as she pulled on her socks:

> These findings have implications for parents and carers of young children engaging together in culturally relevant routines. For example, they indicate the value to children of routinization. Because the 12-months old children found the tasks of eating and dressing already familiar (routinized), they were able simultaneously, in reciprocal interaction with the diversionary strategies offered by their parents, to go beyond these tasks to other activities such as singing. Such multi-focus challenges to infant information processing have a potent part to play in early development.
>
> (Gahan *et al.*, 1994).

Tizard and Hughes (1984: 267) have remarked that 'It is time to shift the emphasis away from what parents should learn from professionals, and towards what professionals can learn from studying parents and children at home.' The view being put forward here is that *both* professionals and parents can learn from one another.

7

MR MICAWBER AND THE MODEL ALL TOGETHER

Mr Micawber maintained that when our resources are greater than the demands made upon us, we function very well; but when the demands (stresses) upon us exceed our resources, we cannot cope. The message from Gowen's (1979) model of childrearing environments is the same as Mr Micawber's. In the see-saw balance of the demands/resources ratio (p. 27), an uptilt in our resources brings benefits to us and to the system of which we are a part. If we are responsible for a child's upbringing, the child too is likely to benefit. When demands pile high upon us, outweighing resources, we function badly and the probabilities worsen for the child.

When we function well, we feel in control of our lives, and we have a high sense of self-esteem. Table 3.1 showed that parents who have a high sense of internal control and self-esteem (Gordon, 1972) are likely to be those who help to increase their young children's resources by exercising a number of behaviours (Hess, 1971) which are related, I have suggested, to dimensions of responsiveness, control and involvement. The resources that children thereby build up are gains in trust, autonomy and initiative.

This book has taken Mr Micawber's resources/demands principle a little further. It has proposed that adult exercise of the same behaviours, at the positive end of the behavioural dimensions, can improve the resources/demands ratio not only for young children, but also for other adults. While stage theorists (e.g. Piaget) have stressed the differences between child and adult development and learning, in this book the increasingly held notion of continuity in development (Bornstein and Sigman, 1986; Catherwood, 1994) has been applied to adult, as well as child, needs for trust, autonomy and initiative. It is not really surprising that humans of any age should require a positive response to the characteristics they bring with them, should require some sense of control over their environment, and should require stimulating involvement with others engaged with them in an enterprise. (These fundamental human needs subsume the needs of, say, professionals and

parents for information and support in their particular jobs, Chapter 2).
Thus, adults enhance the resources of other adults, as well as children,
when they:

- *Promote trust* in others by *responding* to their needs.
- *Promote autonomy* in others by exercising control while fostering their
  independence (*mutual control*).
- *Promote initiative* in others by active *involvement* with them in stimulating ways.

In this book, two bodies of non-stage theory in which there is much
current interest, Vygotskian and empowerment theories, have been
drawn on to account for the ability of adults to promote these changes
in other adults and children. This final chapter consolidates the links
between Vygotskian and empowerment theories and the other major
themes that have recurred throughout the book. We draw together
Vygotskian and empowerment theories, the responsiveness/control/
empowerment model, and the resources/demands ratio.

First, we show, in summary, how interlinking Vygotskian and empowerment theories can help to account for the power of the responsiveness/
control/involvement model to increase the resources of both adults and
children. Second, after the positive stories of resource enhancement in
preceding chapters, we look at a number of professional–parent programs, in the public domain, where the aim of enhancing child resources
has been attempted but not fulfilled. We see whether the failure to
operate at the positive pole of one or another of the three behavioural
dimensions might account for these less successful professional–parent–
child interactions. Third, we draw out implications of the Micawber
principle for our own practice.

VYGOTSKIAN/EMPOWERMENT PERSPECTIVES AND A RESPONSIVENESS/CONTROL/INVOLVEMENT MODEL

In the last three chapters, particular facets of Vygotskian and empowerment theories have been related to the dimensions of responsiveness,
control, and involvement, *considered separately*. In this final chapter,
Vygotskian and empowerment theories are brought together, within a
broad model of learning, to show how they relate to responsiveness/
control/involvement *as a whole*.

The zone of proximal development

Vygotsky's (1978: 86) zone of proximal development, framed in the
context of childhood learning, represents 'the distance between the
actual developmental level as determined by independent problem

solving and the level of potential development as determined through problem solving under adult guidance or in collaboration with more capable peers'. As suggested earlier, Vygotsky's zone of proximal development is applicable also to teaching/learning interactions at all ages, including interactions between parents and professionals. These occasions might include:

- Centre or school links between parents and professionals.
- In-service programs for professionals who will interact with parents as well as children.
- Parent education programs organised by professionals.

Within the zone of proximal development, the concepts of situation redefinition, intersubjectivity and semiotic mediation have been seen to be of particular relevance, and will now be considered *in toto*.

New situation definitions

In the last chapter on involvement, a variety of examples, both from the family day care program and from Stories 7–9, have shown participants moving to internalise new situation definitions through communication with 'more capable' others. Stories from earlier chapters provide similar evidence. For example, in Story 3 (p. 87), Christine, the mother, moves from a sense of inability to read or help her children to read, to a new perception of some important elements of reading, and her ability to actualise them. These new situation definitions she gains from modeling facilitator Prudence.

Intersubjectivity and semiotic mediation

These moves towards new situation definitions are only possible because both facilitator and participant have arrived at a moment of mutual understanding (intersubjectivity) based on what they say to each other (semiotic mediation). In Story 2 (p. 86) we see such a moment occurring for an Aboriginal mother and the non-Aboriginal visitor at a lunch gathering. The Aboriginal mother has felt herself to be the victim of particular school discrimination. The non-Aboriginal mother points out that she has been treated in a similar way. '"Well, maybe we've all got the same trouble with those teachers," said Natalie.' This important insight for both mothers, and others in the group, has been gained only because of their ability to communicate in ways that all can understand.

What these examples from Stories 2 and 3 confirm is Vygotsky's assertion that processes operating first between individuals become processes that are internalised, that is, that interpsychological processes become intrapsychological ones (Vygotsky, 1981). These processes may be further illuminated by complementing Vygotskian with empowerment concepts.

Validation of the learner

While the Vygotskian approach emphasises attentiveness to the learner's situation definition, with a view to replacing it with another (Wertsch, 1984: 13), the empowerment approach advocates attentiveness to learner experience in order to support and validate it (Vanderslice, 1984: 4).

In the stories just cited, both of these processes have occurred. New situation definitions have been arrived at, but some earlier positions have also been supported: in Stories 2 and 3, the parents' powerful entering characteristic of strong advocacy for their children has been affirmed and appropriately resourced by the relevant professionals, Miranda and Prudence.

Cochran (1988) believes such a preventive or maintenance function – that is, the preservation of existing strengths – to be one of the most important features of the empowerment approach, and strongly contrasts it with an approach that attempts to replace existing behaviours with new ones.

While the empowerment and Vygotskian approaches thus differ in their treatment of learners' pre-existing situation definitions, empowerment theorists are not at odds with Vygotsky and his followers in seeking to encourage new situation definitions. In his analysis of the goals of the Family Matters program, Cochran (1988: 27) has emphasised the importance of making available to participants new 'information about children and schools' and encouraging further 'parent–child activities', on the grounds that 'active involvement in the learning of children was a key to success'. Vanderslice (1984: 4), too, specifically includes among criteria of empowering activities the 'provision of new, related knowledge'. In the family day care program, such knowledge was both requested and, as shown in discussing the interview findings, internalised by program participants.

Facilitator empowerment

A major difference in the Vygotskian and empowerment approaches to the role of the facilitator was outlined on p. 79. While in Vygotskian theory, 'the only genuine, lasting situation redefinition that takes place occurs on the part of the child' (Wertsch, 1984: 13) – or learner of any age, in the wider context – empowerment theorists maintain that the facilitator, like the other program participants, is engaged in learning, that is, acquiring new situation definitions, through the processes of genuinely collaborative discussion.

166

In the family day care program, an example is the account given on p. 135 of the finding of a solution to one provider's problem with a child's behaviour. While the facilitator and other members of the group offered a variety of suggestions, the solution finally arrived at by the provider was in part based on these suggestions and was in part a novel initiative of her own from which the facilitator as well as other group members could learn.

To add two final examples of facilitator learning from Stories 1–9, one might instance, in Story 1, the several facilitators – a teacher and some medical personnel – who all gained from the teacher–parent interaction which produced the parent's notebook, a passport, for the first time, to *synchronised* treatment suggestions for a disabled child. In Story 9, we are told that teacher Louise 'had acquired new insights from this experience with her friends'. In particular, after witnessing the effectiveness of linking school-based learning (writing) with home-based enjoyment (gardening), she had developed a new appreciation of the learning potential of the home.

In all these stories, interactional processes operating between participants and facilitator have led to the enhancement of resources over demands. These processes, illuminated by Vgotskian and empowerment perspectives, may be summarised in the model set out in Figures 7.1(a) and (b) representing the effect on learners and facilitator of engaging with one another in the zone of proximal development; for example, taking part in a program such as the family day care program or in learning experiences such as those retold in Stories 1–9. In Figures 7.1(a) and (b) these experiences are seen first from a Vygotskian, then from a combined Vygotskian/empowerment perspective.

From the Vygotskian viewpoint, learners and facilitator enter the zone (the learning experience) at Time 1. Their developmental levels at that time are shown by an open arrow. Over the period of the learning experience they negotiate situation definitions via the processes of intersubjectivity and semiotic mediation. At the end of the

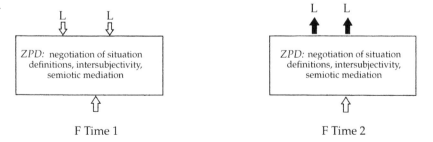

Figure 7.1(a) Learning in the zone of proximal development: Vygotskian perspective

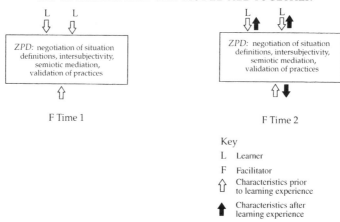

Figure 7.1(b) Learning in the zone of proximal development: Vygotskian and empowerment perspectives

learning experience (Time 2) learners have relinquished their earlier situation definitions and have internalised new ones: ideas, attitudes and reported behaviours (action patterns), represented by the filled arrows.

A combination of Vygotskian and empowerment perspectives adds considerable power to the analysis of the learning experience and its effects. In such a combination, the Vygotskian concepts of situation definition, intersubjectivity and semiotic mediation continue to illuminate, as in Figure 7.1(a), the processes operating within the zone of proximal development. Also, a further empowerment process, that of validation of existing practices, is added. The amalgamation of an empowerment with a Vygotskian perspective permits the demonstration, at Time 2, of some further significant features of teaching and learning:

- Both learners and facilitator have acknowledged and maintained some existing situation definitions (open arrows). The process of attending to existing situation definitions reflects the *responsiveness dimension* of behaviour.
- New situation definitions (filled arrows) have also emerged for both learners and facilitator. This further development of definitions reflects the *involvement dimension.*
- These two diverse outcomes (the retaining of some existing understandings, the adding of new understandings) have been achieved through participants' and facilitator's ongoing exercise, within the zone of proximal development, of situation redefinition, intersubjectivity, semiotic mediation, and validation of some practices. Bringing all these highly varied processes to fruition within the learning experience reflects the operation of the *(mutual) control dimension.*

168

The preceding section and chapters have demonstrated, through a variety of stories, my own and my students', that when professionals and parents act in these ways towards one another as well as towards young children, there are powerful benefits for all three parties, as resources are enhanced. But professionals and parents frequently fail to behave in these ways to one another. Stresses are increased, resources diminished. In the next, penultimate section, we look at some parent–professional programs that have attempted enhancement of childrens' resources, but have not succeeded. Like the more effective programs, these less successful contacts betweeen parents and professionals come in all varieties: for example, in-service programs, centre/school interactions, parent education programs. The examples described are all programs where the presence of a control group gives credibility to program results, and allows firm conclusions to be drawn.

We look first at how these less successful programs have fallen short in one or other of the three behavioural dimensions – how they have demonstrated unresponsiveness, lack of mutual control or insufficient involvement. Then we look at the implications for our own practice.

LESS SUCCESSFUL PROGRAMS AND THE THREE DIMENSIONS

Unresponsiveness to existing situation definitions in an Educational Priority Area program

A glance back at the overviews of the parent-teacher program, the Aboriginal parent/toddler program and the family day care program (Chapter 3) and Stories 1–9 (Chapters 4–6) will show that in every case attempts were made – and fulfilled – to find out from participants what they were bringing with them into the interaction: in other words, what their needs and strengths were.

It has been noted earlier (p. 78) that in professional–parent contacts this does not always happen. As Peters and Kostelnik (1981) have pointed out, irrelevant and ineffective material has often been imposed by professionals on the basis of inferred rather than expressed needs. There is evidence to suggest that parents who find themselves in programs whose agenda does not mesh with their own are likely to leave, if they are able, and/or to suffer lowered sense of self-esteem or control (Rob and Norfor, 1980).

The former reaction (a turning away from the program) has been described by James (1975) in a revealing report on the effects of changes in an Educational Priority Area early intervention program in the north of England in the 1970s. A report on the program as it functioned initially was made by Smith (1975).

A weekly home visiting program for under-three year olds was instituted among mining families in the West Riding of Yorkshire, 'attempting to extend what is already established, rather than introduce new and possibly conflicting ideas' (Smith, 1975: 138). During the visits, which were warmly welcomed by parents, appropriate materials – toys and books – were introduced for the child's discovery and experimentation, the visitor acting both as model in demonstrating ways of encouraging the child's exploration, and as promoter of the mother's participation.

> Once the mothers realised that their children were capable of a great deal more than they had anticipated, they did all they could to encourage the children . . . As children began to enjoy the sessions more, parents became more interested. The idea of learning at home took root, and as the level of interaction between parent and child grew, the children's activities were reinforced.
>
> (Smith, 1975: 145)

Children were not the only beneficiaries, because 'there is a tendency for the visited family to treat the visitor as confidante and informal social worker' (James, 1975: 21). Thus the program was helping to meet the parents' needs both for their children and for themselves.

At the end of the first year, results showed that mothers in the program group, compared with those in the control group, were using significantly fewer negative verbal and physical responses to the children, and that there was less jealousy towards younger babies in program group than in control group children. The program children, too, were 'markedly more verbal, both in spontaneous conversation during the test, and in completing verbal items during the test' (Smith, 1975: 159).

The next year there were changes. The age group of children accepted into the program was raised by a year, and the aims of the program became geared to school learning. From flexible sessions, based on changing parent–child needs, the program adopted a syllabus of 'deliberate, systematic, perceptual and conceptual input' (James, 1975: 24) pre-planned by program personnel and unrelated to parents' particular situations. Instead of wider home/community needs being discussed with the 'confidante/informal social worker', the home visitor was now to devise 'strategies for keeping these distractions to a minimum' (James, 1975: 21).

In the previous program, there was no attempt at formal teaching and parents were not asked to make the child learn particular skills. At the same time, toys or games were left in the home and the parent asked, at the next home visit, for follow-up comments:

All the mothers enjoyed doing this and greeted the home visitor the following week with excited descriptions of how he reacted, how his brothers helped him, or how he had worked it out for himself.

(Smith, 1975: 155)

By contrast, the report on the new program comments:

The technique of introducing 'parental tasks' was persisted with for some time trying several different formats. Sometimes new ideas would be introduced, sometimes a continuation of the session's activity would be suggested. It must be admitted, however, that little enthusiasm could be raised from visitor or parents about continuing the types of activity through to other times in the week on the parents' initiative. Indeed, a good deal of difficulty was found in involving the mothers during the session.

(James, 1975: 29)

From this altered program, marginal differences only were reported between experimental and control groups, both in parental attitudes and in children's test scores. Gains, where they occurred, mostly favoured the control group.

From James' description, one might be tempted to believe that parents deserted (psychologically if not bodily) the new program because of extreme program prescriptiveness. Yet other highly prescriptive programs have demonstrated parent appeal and gains for children. Instances include Karnes' (1969) 'eleven structured toys' program which mothers learnt and then taught to their children, and the program of Moxley-Haegert and Serbin (1983), in which parents were trained to recognise and reinforce specific 'small developmental progressions' in their developmentally delayed infants. Indeed, Ramey *et al.* (1985) have suggested that global training in child development has little effect in changing behaviour, but that specific training related to detailed curriculum may have both short and longer term benefit.

It would seem that it is not prescriptiveness *per se* that is at issue, but whether the prescriptions that a program may offer are responsive to the needs and life situations of the participants (Peters and Kostelnik, 1981). In the case of the participants in the EPA program described by James (1975), it would appear that they were not.

In the first EPA program, activities such as choosing library books and toys with one's child, having fun with them and reporting back about their use were parental endeavours related to particular parental needs and strengths. These endeavours added to parental resources. The second program replaced such parental activities with 'parental tasks' (James, 1975), whose rationale was not clear to parents. These were indeed tasks: they failed to enhance parents' resources, but instead

171

were stresses which added a further burden to the parental demands/ resources ratio (Gowen, 1979, Figure 2.5). It is hardly surprising that child or parent gains were not achieved.

Lack of mutual control: input from facilitators and participants in a health visitor program

In another unsuccessful program (Stevenson *et al.*, 1988), parental needs were carefully captured, at considerable cost, before the program began. Through interviews and questionnaires, parents of young children in an English Health Authority area were assessed to establish those who asserted having behavioural difficulties with their young children. The program then trained health visitors in that area in behavioural management techniques to pass on to the parents during their regular visits to the families. Health visitors had been invited to participate immediately in the training course, or alternatively to delay training for a period. Those who agreed to be a member of either group were randomly allocated to the Train group or the Delay group, the latter thus serving as an equally motivated control group of health visitors.

The program ran for six months before parents were again assessed on their problems and on their contact with their health visitor. The behaviours on which parents (many of them depressed) felt themselves at risk included: self-reported ability to cope with child's behaviour, irritability with child, frequency of smacking child, fear of loss of self-control with child, warmth to child, criticism of child. These behaviours have been incorporated into the widely used Behavioural Screening Questionnaire (Richman and Graham, 1971).

The results of the program demonstrate the fundamental importance of having a control group (in this case made up of both parents and health visitors) against whose performance to evaluate program outcomes. Positive early findings from the group involving the trained health visitors were completely unsubstantiated by the later controlled assessment:

> The initial findings from the study were encouraging in terms of the impact on behaviour problems in the children and on a limited number of parenting measures (Stevenson, 1986). However, the more extensive analysis of the parenting measures . . . and findings from the second group of health visitors before and after training [the Delay Group] have failed to establish any significant effects of the training of health visitors in behaviour management techniques.
>
> (Stevenson *et al.*, 1988: 134)

Indeed, as the authors further note (p. 133): 'For the Delay group of health visitors, any significant differences lie in the direction of their being *less* effective in producing change after being trained.'

In discussing possible reasons for these negative results, the authors wonder if they might be attributable, first, to the health visitors' relatively small numbers, second, to the general rather than specific orientation of their training, or third, to their own lack of a support group. These possibilities might count; but a reading of the report suggests that these problems may feed in to a fourth reason for failure suggested by the authors. This is that the one-to-one approach in the home was less effective than a group approach would have been:

> It may be that the use of these management techniques with groups of mothers possibly at a health clinic might be more effective. This would require the health visitor to adopt a new approach to the advice given to mothers and may also aid the mother to see her problems as the same as those experienced by other mothers and as ones capable of being changed.
>
> (Stevenson *et al.*, 1988: 135)

What is interesting in reading this report is that it is only in this one paragraph that there is an attempt to adopt the viewpoint of the mothers as active agents. At all other times, they are spoken of as recipients of the program, while the direction of influence is presented, by the authors, as flowing exclusively one way. Health visitors need 'an understanding of how to provide effective advice to mothers on problems concerned with their children's behaviour' (p. 125). They 'equip the parents with a framework' (p. 123) 'by providing parents with alternative approaches and strategies' (p. 123). The study is an 'attempt to demonstrate whether it is feasible for . . . health visitors . . . to produce significant changes in selected families on their case loads' (p. 134). It is 'an attempt to establish the preventive value of the dissemination of previously validated techniques' (p. 134), and, now, after the disappointing results, to find out 'What procedures for the delivery of health visitor expertise can facilitate their effectiveness?' (p. 135).

Given that this question is asked, it is odd that there is, in the report, a lack of detailed description of the 'procedures' actually followed in the interactions between health visitors and parents, suggesting that these procedures are in fact not seen as being of fundamental importance to the effectiveness of the program. One comment appears to confirm the unidirectional view of influence suggested in the quotations given above: 'A further consideration in the delivery of primary preventive intervention is that not all health visitors want to become involved in what they see as a didactic approach to giving professional advice' (p. 135).

In summary, the health visitor program seems to exemplify the 'client' approach characterised by Wolfendale (1983: 15; see list, p. 40) which professionals in many areas have brought to their interactions with families. That such approaches to families have indeed been the profess-ional norm is corroborated by Cochran and Woolever (1983: 7), who describe 'the deficit perspective [as] one of the basic tenets of service provision in the United States', and by Edgar (1989: 3), who suggests that, in Australia, '"Services" for families implies a "delivery" of some-thing, by someone, to somebody else. Those in "need" look for "help" and are "serviced" by those with appropriate expertise.' In contrast, Wolfendale (1983: 15) categorises the 'partnership' approach (see list, pp. 40–1). Among the sources of the 'partnership' approach, Powell (1989: 91) includes 'the adoption of the idea that adult change processes involve active roles in program participation'.

'Active roles in program participation' means, on the ground, *evidence of mutual control*. This is what is missing from the account of the health visitor program. Some interesting evidence that parents themselves develop awareness of the importance of shared control comes from Oliver's (1992) study of parents in the Management of Young Children Program. At the beginning and end of the project, the parents were asked to rank the behaviours they valued in the program leaders. At the beginning of the program, parents gave first ranking to leaders who 'have expert knowledge about child development'. The behaviours 'have time to sit and listen' and 'help with talking over a problem' were placed fourth and sixth. As parents' self-esteem and feelings of competence rose, these rankings were reversed. Leaders' preparedness to make 'time to sit and listen' and to 'help with talking over a problem' – behaviours requiring parent as well as leader input – now ranked first and second. Leaders 'having expert knowledge' slipped from parents' first choice to fifth. Oliver (1992) suggests that:

> This change in ranking has importance for leaders if they are to become aware of behaviours and approaches considered important and helpful by parents. The importance of presenting these leader-ship behaviours within programs is stressed by Rodd and Holland (1989) as a strategy for leaders to develop in order to prevent the depowerment and deskilling of parents.
> . . . A non-judgmental and acceptance approach by program leaders gave parents enough confidence and self-awareness to attempt to implement some of the learned skills.
>
> (Oliver, 1992: 81)

In the health visitor program, the techniques being promoted by the visitors – in the absence of mutual control – may well have been seen by already depressed parents as further demands upon them. Evidence from the results, namely that parents did, if anything, better without the behavioural management techniques of the trained health visitors, suggests that their resources/demands ratio (Gowen, 1979, Figure 2.5) was diminished, not enhanced.

As Bronfenbrenner (1974) long ago wrote:

> By communicating to the parent that someone else can do it better, that he or she is only an assistant to the expert who is not only more competent but actually does the job, some social agencies, schools, and even intervention programs undermine the principal system that not only stimulates the child's development but can sustain it through the period of childhood and adolescence.
>
> (Bronfenbrenner, 1974: 32)

Insufficient involvement: the exchange of feedback

As we have seen, Stevenson *et al.* (1988) have suggested that group rather than one-to-one interaction with health visitors would have added to the likelihood of change among the mothers. I would amend this suggestion to read: 'Group *as well as* one-to one interaction would have added to the likelihood of change.' It is precisely in this culminating dimension of professional–parent involvement, made possible if the dimensions of responsiveness and mutual control are activated, that failure to capitalise on the possibilities of parent–professional interactions may occur. In the family day care program described in this book, I believe that such failure did, in part, occur. Explanation of this suggestion will follow on p. 177. First, however, let us consider the evidence which would support the suggestion of Stevenson *et al.* that group interaction would have been beneficial to their project.

Group feedback

On p. 107 evidence was cited of the effectiveness of information processing in groups rather than in individual work (Johnson and Johnson, 1985: 5). This aspect of the involvement dimension is exemplified in the family day care program. In the small group discussion format participants were able to recast their definitions of such concepts as 'independence' and 'accomplishment' so as to apply these terms and their own related behavioural options to a wider range of practical situations than formerly. They did this by negotiating definitions with other participants (including the facilitator) within the zone of proximal development (the program), trying out their amended definitions in particular situations in the field (the family day care homes), and subsequently returning to the zone for further negotiation. What had been formed here was a group feedback loop: the successful operation of the repeated, circular processes of talk, action and re-talk.

The marked differences between program and control group participants in the quality and quantity of their responses (situation definitions) at the end of the program suggests that, as Logan (1990: 15) asserts, 'talking about what you do with your colleagues' may be one of the most valuable forms of in-service education. McLean (1991b: 19), too, has written of the importance, in adult learning, of group exchange of 'stories of practice [which enable] students to imagine themselves in the situation; and to see connections between the ideas and their own experience'.

Frequency and regularity of feedback

In such interactive learning, the extent to which contact between participants is frequent and regular obviously affects the mutual responsiveness developed within the group. Involved here are the Vygotskian processes of intersubjectivity and semiotic mediation discussed by Bruner (1985) in relation to adult–child formated learning. In describing the setting in which such learning can best take place as 'familiar and routinized', 'a highly known microcosm . . . where the adult can most easily calibrate his or her intentions about what the child means' (p. 27), Bruner is drawing attention to conditions highly favourable to the building up of intersubjectivity and semiotic mediation through mutually meaningful language.

Such conditions for the development of mutual responsiveness are as applicable to adult as to child learning. As the family day care providers met week by week in a group which, like Bruner's formated learning settings, had become familiar and comfortable, the frequency and regularity of the feedback they received enabled participants to interpret one another's signals with increasing ease. Thus they were able to pay maximum attention to other participants' recounted experiences and to the new information they were encountering. Where dyads or groups meet infrequently, time is required for intersubjectivity to be reestablished before issues can be taken up where they were last left off (Leler, 1980).

Regularity and frequency of contact between all the players in professional/parent programs are factors of great importance, often overlooked. Writing of their home visiting program with poor urban children in Jamaica, Powell and Grantham-McGregor (1989) have observed that children who were visited every two weeks scored higher on post-tests than children visited monthly, while children visited weekly scored substantially higher still.

Discussing the disappointing results of the parent education component of another early intervention program, Project CARE, Wasik et al. (1990) have noted the less than optimal intensity (frequency and regularity) of scheduling of sessions and of the training and supervision of facilitators.

Individualised feedback and practice: the family day care program

Frequent, regular contact is an important aspect of the involvement dimension not only in group functioning, but also in one-to-one inter-action. Here, too, the family day care program serves as an example.

So far in this book, the family day care program has been presented as one which fulfilled the Micawber principle, enhancing both the pro-viders' and the children's resources. At the end of the program striking gains were reported by providers in their responsiveness to, guidance of and involvement with children, and the children, too, were more respon-sive and vocal to their carers. But other observed behaviours were not significantly different from those of the control group, and in this respect the family day care program was only partially successful. The following section on individualised feedback in the real world offers an explan-ation.

What the family day care group discussion made possible, so Vygots-kian and empowerment perspectives would suggest, were processes of attentiveness to and validation of participants' situation definitions, along with maximum opportunity for the negotiation of new definitions within the zone of proximal development. One way in which these definitions were negotiated was, as noted earlier (p. 175), through the establishment of a feedback loop whereby experiences in the family day care homes were regularly reviewed by the group in the discussion sessions. Talk in the group led to action in the family day care homes and back to further talk within the group.

For observed behavioural change among providers to have been unequivocally demonstrated, however, more than a feedback loop from home to discussion group may have been required. A reading of Bronfenbrenner's (1979: 215) second hypothesis (p. 122) implies that the marked changes in providers' attitudes and reported behaviours achieved through off-site group interchange (away from the family day care homes) might have been powerfully augmented had the zone of proximal development extended to on-site, one-to-one interchange in the homes themselves: the practice teaching situation.

Peters and Kostelnik (1981) are among those who have drawn atten-tion to the limitations of classroom training for day care personnel, given the difficulty trainees may have in transferring the skills learnt in train-ing sessions to the actual day care setting. Johnson and Johnson (1985), too, have identified complexities present in the actual setting not found in the classroom. Such reports support the implication of Bronfenbrenner's hypothesis (1979: 215), namely that the developmental potential of adult–adult links is enhanced where a facilitative program member not only acts as a support to participants within the discussion group (or mesosystem), but actually moves in to the microsystem, interacting (in the present case) in the home setting with both provider and child (see Bronfenbrenner's ecological model, p. 9).

In the family day care program, it had been hoped that students undertaking an Associate Diploma in Child Care would be able to play this role of facilitative program member, visiting the homes of one group of providers and engaging 'in joint activity' (Bronfenbrenner, 1979: 215) with them and the children. Numbers, however, did not permit the formation of this group, and the two to three visits which students, as part of their course, made to program group providers did not take place on the frequent and regular basis discussed earlier as an important factor in learning in the zone of proximal development (Bruner, 1985).

The potential benefits of extending the program's group links to one-to-one interaction in the home may be glimpsed in the summary given by one student of a visit to a provider and the three children in her care. This was a provider who initially scored low in overall satisfaction in the job. The student's report records the fun that she, the provider and the three children had with bubbles made and blown on a windy day 'so the bubbles really moved', with wire twists used as bubble pipes. The student's understanding of her role in widening horizons not just for the children but also for the provider is brought out in her statement of objectives and requirements:

- To support the provider in viewing her own work as an important occupation requiring special planning and preparation skills.
- To provide wire twists and small plastic containers to add detergent to, so that children can blow bubbles, and provider can see how simple some activities are to provide.

Evaluating the activity, the student recorded changes in the provider:

> I think Jill was amazed that a 'trained' person should come up with an idea which was so simple. She had not been aware of the possibilities of improvising – thinking she had to have all the 'right' equipment to be able to offer activities . . . I modelled things to talk about with the bubbles with the children and the things they could be taught in the process (e.g. not blowing in each other's faces) and Jill picked up on these very quickly and added a lot.

Several weeks later, after a workshop session in the family day care program, the provider asked the student to bring to her final visit some ideas about paper bag puppets that could be made with the children. The student reported:

The activity worked very well, with the provider picking up on the opportunity to use lots of language in making the puppet – Where is the nose going to go? How many eyes? – and the children responding very well, as well as the language used when actually playing with the puppet. The children made three puppets each. The last one had straw whiskers and was a cat so we talked about lots of animal noises. I had books with other ideas for puppets which the provider and I looked at together.

At the end of her report the student noted some changes in the provider's attitudes which she attributed to the program:

Jill is much more positive and self-confident than before. Since starting the course she is not so worried about Warren's development rate as she can see areas he is learning in all the time. He is managing an open drink cup now, is happy to run barefoot now and still achieving a lot physically. Prior to the evening classes Jill could not see these developments, only what he was not achieving.

In the extracts from the student's report, one may see how an individualised practice teaching experience would, if frequently and regularly repeated, potentiate the benefits of the group learning experience. The interaction of the two elements of supervised practical experience with formal child development training has been shown by Snider and Fu (1988) as having significantly greater influence than either element alone on the knowledge of developmentally appropriate practice demonstrated by child care personnel. Lampert and Clark (1990), too, have argued the importance, in educating those who interact with children, of not only providing 'knowledge of general tendencies and associations' but also encouraging thinking 'in ways that are highly responsive to the social details of particular problem situations and integrated with action' (p. 22).

The student reports of home visits set out above illustrate the dictum of Lampert and Clark (1990: 22) that 'expertise is contextual', a dictum that can be supported from both empowerment and Vygotskian viewpoints. An empowerment perspective would suggest that it is only by becoming familiar with program participants' own contexts that facilitators are in a position to 'validate participants' experience and knowledge' (Vanderslice, 1984: 4). In the group meetings that took place in the family day program the facilitator met participants in their own contexts only vicariously, through their recounted experiences. In the home visit the student and participant were able to experience the context and build on it directly.

From a Vygotskian point of view, the presence of facilitator and participant together in the actual rather than the vicarious context confers a further advantage: it enables interaction to be precisely tailored to specific features of the environment and specific needs of the persons involved in the interaction, exactly the requirements for responsive adult behaviour towards children entering the zone of proximal development that observers of parent–child interaction have described (Rogoff *et al.*, 1984; Saxe *et al.*, 1987; Wertsch and Stone, 1985).

In the home visit situation described above, the student's 'scaffolds, models, and direct instruction' (Cazden, 1983) were employed in relation not only to the children's learning but also that of the provider. The blowing of the wind as the bubbles were let loose enabled teaching to take place about the benefits of not puffing in others' faces, a prompt from which the provider, as well as the children, could learn. The fashioning of the puppet cat's whiskers set the scene for the modelling of animal noises by the student, a further hint or prop (Bruner, 1985) to both children and provider. Relevant and wide-ranging as were the experiences recounted by providers within the discussion group sessions, they could not provide the specific opportunities for provider–facilitator joint activity which studies by Peters and Kostelnik (1981) and Ramey *et al.* (1985) have linked with effectiveness in training programs.

Thus in addition to the general provider responsiveness which appears (Chapter 5) to have been supported by the program, specific behaviours, identified in Chapter 6 as important for development (for example giving information, asking questions, focusing attention on resources) may well have been enhanced by a regular and frequent home visiting component.

In terms of Gowen's (1979) model (which we saw in Figure 2.5), such an extension of program involvement could have provided further sources of reinforcement for providers in the family day care program. Figure 7.2, which indicates these sources, shows the potentially powerful combination of influences created in programs in which facilitators are able to 'engage in joint activity and primary dyads' (Bronfenbrenner, 1979: 215) with adults and children in home visits, as well as interacting with adults in group sessions. Such programs would have two locations. First, the discussion group, held outside the family day care home, is shown in Figure 7.2 as constituting part of the providers' extra-household resources. Second, the home visit is shown as part of the 'family day care childrearing environment'.

In such an extended family day care program (Figure 7.2) resources could be enhanced in the following ways:

1 The facilitator in the group setting interacts with other resources (e.g. knowledge and attitudes) to enhance the provider's 'demands/ resources ratio'.

2 The facilitator in the home context (shown in Figure 7.2 as 'family day

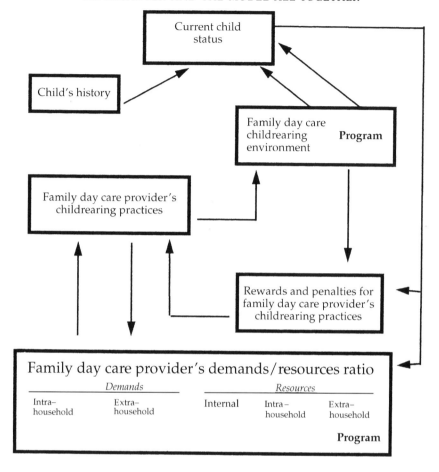

Figure 7.2 In-service program for family day care incorporating group discussion and home visiting components
Source: adapted from Gowen, 1979

care childrearing environment') interacts directly with the child, thus providing a model for the provider. The student, in the home visit described earlier, modelled the use of language with the children; the provider 'picked up on this', adding more language of her own. In Figure 7.2, such a process is illustrated by the feedback loop leading from 'child status' to the provider's 'demands/resources ratio'.

3 Still in the home context, the facilitator also interacts directly with the provider, thus becoming an immediate source of reinforcement or 'reward for the provider's childrearing practices'. As the student and provider together helped the children to make bubbles and construct

puppets, the provider was able 'to see how simple some activities are to provide'.

4 In addition to the effects mentioned in 2 and 3, the cumulative effects of the dual-siting of the program in home and group settings feed through the system. Thus further loops from the enriched 'child status' feed back as 'rewards for the provider's childrearing practices' and as still further enhancement of the provider's balance of 'resources over demands'.

The Micawber view of such enhancement of the balance of resources so that they outweigh demands is emphatic: 'result happiness'. In the family day care program described in this book, that happiness was only partial. There were more positive provider attitudes and reported behaviours, which would seem to be the result of factor 1 above: participation in the group discussion sessions and a consequent change in situation definitions. The student's report underlines this (in particular the portion in italics):

> Jill is much more positive and self-confident than before. Since starting the course she is not so worried about Warren's development rate as she can see areas he is learning in all the time . . . *Prior to the evening classes Jill could not see these developments, only what he was not achieving.*

As for the other factors associated with Figure 7.2, it appears that the home visiting component (occasional student visits) was not frequent or regular enough for effects 2, 3 and 4 to be reflected in significant change in specific behaviours observable at the end of the program.

Thus in the family day care program, findings suggest that the dimension where functioning was less than optimal was that of involvement. There was a need, it appears, to augment the interchange offered within the group setting with the powerful reinforcements available when program personnel are able to meet providers and children in individual family day care homes. The incorporation of such a supervised practice component, operating on the frequent and regular basis discussed earlier, could increase still more the likelihood of a positive tilting of the balance of resources to demands in the lives of caregivers and children.

IMPLICATIONS FOR PRACTICE: THE MICAWBER PRINCIPLE

The EPA, health visitor and family day care programs reviewed in this section have all been in-service programs. Arising from the Vygotskian and empowerment perspectives drawn together in this chapter, the following implications emerge for in-service programs involving parents and professionals:

1 The importance of not only tapping participants' existing positions or situation definitions to discover needs (Wertsch, 1984) but also of validating participants' existing strengths (Cochran, 1988).
2 The necessity of negotiating these situation definitions through the processes of intersubjectivity and semiotic mediation, that is, allowing much time for open discussion between participants and facilitator (Powell, 1989; Vanderslice, 1984).
3 The consequent *semi*-structuring of programs (Watts and Henry, 1978) to allow for input from both facilitator and participants.
4 The value of complementing frequent and regular facilitator–participant group meetings with an individualised practice component also involving program personnel (Lampert and Clark, 1990; Snider and Fu, 1988) to introduce new situation definitions.

It is possible to view these criteria for effective in-service programs for caregivers as manifestations, in the facilitator-participant arena, of precisely the dimensions that this book has suggested characterise caregiving interactions in general. Thus:

● Criterion 1, sensitivity to participants' existing situation definitions, embodies *the responsiveness dimension.*
● Criteria 2 and 3, comprising a semi-structured format arrived at through input from facilitators and participants, reflect *the control dimension.*
● Criterion 4, introduction of new situation definitions and facilitator participation in group and individual interactions, relates to *the involvement dimension.*

In seeking reasons why, in some programs aiming for change in child-rearing behaviour, results have not matched rosy hopes of effectiveness, we need to look first at how the programs have fulfilled both the criteria set out above and the dimensions these criteria represent.

The second EPA, the health visitor and the family day care programs all operated at the negative pole of one of the three caregiving dimensions. In the second EPA program (as opposed to the first), the needs of the parents were not elicited, so that *responsiveness* in the first program turned to unresponsiveness. In the health visitor program, the measures that the visitors described as didactic appear to have left little room for visitors and parents to exercise *mutual control*. Rather, control appears to have been one-way, and thus ineffective. In these two programs, demands on parents increased, rather than resources. The family day care program, strong in responsiveness, mutual control and group exchange of feedback, was singularly weak in the one-to-one practice area of the *involvement* dimension. By building in such a component, the gains made in the program might have been dramatically potentiated, and enhanced resources might further have outweighed demands. In all cases, the professionals engaged in planning the programs might have done a more effective job had they been able to implement the three dimensions of the caregiving model.

In sum, these dimensions and the resources associated with them might be depicted as in Figure 7.3. In this model, when the two adults in the parent/professional/child group offer each other, as well as the child, responsiveness, mutual control and involvement, all three members of the group are better able to reach out towards the challenges (or resources) of trust, autonomy and initiative. The resultant impetus from each individual to resource is shown by a single line. The positive adult

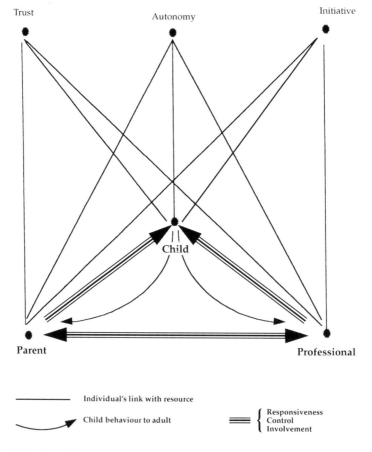

Figure 7.3 Three dimensions of adult caregiving behaviour and their associated resources

behaviours belonging to the three dimensions shown in the model are operationalised in Table 3.1. The child's behaviours towards each adult are shown as separate loops since they are not part of the adult behavioural system presented in Table 3.1. Nevertheless, as shown throughout this book, they are reciprocating behaviours which feed in to the adults' capacity for further responsiveness, mutual control and involvement.

From the drawing together, not only in this chapter but throughout the book, of the elements of this model, what can professionals and parents learn that is of use in the real world?

First, there is a message about its breadth of application. The focus of the last section has been on in-service: in-service programs for parents at home, family day care providers in a group. Some professionals may see such programs as being simple to set up, aimed at easy-to-reach, sitting-duck targets, unlike the parents they find themselves unable to work with or even contact: alienated parents, bossy parents, parents from inaccessible cultural groups, tired working parents, angry or withdrawn parents. But Stories 1–9 give the lie to any suggestion that the three dimensional model has a narrow range of application. In these stories, the contacts between parents and professionals have gone far beyond formal in-service programs. They have been about real interaction in the real world, and they have included alienated parents (Story 3), bossy parents (Story 5), culturally inaccessible parents (Story 4), tired working parents (Stories 7 and 8), angry (indigenous) parents (Story 2). In each of these stories, application of the elements of the three dimensional model has produced good outcomes, that is, in each story the resources/demands ratio has been improved for the child(ren), the parent(s) and the professional(s): a win-win-win situation.

Herein lies a second message for professionals and parents. This is a model helpful to all participants. The dimensions of the model are activated in the interests of a child or children by either a professional or a parent. In the selection of stories in this book the honours in this respect are almost equally shared. In Stories 1–9, professionals initiate the interactions in five cases by approaching a parent or parents (Stories 3, 4, 5, 7 and 8) while parents are the initiators in four (Stories 1, 2, 6 and 9). One adult or set of adults sees the advantages to the child of 'bringing together the two halves of the child's world' (Bronfenbrenner, 1974), either meeting a need or validating a strength in the other adult or set of adults. For themselves, the critical outcome is a positive: their own needs are met and/or strengths validated. It is worthwhile to check Stories 1–9 to test this claim. Thus professionals, who have little time to spare, will find that time spent in responsive mutual control and involvement with parents is more than repaid, because their own professional resources (like parental resources) of information and support are thereby augmented.

This finding leads naturally on to the third message, in the form of a question: if it is so valuable to behave in this way, why is it not done more often? There are several answers to this.

One is that it is in fact done quite often, though not as often as it should be. As was noted on p. 97, many parents intuitively behave to their children in the facilitative ways categorised by Hess (Table 3.1) and should be far more widely recognised for doing so. Likewise, many professionals (teachers and care providers) meet young children's needs, and support their strengths (see the Munro Centre description, p. 16), in ways which repudiate Leach's (1994) denigration of all non-parental care of very young children. Further, as shown in Stories 1–9, which are all unsurprising, common sense, non-outlandish stories, parents and professionals do help one another at times.

However, such occasions tend to be quite infrequent in many places, because, since the advent of universal education in the west, 'there developed, among some teachers at least, a view that they were the experts and that they alone could and should provide the learning settings for the children' (Watts and Henry, 1978: 5). This attitude has led to the unfacilitative 'client relationship' (Wolfendale, 1983) existing between parents and professionals, which the 'partnership relationship' (Wolfendale, 1983) is only slowly beginning to replace. As Bronfenbrenner (1989; Figure 1.1) has pointed out, sociohistorical conditions underlie and constantly constrain our practice.

Adding to the historical difficulty of parents and professionals seeing one another as people with 'equal strengths and equivalent expertise' (Wolfendale, 1983: 15) has been the clearly unequal position of many mothers, housebound non-earners to whom independent, earning professionals find it difficult to accord equal respect (Chapter 1).

But the major reason, I believe, why we parents and professionals often fail to bring to our contacts with one another the effective relationships which many of us have with young children is that, to recall Bruner's (1957) fish, we are the last to know water. We are surrounded in the human shoal by other adults whom we take for granted and with whom we do not much wish to collaborate. We are used to the status quo, and sporadic calls for more cooperation (from education systems, for example, Ministerial Consultative Council on Curriculum, 1992) have little effect on our day-to-day behaviour. We do not see that, by directing some energy outwards, we could change the movement of the currents to make resources flow our way and flow, too, both to the children we care for and to the parents or professionals who are our opposite numbers.

Yet business and industry have begun to see the benefit of more collaboration among the stakeholders in an enterprise (Griffin, 1993), and caregiving/education should not be left behind.

Like the water surrounding the fish, the elements of the caregiving model presented in this book are so obvious that they are frequently unnoticed. So they are often unimplemented. They might be symbolised by the variable of 'maternal position during interaction with an infant' which underlay an early project of Crittenden (1981). In this project with 33 mothers and their infants, at risk for developmental delay, one-minute videotapes of the mothers seated on a rug with their infants showed that maternal position during interaction (facing, besides, or behind) was strongly related to the frequency of maternal interactional behaviour and also to measures of infant communication and cognitive development. At weekly group meetings over four months:

> Intervention consisted of replaying weekly videotapes for the entire group to observe and discuss. Emphasis was focused on the mother's position relative to her baby and its effect on her own and her baby's behaviour. Discussions as well as modelling and role playing were used to help the mothers learn to change their position during interaction.
>
> (Crittenden, 1981: 4)

At the end of the project a significant increase was reported in the number of mothers consistently facing their babies, as well as significant improvements in both maternal interactive behaviour and infant developmental measures. Improvements in both areas were associated with maternal improvement in position. The framers of the program also learnt much about ways of encouraging change in human behaviour.

In this study Crittenden called the variable of maternal position 'conceptually simple while, at the same time, functionally complex'. The elements of the responsiveness/control/involvement model are similarly conceptually simple while at the same time functionally complex. It is easy to see that it would be useful to find out (not guess) what someone's needs and strengths are, to give that person a chance to meet some of the needs and exercise the strengths while not overlooking our own similar requirements, and to keep in touch during the process to expand mutual perspectives. Putting these conceptually simple, functionally complex tasks into practice seems hard, but not too hard, as Stories 1–9 have shown.

To change the metaphor from fish in water to a boat on water, what this book offers is a chart of the navigational features to look for and some pointers as to how we might negotiate them for the benefit of us all, together. Like any voyage, this one takes time. Some of the stories in this book occupied a day, others have extended over months. The usefulness of the model of responsiveness, mutual control and involvement is that, despite one or many failures, such a model allows us to try again. Recalling the downs and ups of Mr Micawber's life, that is essentially his message to us; that, and his wise insistence on keeping the long view. He was not talking about enhancing resources over a day or a week. As he said, '*Annual* income. . .'

QUESTIONS

The following sets of questions or problems, which relate to each of the chapters, appear at this point in order not to disrupt the flow of the chapters. The questions may be considered by individuals or they may serve as discussion material for small groups.

CHAPTER 1

Question 1.1

(a) Families are changing, as they have always done. What meaning does the term 'traditional family' have for you?
(b) From your reading find two references, each implying a different meaning for the word 'traditional'. What characteristics of family diversity are included in each reference?

Question 1.2

This chapter contains references to the similarities of parents and other caregivers. There are also references to the differences between them. Weigh up these conflicting references. What effects do you see the suggested differences and similarities having in the care of young children?

CHAPTER 2

Question 2.1

Observe a toddler interacting with an adult he/she is attached to. What evidence do you see in the adult's behaviour of the two factors that Schaffer (1971) described as fostering attachment? These factors are p. 13): 'in the first place the individual's responsiveness to the infant's signals for attention, and in the second place, the amount of interaction which the adult spontaneously initiated with the infant'.

Question 2.2

As Rogoff (1990: 5) points out, 'Piaget's primary focus was on the individual rather than on the aspects of the world that the child struggles to understand or on how the social world contributes to individual development.'

Piaget's focus on the individual child continues to underlie much of what occurs in early childhood care and education. On the other hand (p. 24), Edgar (1993: 8) maintains that stressing individual mastery 'flies in the face of how children actually learn and is mocked by the real world outside the school. Children learn and grow in competence with other people – mother, father, siblings, friends. Few tasks are done alone.'

Make a diary over one day of the activities of a young child with free access to other members of a family. Note how many 'tasks are done alone', how many with others, including adults.

Question 2.3

This chapter notes (p. 25) that:

> Erikson (1950) has pointed out that the challenge of meeting needs is never finally resolved. Meeting the needs that are fundamental to young children's productive lives – needs for trust (confidence), autonomy (a sense of power and independence) and initiative (ability to carry through new ideas) – remains a challenge for adults as well.

Do you agree? Make a diary over one day of your own needs. Can you categorise them in terms of these three domains – or combinations thereof?

CHAPTER 3

Question 3.1

Table 3.1 sets out the parental behaviours that Robert Hess (1971) found were correlated with young children's capacity for personal, social and intellectual wellbeing. (The same table shows the similar findings from Amato's later review relating to parents and their school-age children.)

190

(a) Observe a young child and parent who are getting on well (or badly) together. How many of the behaviours mentioned by Hess do you observe in the case of the well functioning dyad (or do not observe in the case of the unhappy pair)?

(b) Make similar observations of a young child and adult, where the adult is a non-parental careprovider. How many of Hess's behaviours do you observe (or not)?

(c) Do your findings from these two sets of observations – (a) and (b) – add anything to your conclusions in Question 1.2 about the similarities or differences between young children's parents and caregivers?

Question 3.2

(a) Try out the playdough game (p. 62) with a group of people. The results are more impressive if the participants have just undergone a slightly stressful experience such as the trust walk described in the logbook.

(b) You and your colleagues will find the sequence of results stimulating to discuss. Do these results add anything to your conclusions (Question 2.3) about adult, as well as children's, needs?

CHAPTER 4

Question 4.1

Responsiveness begins with the identification of situation definitions: the cues that we and others emit. Some of these cues are needs. By 'listening blatantly' (McLean, 1991a) we may discover what our own needs and the needs of others are. Behind the following statements made by teachers lie a series of needs: needs of the teachers, needs of children, needs of parents:

(a) I'd like to have parents coming in to help in my classroom, but some parents are just not interested.

(b) Some parents don't feel comfortable inside a pre-school.

(c) Some parents work, they're not available.

(d) Some teachers don't have the skills to relate to parents.

(e) I'd like to see parents involved in program planning, but they don't know enough to begin.

Implied in response (a) is the children's need to have more one-to-one support for their learning. The teacher's need is to have more resources available in the classroom. The parent's need is to feel welcomed as part of a team. Being 'not interested' may mean being unaware of the

Table Q.1

Parent–teacher program	Needs to satisfy		
	For children	For parents	For teacher
(a) Parents come into classroom to help children.	Need for support from attentive, engaged adults. Need for achievement through feedback.	Need for enhanced self-esteem, sense of control. Need to foster own child's development. Need for support as part of team.	Need for optimal fostering of children's achievement. Need for support as part of team. Need for augmented resources and information.
(b) Parents feel comfortable in the preschool.			
(c)			
(d)			
(e)			

advantages of participation (higher achievement for the child, enhanced self-esteem for the parent). The teacher can find this out only by establishing a relationship which allows her/him to listen to the parent.

In examples (a), (b), (c) and (e) let us assume that parents have conveyed their situation definitions to the teacher. That is, their needs have been expressed, not merely inferred.

As noted on p. 93 of this chapter, satisfying needs takes time and not all needs may be completely satisfied, especially when several sets are involved. A very useful first step is to set out the broad categories of needs of all participants, from which the realistic goals of your intervention will emerge. Copy and complete Table Q.1 above, describing the needs which arise from responses (b) to (e).

CHAPTER 5

Question 5.1

In looking at the dimension of control as illustrated in Stories 4, 5 and 6, we have paid particular attention to the useful effects of the exercise of *mutual* control. The foundation for mutual control (the capacity of all participants to contribute) has been laid by the prior exercise of responsiveness by at least one person in each story.

Read again Stories 4, 5 and 6 to determine:

(a) The person(s) demonstrating responsiveness.
(b) Examples of warmth.
(c) Examples of high regard.
(d) Examples of attentiveness and engagement.

Question 5.2

This chapter has asserted (p. 125) that, 'as social conditions change, and as groups of people come into contact with others, values shift both between and within groups and individuals'. The value orientations emphasised in this chapter have been those relating to the authority figure, the group and the individual. Reflecting on your own life, can you think of one or more occasions when you recall changing from one to another of these orientations? In such a shift, can you identify:

(a) A change of social conditions?
(b) Contact with a new group of people?

CHAPTER 6

Question 6.1

Table 6.1 lists examples of strategies reported by family day care providers as being successful in encouraging a sense of accomplishment in the 0–3 children in their care. You will find in these strategies differing elements of the dimensions of responsiveness, control and involvement. Can you categorise them?

Question 6.2

For Question 5.1 you checked through Stories 4, 5 and 6 to see how, in addition to control, they incorporated the dimension of responsiveness.

Having read this chapter on involvement, look again at Stories 7, 8 and 9, for evidence of the dimensions of responsiveness and control. Watch for the specific behaviours that operationalise these dimensions, that is:

(a) Responsiveness – warmth, high regard, attentiveness and engagement.

(b) (Mutual) control – consistent, explanatory rather than arbitary strategies, encouragement of independence.

Question 6.3

- Question from a professional:
  'How can professionals and parents reach intersubjectivity through
  semiotic mediation?'
- Answer from a parent:
  'Please talk to us in a language we can understand' (Anderson, 1984).

The professional's question and the 'gross and fine motor skills' role-
play on p. 141 show how hard it is for professionals to do what the
parent requests. Used in communication with the initiated, professional
language allows us to pack much into little. Used in communication
with the uninitiated, it is impolite and counterproductive.

(a) Compose some items to be used in a newsletter, demonstrating:
    (i) The unsuitable use of jargon.
    (ii) The acceptable use of everyday language.
(b) Try these out with other parents/professionals.

CHAPTER 7

Question 7.1

In the main this book has examined the positive effects on children,
parents and professionals of exercising responsiveness, control and
involvement, as operationalised in the behaviours proposed by Hess
(1971) in Table 3.1. Chapter 7, however, presents some of the negative
results which follow when one or another of these dimensions is not
exercised, or is imperfectly exercised.

All around us examples abound of the distressing results of the failure
by adults to practise the positive behaviours constituting these dimensions. You will find it instructive to consider some examples, from your
experience, of:

(a) The negative exercise of these dimensions.
(b) Negative outcomes.

Question 7.2

At various points in this book, we have noted Bronfenbrenner's (1979:
215) proposal that 'the developmental potential of a setting is increased

as a function of the number of supportive links existing between that setting and other settings.' A major function of the book has been to build a picture of the behavioural dimensions that make up the supportive links involving young children.

Look back to Bronfenbrenner's ecological model of educational environments (Figure 1.1). The links referred to by Bronfenbrenner constitute the mesosystem: the potential connections between the elements of the microsystem influencing the individual at the centre of the model.

Think of a young child you know and the figures from that child's microsystem who exert some influence on his/her development, e.g. a mother, a father, a family friend, a teacher, a child care worker.

(a) What supportive links are there between the settings containing these figures?
(b) Do most mothers have more supportive links with other influencers of the child than fathers do? If so, how does this affect each parent's ability to parent?
(c) If you are one of the figures in the child's microsystem, what can you do to enhance the links?

APPENDICES

APPENDIX 1

Appendix 1 Interview questions related to dimensions of caregiver behaviour

Caregiving variables	*Interview questions*
Responsiveness	
Warm affective relationship towards child	1 What specially appeals to you about being a family day care provider?
High regard for child	2 Thinking of the under three year olds, what are the things about them that you enjoy most?
	3 And least?
Attentiveness to and engagement with child	4 Children keep changing all the time. Are there any particular changes you've noticed in the children lately?
	5 What do the children seem to enjoy doing most when they're here with you?
	6 What sorts of things do *you* most enjoy doing with them?
Control	
Consistency of discipline	7 What do you think about rules and limits for young children? What sorts of things should they be allowed to do, and what not?
	8 Can you think of any occasion lately when something happened that wasn't allowed? What did you do then? Do you feel that that way of handling the situation worked? What would you do another time? (Same thing? Something else?)
Explanatory control	9 How do the children get on together?
	10 Do you think a provider can help them behave cooperatively to one another? How?
Encouragement of independence	11 How old do you think children are when they start trying to do things for themselves – without having to be helped?
	12 How do you think providers can encourage children to try things on their own?

196

Caregiving variables	Interview questions
Involvement	
Encouragement of achievement	13 You know how children can look pleased with themselves at being able to do something really well. How old do you think children are when they start being pleased with themselves and their accomplishments?
	14 Do you think providers can help them feel pleased at really accomplishing something? How?
Maximisation of verbal interaction	15 Some people talk to their children quite a bit, others don't think this is important. What do you think about talking to children and telling them about things that are happening?
	16 What about explaining to children how to do things – how things work? How early do you think that's possible?
	17 How old do you think children are when they can start taking part in a conversation with grown-ups?
Teaching behaviour	18 Some people think it's important to read or look at books with young children, some don't. What do you think?
	19 Family day care children learn a lot of things from their parents. What sort of things do you feel they're learning from *you*?
Diffuse intellectual stimulation	20 Let's think about all the ways the children keep busy while they're here with you. What things are there now in the house that they use in their activities?
Presage variables	
Satisfaction with family day care	21 Has working in family day care been what you hoped it would?
Self-esteem	22 How do you feel about the things you've done as a day care mother? Have they measured up to your expectations?
Locus of control	23 Finally, do you feel that you're on top of things – or do you feel things are getting on top of you?

Appendix 2 Provider behaviour observation schedule

Behavioural dimension	*Codes*
Responsiveness	
Warm affective relationship towards child	F Appreciate
	F Denigrate
High regard for child	F Phatic
Attentiveness to and engagement with child	D Responsive interaction
	F Non-responsive move:
	• Interrupt subject
	• Reject subject
	• Ignore subject
Control	
Consistency of management	F Physical control (no utterance)
Explanatory control	F Verbal direction (no explanation) – may
Encouragement of independence	include physical control
	F Information (associated with direction)
	F Encourage independence
	F Facilitate harmonious relations involving subject
	F Foster disharmony involving subject
Involvement	
Encouragement of achievement	F Encourage achievement
	F Question
Maximisation of verbal interaction	F Repetition/extension
	F Information (not associated with direction)
Teaching behaviour	F Foster imagination
Diffuse intellectual stimulation	F Focus attention on resource
	D Physical care

Note: F = Frequency; D = Duration

APPENDIX 3

Appendix 3 Child behaviour observation schedule

Behavioural dimension	*Codes*
Personality dimension	
Active outgoingness	D Purposeful self-initiated locomotion
	D Mastery activity
	D Procure object
	D Large muscle activity
	D Non-involved
Social dimension	
Social warmth and	F Procure service
cooperation	F Prosocial
	D Responsive interaction
	• With adult
	• With child(ren)
	• With adult/child(ren)
	F Resist
	F Aggress
Cognitive dimension	F Utterance:
Competence in intellectual	• To self
functioning	• To adult
	• To child(ren)
	F Observe/listen
	D Pretend
	F Imitate:
	• Adult
	• Child(ren)
	D Physical function

Note: D = Duration; F = Frequency

APPENDIX 4

Appendix 4 Provider interview: responsiveness; group × occasion – mean scores and interactions

No.	Caregiving variable	Mean frequency of response					
		Pre-program		Post-program		F	P
		Program group	Control group	Program group	Control group		
1	Appeal of family day care	2.3 (1.1)	2.5 (1.0)	2.2 (1.1)	2.0 (0.9)	1.14	0.2922
2	Like about children	2.2 (1.2)	2.4 (0.9)	2.8 (1.6)	2.4 (1.0)	2.92	0.0952
3	Dislike about children	0.9 (0.6)	1.0 (1.0)	0.7 (0.5)	1.1 (0.8)	1.30	0.2604
4	Changes in children	2.8 (1.6)	2.9 (2.1)	6.1 (3.2)	3.3 (1.5)	8.80	0.0051
5	Children enjoy	3.6 (2.4)	4.2 (1.7)	7.4 (3.6)	4.3 (1.8)	13.08	< 0.001
6	Enjoy with children	2.1 (1.2)	2.3 (1.3)	5.1 (1.7)	3.1 (1.6)	12.70	0.001

APPENDIX 5

Appendix 5 Provider interview: control; group × occasion – mean scores and interactions

No. Caregiving variable	Mean frequency of response					
	Pre-program		Post-program		F	P
	Program group	Control group	Program group	Control group		
7 Rules for children	2.7 (1.0)	2.4 (1.0)	2.3 (0.8)	2.7 (0.8)	3.66	0.0628
8 Control strategies	1.8 (0.7)	1.6 (1.0)	2.0 (0.6)	2.4 (1.1)	5.77	0.0210
9 Children get on	1.6 (0.7)	1.5 (0.5)	1.2 (0.4)	1.2 (0.4)	0.07	0.7877
10 Cooperation strategies	2.0 (1.0)	2.2 (1.6)	4.3 (1.8)	2.0 (1.2)	20.96	< 0.001
11 Age independence	17.8 (8.6)	17.7 (10.4)	3.9 (4.80)	16.1 (11.3)	10.18	0.0031
12 Independence strategies	1.6 (0.7)	1.7 (0.9)	3.2 (0.9)	1.9 (0.7)	15.29	< 0.001

APPENDIX 6

Appendix 6 Provider interview: involvement; group × occasion – mean scores and interactions

No.	Caregiving variable	Mean frequency of response					
		Pre-program		Post-program		*F*	*P*
		Program group	Control group	Program group	Control group		
13	Age accomplishment	16.4 (7.8)	15.6 (10.2)	6.8 (6.2)	17.6 (10.7)	23.93	< 0.001
14	Accomplishment strategies	1.7 (0.9)	2.0 (0.8)	3.4 (1.0)	2.1 (1.1)	21.12	< 0.001
15	Talk important	2.8 (1.4)	3.0 (2.3)	3.9 (2.1)	3.1 (2.3)	3.04	0.0887
16	Age understanding	19.3 (9.6)	18.0 (8.6)	10.1 (8.4)	17.8 (8.8)	19.79	< 0.001
17	Age conversation	20.0 (7.3)	18.4 (10.2)	12.2 (9.8)	21.2 (10.9)	15.90	< 0.001
18	Books important	2.3 (1.5)	2.7 (1.8)	5.1 (3.1)	2.6 (1.7)	12.71	0.001
19	Learning from family day care	4.0 (1.8)	4.1 (1.9)	7.7 (3.2)	5.3 (2.8)	9.78	0.0033
20	Keeping busy	8.7 (2.8)	10.9 (3.5)	11.8 (3.0)	10.6 (3.5)	9.19	0.0040

APPENDIX 7

Appendix 7 Child behaviour: durational scores as percentages of total time

Variable	Mean scores as percentages of total time			
	Pre-program		Post-program	
	Program group	Control group	Program group	Control group
Personal				
Purposeful self-initiated locomotion	7.40	5.40	6.80	7.50
Mastery activity	41.00	44.10	42.20	43.40
Procure object	0.33	0.56	0.39	0.67
Large muscle activity	1.78	1.56	0.50	2.40
Non-involved	4.25	2.38	1.89	3.00
Social				
Responsive interaction with adult	32.50	22.00	29.50	19.20
Responsive interaction with child(ren)	5.60	3.80	4.30	8.20
Responsive interaction with adult/child(ren)	2.10	2.20	4.30	3.60
Cognitive				
Observe/listen	16.50	19.50	15.60	17.30
Pretend	1.06	0.78	3.89	3.53
Physical function	13.10	16.20	14.00	18.80

APPENDIX 8

Appendix 8 Provider interview: presage variables; group × occasion – mean scores and interactions

Response scores: means and standard deviations

No. Caregiving variable	Pre-program		Post-program		F	P
	Program group	Control group	Program group	Control group		
21 Satisfied with family day care?						
• Positive factors	1.1 (1.3)	1.2 (1.2)	1.7 (1.6)	1.1 (1.1)	1.71	0.2267
• Negative factors	0.6 (1.4)	0.6 (1.0)	1.1 (1.6)	1.1 (1.7)	0.04	0.8347
22 Self-esteem in family day care?						
• Positive factors	1.7 (1.5)	2.0 (2.1)	2.5 (1.8)	1.7 (1.5)	1.51	0.2259
• Negative factors	1.3 (2.0)	1.4 (1.8)	0.5 (1.0)	0.6 (1.2)	0.01	0.9379
23 On top of things?						
• Positive factors	1.3 (1.4)	1.4 (1.4)	2.3 (2.7)	1.1 (1.3)	3.00	0.0910
• Negative factors	1.4 (1.6)	0.9 (1.0)	0.7 (0.9)	1.3 (1.4)	4.51	0.0400
Overall satisfaction	4.2 (2.7)	4.6 (2.9)	6.6 (3.9)	4.0 (2.9)	4.46	0.0411
Overall dissatisfaction	3.2 (2.7)	2.9 (2.3)	2.3 (2.3)	3.0 (2.6)	1.64	0.2075

REFERENCES

a'Beckett, C. (1988) 'Parent/staff relationships', in A. Stonehouse (ed.) *Trusting Toddlers*, Canberra: Australian Early Childhood Association.

a'Beckett, C., Ashby, G., Gahan, D., Henry, M. and Piscitelli, B. (1988) *Report to the Munro Centre*, Kelvin Grove: Brisbane College of Advanced Education.

Adler, R. B., Rosenfeld, L. B., and Towne, N. (1983) *Interplay*, New York: Holt, Rinehart & Winston.

Ainsworth, M. D. S. (1967) *Infancy in Uganda: Infant Care and the Growth of Love*, Baltimore: Johns Hopkins Press.

Ainsworth, M. D. S. and Bell, S. M. (1970) 'Attachment, exploration and separation: illustrated by the behavior of one-year-olds in a strange situation', *Child Development* 141, 49–67.

Ainsworth, M. D. S. and Bell, S. M. (1974) 'Mother–infant interaction and the development of competence', in K. J. Connolly and J. S Bruner (eds) *The Growth of Competence*, New York: Academic Press.

Ainsworth, M. D. S., Bell, S. M. and Stayton, D. J. (1974) 'Infant–mother attachment and social development: Socialisation as a product of reciprocal responsiveness to signals', in M. P. M. Richards (ed.) *The Integration of a Child into a Social World*, New York: Cambridge University Press.

Ainsworth, M. D. S., Blehar, M., Waters, E. and Wall, S. (1978) *Patterns of Attachment*, Hillsdale, NJ: Erlbaum.

Alley, T. (1983) 'Growth-produced changes in body shape and size as determinants of perceived age and adult caregiving', *Child Development*, 54, 241–8.

Amato, P. (1987) *Children in Australian Families: The Growth of Competence*, Sydney: Prentice-Hall.

Anderson, R. (1984) 'Parents in the early childhood system', paper presented at Queensland Creche and Kindergarten Association In-service Seminar for Teachers, Brisbane.

Aries, P. (1962) *Centuries of Childhood*, London: Jonathan Cape.

Australian Bureau of Statistics (1993) *Women in Australia*, catalogue no. 4113.0, Canberra: Australian Bureau of Statistics.

Bales, R. F. (1950) *Interaction Process Analysis: A Method for the Study of Small Groups*, Cambridge, MA: Addison-Wesley.

Bandura, A. (1977) *Social Learning Theory*, Englewood Cliffs, NJ: Prentice-Hall.

Barker, R. G. and Gump, P. V. (1964) *Big School, Small School*, Stanford, California: Stanford University Press.

Baumrind, D. (1971) 'Current patterns of parental authority', *Developmental Psychology* 4 (Monograph 1), 1–103.

Bell, R. Q. (1974) 'Contributions of human infants to care giving and social interaction', in M. Lewis and L. Rosenblum (eds) *The Effect of the Infant on Its Care Giver*, New York: Wiley.

Bell, S. M. and Ainsworth, M. D. S. (1972) 'Infant crying and maternal responsiveness', *Child Development* 43, 1171–90.

Belsky, J. (1984) 'The determinants of parenting: a process model', *Child Development* 55, 83–96.

Belsky, J. (1986) 'Infant day care: a cause for concern', *Zero to Three*, Bulletin of the National Center for Clinical Infant Programs, 6, 5, 1–7.

Belsky, J. and Rovine M. (1988) 'Nonmaternal care in the first year of life and the security of infant–parent attachment', *Child Development* 59, 157–67.

Berger, E. H. (1995) *Parents as Partners in Education*, Englewood Cliffs, NJ: Prentice-Hall.

Berger, K. S. (1988) *The Developing Person through the Life Span*, New York: Worth.

Berk, L. E. (1994) *Child Development* (third edition), Boston: Allyn and Bacon.

Berthelsen, D. (1994) 'Socialisation and family relationships', in G. Boulton-Lewis and D. Catherwood (eds) *The Early Years*, Melbourne: Australian Council for Educational Research.

Bornstein, M. H., and Sigman, M. D. (1986) 'Continuity in mental development from infancy', *Child Development* 57, 251–74.

Bowlby, J. (1953) *Child Care and the Growth of Love*, Harmondsworth: Penguin.

Bowlby, J. (1969) *Attachment and Loss*, vol. 1, *Attachment*, New York: Basic Books.

Bowlby, J. (1973) *Attachment and Loss*, vol. 2, *Separation: Anxiety and Anger*, London: Hogarth.

Bowlby, J. (1980) *Attachment and Loss*, vol. 3, *Loss, Sadness and Depression*, New York: Basic Books.

Brackbill, Y. (1967) 'The use of social reinforcement in conditioned smiling', in Y. Brackbill and G. C. Thompson (eds) *Behavior in Infancy and Early Childhood*, New York: Free Press.

Bradley, R. H. and Caldwell, B. M. (1984) 'The relation of infants' home environments to achievement test performance in the first grade: a follow-up study', *Child Development* 55, 803–9.

Bradley, R. H., Caldwell, B. M. and Rock, S. L. (1988) 'Home environment and school performance: a ten-year follow-up and examination of three models of environmental action', *Child Development* 59, 852–67.

Braun, L. A., Coplon, J. K., and Sonnenschein, P. C. (1984) *Helping Parents in Groups: A Leader's Handbook*, Boston, MA: Wheelock College.

Bredekamp, S. (1987) *Developmentally Appropriate Practice in Early Childhood Programs Serving Children from Birth through Age 8*, Washington, DC: National Association for the Education of Young Children.

Bretherton, I. (1985) 'Attachment theory: retrospect and prospect', in I. Bretherton and E. Waters (eds) *Growing Points of Attachment Theory and Research*, monograph of the Society for Research in Child Development, vol. 50, 3–38, Chicago: University of Chicago Press.

Bronfenbrenner, U. (1969) 'Motivational and social components in compensatory education programs', in E. Grotberg (ed.) *Critical Issues in Research Relating to Disadvantaged Children*, Princeton, NJ: Educational Testing Service.

Bronfenbrenner, U. (1974) *A Report on Longitudinal Evaluations of Pre-school Programs*, vol. 2, *Is Early Intervention Effective?* Washington, DC: US Department of Health, Education and Welfare.

Bronfenbrenner, U. (1976) 'The experimental ecology of education', *Teachers College Record* 79(2), 157–204.

Bronfenbrenner, U. (1979) *The Ecology of Human Development: Experiments by Nature and Design*, Cambridge, MA: Harvard University Press.

Bronfenbrenner, U. (1989) 'Ecological systems theory', in R. Vasta (ed.) *Annals of Child Development*, vol. 6, pp. 187–251, Greenwich, CT: JAI Press.

Bronfenbrenner, U. (1994) 'A new head start for Head Start', *New Horizons in Education* 91, December.

Brownell, C. (1990) 'Peer social skills in toddlers: competencies and constraints illustrated by same-age and mixed-age interaction', *Child Development* 61, 837–48.

Bruner, J. (1957) 'On going beyond the information given', in *Cognition: The Colorado Symposium*, Cambridge, MA: Harvard University Press.

Bruner, J. S. (1975) 'The ontogenesis of speech acts', *Journal of Child Language* 2, 1–19.

Bruner, J. S. (1985) 'Vygotsky: a historical and conceptual perspective', in J. Wertsch (ed.) *Culture, Communication and Cognition: Vygotskian Perspectives*, Cambridge: Cambridge University Press.

Buber, M. (1965) *Between Man and Man*, New York: Macmillan.

Burchinal, M., Bryant, D., Lee, M. and Ramey, C. (1992) 'Early day care, infant–mother attachment, and maternal responsivness in the infant's first year', *Early Childhood Research Quarterly* 7, 383–96.

Caldwell, B. M. (1974) In *Child's Play and the Real World* (motion picture), San Francisco: Davidson Films.

Caldwell, B. M. and Bradley R. H. (1978) *Manual for the Home Observation for Measurment of the Environment*, Little Rock: University of Arkansas at Little Rock.

Campbell, W. J. (1990) 'Class sizes revisited', *New Horizons in Education* 83, 20–30.

Campbell, W. J. (1995) 'Alchemy reversed: turning gold into base metals', paper delivered to World Education Fellowship, Queensland, March.

Carew, J. V. (1980) 'Experience and the development of intelligence in young children at home and in day care', *Monographs of the Society for Research in Child Development* 45 (6–7, serial no. 187).

Catherwood, D. (1994) 'The origins of thinking: perception and cognition in early childhood', in G. Boulton-Lewis and D. Catherwood (eds) *The Early Years*, Melbourne: Australian Council for Educational Research.

Cazden, C. B. (1983) 'Adult assistance to language development: scaffolds, models, and direct instruction', in R. P. Parker and F. A. Davis (eds) *Developing Literacy: Young Children's Use of Language*, Newark, DE: International Reading Association.

Clarke-Stewart, K. A. (1987) 'Predicting child development from child care forms and features: the Chicago study', in D. A. Phillips (ed.) *Quality in Child Care: What Does Research Tell Us?* Washington, DC: National Association for the Education of Young Children.

Cochran, M. M. (1987) 'The parental empowerment process: building on family strengths', *Equity and Choice* 4(1), 9–23.

Cochran, M. M. (1988) 'Parental empowerment in family matters: lessons learned from a research program', in D. R. Powell (ed.) *Parent Education as Early Childhood Intervention*, Norwood, NJ: Ablex.

Cochran, M. M. and Woolever, F. (1983) 'Beyond the deficit model: the empowerment of parents with information and informal supports', in I. Sigel and L. Laosa (eds.) *Changing Families*, New York: Plenum Press.

Crittenden, P. M. (1981) 'Abusing, neglecting, problematic and adequate dyads: differentiating by patterns of interaction', *Merrill-Palmer Quarterly* 27, 1–19.

REFERENCES

Crittenden, P. M. (1985) 'Social networks, quality of childrearing, and child development', *Child Development* 56, 1299–313.

Crowe, B. (1973) *The Playgroup Movement*, London: Allen and Unwin.

de Charms, R., Carpenter, V. and Cuperman, A. (1965) 'The "origins–pawns" variable in person perception', *Sociometry* 28, 241–58.

de Mause, L. (1974) *The History of Childhood*, New York: Psychohistory Press.

Demo, D. H. and Acock, A. C. (1993) 'Family diversity and the division of domestic labour. How much have things really changed?', *Family Relations* 42, 323–31.

Dennis, W. (1973) *Children of the Crèche*. New York: Appleton-Century-Crofts.

Derman-Sparks, L. (1989) *Anti-Bias Curriculum: Tools for Empowering Young Children*, Washington, DC: National Association for the Education of Young Children.

de Vaus, D. A. (1985) *Surveys in Social Research*. Sydney: Allen and Unwin.

DeVries, R. and Kohlberg, L. (1990) *Constructivist education: overview and comparison with other programs*, Washington, DC: National Association for the Education of Young Children.

DeVries, R., Reese-Learned, H. and Morgan, P. (1991) 'Sociomoral development in direct instruction, eclectic and constructivist kindergartens: a study of children's enacted interpersonal understanding', *Early Childhood Research Quarterly* 6(4), 449–71.

Donovan, W. L. and Leavitt, L. A. (1978) 'Early cognitive development and its relation to maternal physiologic and behavioral responsiveness', *Child Development* 49, 1251–4.

Doorly, E. (1936) *The Insect Man*, London: Heinemann.

Edgar, D. (1981) 'A new task for parents?', *Australian Journal of Early Childhood* 6(2), 4–8.

Edgar, D. (1989) 'Cross-roads for family policy', *Family Matters* 24, August, 2–4.

Edgar, D. (1993) 'Competence in children', *Family Matters* 36, December, 7–10.

Erikson, E. H. (1950) *Childhood and Society*, New York: Norton.

Everingham, C. (1994) *Motherhood and Modernity*, Sydney: Allen and Unwin.

Ferguson, J. and Solomon, R. (1984) *A Toddler in the Family: A Practical Australian Guide for Parents*, Brisbane: University of Queensland Press.

Fosburg, S. (1982) 'Family day care: the role of the surrogate mother', in L. M. Laosa and I. E. Sigel (eds) *Families as Learning Environments for Children*, New York: Plenum Press.

Freud, S. (1961) *Civilization and its Discontents* (translated and edited by James Strachey), New York: Norton.

Fuller, F. F. (1969) 'Concerns of teachers: a developmental conceptualization', *American Educational Research Journal* 6, 207–26.

Gahan, D., Broughton, B., McDonell, J. and Henry, M. (1994). 'Infant development in the context of everyday activities', paper presented at the Twentieth Triennial Conference of the Australian Early Childhood Association, October, Perth.

Glezer, H. (1991) 'Juggling work and family commitments', *Family Matters* 28, April, 6–10.

Goodnow, J. and Burns, A. (1985) *Home and School: A Child's Eye View*, Sydney: Allen and Unwin.

Goossens, F. A. and van IJzendoorn, M.H. (1990) 'Quality of infants' attachments to professional caregivers: relation to infant–parent attachment and daycare characteristics', *Child Development* 61, 832–7.

208

Gordon, I. J. (1972) 'What do we know about parents as teachers?', *Theory into Practice* 11(3), 146–9.

Gordon, I. J. (1975) *The Florida Parent Education Early Intervention Projects: A Longitudinal Look*, Urbank: University of Illinois Press.

Gordon, I. J. (1977) 'Parent education and parent involvement: retrospect and prospect', *Childhood Education* 54, 71–9.

Gordon, I. J., Olmsted, P. P., Rubin, R. I., and True, J. H. (1979) 'How has Follow Through promoted parent involvement?' *Young Children* 34(5), 49–53.

Gowen, J. W. (1979) 'Poverty related developmental delay: is parent education the answer?', paper presented at the Ira J. Gordon Memorial Conference on Parent Education and Involvement, University of North Carolina.

Griffin R. W. (1993). *Management* (fourth edition), Boston: Houghton Mifflin.

Gump, P. V. (1964) 'Environmental guidance of the classroom behavioral system', in B. J. Biddle and W. J. Ellena (eds) *Contemporary Research on Teacher Effectiveness*, New York: Holt, Rinehart & Winston.

Halpern, R. and Larner, M. (1988) 'The design of family support programs in high-risk communities: lessons from the Child Survival/Fair Start initiative', in D. R. Powell (ed.) *Parent Education as Early Intervention*, Norwood, NJ: Ablex.

Hanks, H. and Stratton, P. (1988) 'Family perspectives on early sexual abuse', in K. Browne, C. Davies and P. Stratton (eds) *Early Prediction and Prevention of Child Abuse*, Chichester: John Wiley.

Harper, J. and Richards, L. (1986) *Mothers and Working Mothers*, Melbourne: Pelican Books.

Henry, M. B. (1969) *Up and Doing: Creative Activities for Home and School*, Sydney: Hodder and Stoughton

Henry, M. B. (1980) *Developing Together: An Inala Program for Aboriginal Parents and Infants*, Brisbane: Queensland Department of Education.

Henry, M. B. (1981) 'The development of a parent education program with young urban Aboriginal mothers and their infants', unpublished Masters thesis, Brisbane: University of Queensland.

Henry, M. B. (1984) 'Expanding caregiver perspectives on parent involvement', *Handbook for Day Care*, Watson, ACT: Australian Early Childhood Association.

Henry, M. B. (1986) 'Parents and professionals working together', in B. Raward and J. Ferguson (eds) *Early Childhood: Ideals/Realities*, Canberra: Australian Early Childhood Association.

Henry, M. B. (1988) 'The dimensions of parental behaviour: some implications for professionals', *Australian Journal of Early Childhood* 13(2), 3–12.

Henry, M. B. (1990) 'More than just play: the significance of mutually directed adult–child activity', *Early Child Development and Care* 60, 35–51.

Henry, M. B. (1992) 'An in-service program in family day care: supporting the development of young children and their care providers', unpublished PhD thesis, Brisbane: University of Queensland.

Hess, R. D. (1969) 'Parental behavior and children's school achievement: implications for Head Start', in E. Grotberg (ed.) *Critical Issues in Research Relating to Disadvantaged Children*, Princeton, NJ: Educational Testing Service.

Hess, R. D. (1971) 'Community involvement in day care', *Day Care: Resources for Decisions*, Washington, DC: US Office of Economic Opportunity.

Hock, E., De Meis, D. and McBride, S. (1988). 'Maternal anxiety: its role in the balance of employment and motherhood in mothers of infants', in A. E. Gottfried and A. W. Gottfried (eds) *Maternal Employment and Children's Development: Longitudinal Research*, New York: Plenum Press.

209

Isaacs, P. (1995) 'Tribalism and the liberal ideal', a paper presented at the conference *Social Development between Intervention and Integration*, Copenhagen, March.

Isabella, R. and Belsky, J. (1991) 'Interactional synchrony and the origins of infant–mother attachment: a replication study', *Child Development* 62, 373–84.

James, T. E. (1975) *West Riding EPA Project Follow-Up Studies*, Department of Social and Administrative Studies, Oxford University.

Johnson, D. W. and Johnson, R. T. (1985) 'Nutrition education: a model for effectiveness, a synthesis of research', *Journal of Nutrition Education* 17(2), Supplement.

Karnes, M. B. (1969) *Research and Development Program on Pre-school Disadvantaged Children: Final Report*, Washington, DC: US Office of Education.

Katz, L. G. (1972) 'Developmental stages of pre-school teachers', *Elementary School Journal* 73, 50–54.

Katz, L. G. (1980) 'Mothering and teaching: some significant distinctions', in L. G. Katz (ed.) *Current Topics in Early Childhood Education*, vol. 3, Norwood, NJ: Ablex.

Kean, J. (1994) 'Children's temperaments and their relation to behaviour and emotion across different contexts', unpublished PhD thesis, Brisbane: University of Queensland.

Kelly, G. A. (1955) *The Psychology of Personal Constructs*, vol. 1, *A Theory of Personality*, New York: Norton.

Kelly, J. (1986) 'Day care: an unfortunate necessity or a desirable community resource?', *Australian Journal of Early Childhood* 11(1), 3–9.

Kemper, T. D. (1968) 'Reference groups, socialization and achievement', *American Sociological Review* 3(1), 323–43.

Kluckhohn, F. R. and Strodtbeck, F. L. (1961) *Variations in Value Orientations*, New York: Row, Peterson.

LaForge, R. and Suczek, R. (1955) 'The interpersonal dimension of personality: an interpersonal checklist', *Journal of Personality* 24, 94–112.

Lamb, M. (1976) *The Role of the Father in Child Development*, London: John Wiley.

Lamb, M. and Oppenheim, D. (1989) 'Fatherhood and father–child relationships: five years of research', in S. Cath, A. Gurwitt and L. Gunsberg (eds) *Fathers and their Families*, Hillsdale, NJ: Analytic Press.

Lampert, M. and Clark, C. M. (1990) 'Expert knowledge and expert thinking: a response to Floden and Klinzing', *Educational Researcher* 19(5), 21–3.

Leach, P. (1994) *Children First*, Harmondsworth: Penguin.

Leler, H. (1980) 'Approaches designed to strengthen families', paper presented at the World Congress of the International Federation for Parent Education, Mexico.

Levenstein, P. (1970) 'Cognitive growth in preschoolers through verbal interaction with mothers', *American Journal of Orthopsychiatry* 40, 426–32.

Lewis, M. and Feiring, C. (1982) 'Some American families at dinner', in L. M. Laosa and I. E. Sigel (eds) *Families as Learning Environments for Children*, New York: Plenum Press.

Logan, L. (1990) 'Helping teachers grow professionally', *Newsletter of the Early Childhood Teachers Association*, Queensland, December.

Long. F., Peters, D. L. and Garduque, L. (1985) 'Continuity between home and day care: a model for defining relevant dimensions of child care', in I. Sigel (ed.) *Advances in Applied Developmental Psychology*, vol. 1, Norwood, NJ: Ablex.

Maccoby, E. E. (1980) *Social Development*, New York: Harcourt Brace Jovanovich.

Maccoby, E. E. and Martin, J. A. (1983) 'Socialisation in the context of the family:

parent–child interaction', in P. E. Mussen (ed.) *Handbook of Child Psychology* (third edition), New York: Wiley.

McCartney, K. (1984) 'Effect of quality of day care environment on children's language environment', *Developmental Psychology* 20(2), 244–60.

McGraw, K. O. (1987) *Developmental Psychology,* San Diego: Harcourt Brace Jovanovich.

McLean, S. V. (1986) 'Facilitating social interaction: ideal or reality?', *Early Childhood: Ideals/Realities,* vol. 2, proceedings of the 17th National Conference of the Australian Early Childhood Association, Brisbane, September, 1985.

McLean, S. V. (1991a) *The Human Encounter: Teachers and Children Living Together in Pre-schools,* London: Falmer Press.

McLean, S. V. (1991b) 'Teachers' work: the use of stories of practice in two preservice teacher education programs', paper presented at the Australian Early Childhood Association Conference, Adelaide, SA.

McNamara, C. (1979) *Trailing the Twentieth Century,* Sydney: Mitchell Library.

McNamara, C. (1967) 'The discussion group method', in C. McNamara and M. Henry, *Parents and Children,* Sydney: Angus and Robertson.

Martin, K. (1979) 'Aboriginal parent/infant playgroup', *The Aboriginal Child at School* 7(3), 24.

Maslow, A. (1954) *Motivation and Personality,* New York: Harper and Row.

Massey, D. (1995) 'What rights and wrongs are we to teach?', *New Horizons in Education* 93, December.

Midwinter, E. (1973) *Patterns of Community Education,* London: Ward Lock.

Ministerial Consultative Council on Curriculum (1992) *Early Childhood Education Project,* Ministerial Consultation and Research Series no. 7, Queensland Department of Education.

Monrad, D. M. (1978) 'An investigation of the cognitive and affective components of maternal teaching style', unpublished doctoral dissertation, Department of Psychology, Johns Hopkins University, Baltimore.

Moxley-Haegert L. and Serbin L. A. (1983) 'Developmental education for parents of delayed infants: effects on parental motivation and children's development', *Child Development* 54, 1324–31.

Nedler, S. and McAfee, O. (1979) *Working with Parents,* Belmont, California: Wadsworth.

Ochiltree, G. (1994) *Effects of Child Care on Young Children: Forty Years of Research,* Melbourne, Australian Institute of Family Studies.

Oliver, D. M. (1992) 'Leading towards empowerment', unpublished Masters thesis, Brisbane: Queensland University of Technology.

Open University (1979), *The First Years of Life,* London: Ward Lock.

Oppenheim, D., Sagi, A. and Lamb, M. E. (1988) 'Infant–adult attachments on the kibbutz and their relation to socioemotional development four years later', *Developmental Psychology* 24(3), 427–33.

Perry, R. (1994) 'Social justice in early education', in G. Halliwell (ed.) *Early Childhood Perspectives on Assessment, Justice and Quality,* Canberra: Australian Curriculum Studies Association, 20–25.

Peters D. L. and Kostelnik, M. J. (1981) 'Current research in day care personnel preparation', *Advances in Early Education and Day Care* 2, 29–60.

Petit, D. (1980) *Opening Up Schools* Harmondsworth: Penguin.

Piaget, J. (1952) *The Origins of Intelligence in Children,* New York: International Universities Press.

Piaget, J. (1954) *The Construction of Reality in the Child,* New York: Basic Books.

Powell, C. and Grantham-McGregor, S. (1989) 'Home visiting of varying frequency and child development', *Pediatrics* 84, 157–64.

Powell, D. R. (1989), *Families and Early Childhood Programs*, Washington, DC: National Association for the Education of Young Children.

Powell, D. R. and Eisenstadt J. W. (1988) 'Informal and formal conversations in parent discussion groups: an observational study', *Family Relations* 37, 166–70.

Powell, D. R. and Stremmel, A. J. (1987) 'Managing relations with parents: research notes on the teacher's role', in D. L. Peters and S. Kontos (eds) *Continuity and Discontinuity of Experience in Child Care*, Norwood, NJ: Ablex.

Power, T. J. (1985) 'Perceptions of competence: how parents and teachers view each other', *Psychology in the Schools* 22, 68–78.

Prescott, E. (1978) 'Is day care as good as a good home?', *Young Children*, January, 13–19.

Ramey, C. T., Bryant, D. M. and Suarez, T. M. (1985) 'Pre-school compensatory education and the modifiability of intelligence: a critical review', in D. Detterman (ed.) *Current Topics in Human Intelligence*. Norwood, NJ: Ablex.

Rheingold, H. L. (1982) 'Little children's participation in the work of adults, a nascent prosocial behavior', *Child Development* 53, 114–25.

Richman, N. and Graham, P. (1971) 'A behavioural screening questionnaire for use with three year old children', *Journal of Child Psychology and Psychiatry* 12, 5–53.

Rob, M. and Norfor, J. (1980) 'Parenting: can skills be learned?', *Australian Journal of Social Issues* 15(3), 189–93.

Rodd, J. and Holland, A. (1989) 'Recognizing and respecting family diversity: models of parent education', *Australian Journal of Sex, Marriage and Family* 10, 4, 172–9.

Rogoff, B. (1990) *Apprenticeship in Thinking: Cognitive Development in Social Context*, New York: Oxford University Press.

Rogoff, B. and Gardner, W. (1984) 'Adult guidance of cognitive development', in B. Rogoff and J. Lave (eds) *Everyday Cognition: Its Development in Social Context*, Cambridge, MA: Harvard University Press.

Rogoff, B., Malkin, C. and Gilbride, K. (1984) 'Interaction with babies as guidance in development', in B. Rogoff and J. V. Wertsch (eds) *Children's Learning in the 'Zone of Proximal Development'*, San Francisco: Jossey-Bass.

Ruff, H. A., Lawson, K. A., Parrinello, R. and Weissberg, R. (1990) 'Long-term stability of individual differences in sustained attention in the early years', *Child Development* 61, 60–75.

Russell, G. (1983) *The Changing Role of Fathers*, St Lucia: University of Queensland Press.

Russell, G. (1984) 'The theory and practice of shared responsibility for parenting', Australian Research Grants funded project, Macquarie University, Sydney.

Russell, G. (1994) 'Sharing the pleasures and pains of family life', *Family Matters*, 37, April, 13–19.

Rutter, M. (1981) 'The city and the child', *American Journal of Orthopsychiatry* 51, 610–25.

Santrock, J. and Yussen S. (1992) *Child Development* (fifth edition), Dubuque, IA: William C. Brown.

Saxe, G. B., Guberman, S. R. and Gearhart, M. (1987) 'Social processes in early number development', *Monographs of the Society for Research in Child Development* 52(2, serial no. 216).

Schaefer, E. S. (1982) 'Professional support for family care of children', in H. M. Wallace, E. M. Gold and E. F. Lis (eds) *Maternal and Child Health Practices:*

Problems, Resources and Methods of Delivery, Springfield, Illinois: Charles C. Thomas.

Schaefer, E. S. (1987) 'Parental modernity and child academic competence: toward a theory of individual and societal development', *Early Child Development and Care* 27, 373–89.

Schaffer, H. R. (1971) *The Growth of Sociability*, Harmondsworth Penguin.

Schaffer, H. R. and Emerson, P. E. (1964) 'The development of social attachments in infancy', *Monographs of the Society for Research in Child Development* 29(3, serial no. 94).

Schneider-Rosen, K. and Wenz-Gross, M. (1990) 'Patterns of compliance from eighteen to thirty months of age', *Child Development* 61, 104–12.

Schools Council (1968) *Enquiry into Young School Leavers*, London: Her Majesty's Stationery Office.

Schroeder, C. S. (1979) 'Psychologists in a private pediatric practice', *Journal of Pediatric Psychology* 4, 5.

Sebastian-Nickell, P. and Milne, R. (1992) *Care and Education of Young Children*, Melbourne: Longman Cheshire.

Shorter, E. (1976) *The Making of the Modern Family*, Glasgow: Fontana-Collins.

Siegler, R. S. (1983) 'Information processing approaches to development', in P. H. Mussen (ed.) *Handbook of Child Psychology*, vol. 1, *History, Theory, and Methods*, New York: Wiley.

Skeels, H. (1966) 'Adult status of children with contrasting early life experiences', *Monographs of the Society for Research in Child Development*, 31(3).

Skinner, B. F. (1953) *Science and Human Behavior* New York: Macmillan.

Smith, G. (1975) *Educational Priority*, vol. 4, *EPA The West Riding Project*, London: Her Majesty's Stationery Office.

Snider, M. H. and Fu, V. R. (1988) 'The effects of specialized education and job experience on early childhood teachers' knowledge of developmentally appropriate practice', unpublished paper, Department of Family and Child Development, Virginia Polytechnic Institute and State University.

Sparling, J. and Lewis, I. (1979) *Learningames for the First Three Years*, New York: Walker.

Spitz, R. A. (1945) 'Hospitalism: an inquiry into the genesis of psychiatric conditions in early childhood', *Psychoanalytic Study of the Child* 1, 53–74.

Sroufe, L. A. (1985) 'Attachment classification from the perspective of infant–caregiver relationships and infant temperament', *Child Development* 56, 1–4.

Staines, J. W. (1974) 'Pre-school: is it too late?', *New Horizons in Education* 52, 29–38.

Stayton, D. J., Hogan, R.T. and Ainsworth, M. D. S. (1971). 'Infant obedience and maternal behavior: the origins of socialisation reconsidered', *Child Development* 42, 1057–69.

Stevenson, J. (1986) 'Developing parenting skills through health visitors', paper presented at the Development Section, British Psychological Society Annual Conference, September, University of Exeter.

Stevenson, J., Bailey, V. and Simpson, J. (1988) 'Feasible intervention in families with parenting difficulties: a primary preventive perspective on child abuse', in K. Browne, C. Davies and P. Stratton (eds) *Early Prediction and Prevention of Child Abuse*, Chichester: John Wiley.

Tizard, B. and Hughes, M. (1984) *Young Children Learning: Talking and Thinking at Home and at School*, London: Fontana.

Tizard, B., Mortimore, J. and Burchell, B. (1983) *Involving Parents in Nursery and Infants Schools*, Ypsilanti, Michigan: Hi-Scope.

213

REFERENCES

Triandis, H. C. (1964) 'Exploratory factor analysis of the behavioral component of social attitudes', *Journal of Abnormal and Social Psychology* 68, 420–30.

Vanderslice, V. (1984) *Communication for Empowerment: A Facilitator's Manual of Empowering Teaching Techniques*, Family Matters Project, Cornell University.

Vygotsky, L. S. (1978) *Mind in Society: The Development of Higher Psychological Processes*, Cambridge, MA: Harvard University Press.

Vygotsky, L. S. (1981) 'The genesis of higher mental functions', in J. V. Wertsch (ed.) *The Concept of Activity in Soviet Psychology*, Armonk, New York: Sharpe.

Wasik, B. H., Ramey, C. T., Bryant, D. M. and Sparling, J. J. (1990) 'A longitudinal study of two early intervention strategies: Project CARE', *Child Development* 61, 1682–96.

Watts, B. H. (1970) 'Achievement-related values in two Australian ethnic groups', in W. J. Campbell (ed.) *Scholars in Context: The Effects of Environment on Learning*, Sydney: John Wiley.

Watts, B. H. and Henry, M. B. (1978) *Focus on Parent/Child: Extending the Teaching Competence of Urban Aboriginal Mothers*, Canberra: Australian Government Publishing Service.

Watts, B. H. and Patterson, P. (1984) *In Search of Quality. Home and Day Care Centre: Complementary Environments for the Growing Child*, Brisbane: Lady Gowrie Child Centre.

Wertsch, J. V. (1984) 'The zone of proximal development: some conceptual issues', in B. Rogoff and J. V. Wertsch (eds) *Children's Learning in the 'Zone of Proximal Development'*, San Francisco: Jossey-Bass.

Wertsch, J. V. and Stone, C. A. (1985) 'The concept of internalization in Vygotsky's account of the genesis of higher mental functions', in J. V. Wertsch (ed.) *Culture, Communication and Cognition: Vygotskian Perspectives*, Cambridge: Cambridge University Press.

White, B. L. (1975) 'Critical influences in the origins of competence', *Merrill-Palmer Quarterly* 21(4), 243–66.

White, B. L., Kaban, B. and Attanucci, J. (1979) *The Origins of Human Competence: Final Report of the Harvard Pre-school Project*, Toronto: Lexington Books.

White, R. W. (1959) 'Motivation reconsidered: the concept of competence', *Psychological Review* 66, 297–333.

Wolfendale, S. (1983) *Parental Participation in Children's Development and Education*, New York: Gordon and Breach.

Zeuli, J. P. (1986) 'The use of the zone of proximal development in everyday and school contexts: a Vygotskian critique', paper presented at the 70th Annual Meeting of the American Educational Research Association, San Francisco.

INDEX

215